Deer Hunters' Almanac

FROM THE PUBLISHERS OF DEER & DEER HUNTING MAGAZINE

© 1992 by
Krause Publications, Inc.

Published by

**krause
publications**

700 E State St., Iola, WI 54990-0001

Printed in the United States of America

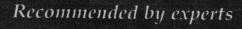

Contents

Be part of '94 Almanac

If you have articles, stories or original photos that would be of interest to white-tailed deer hunters and would like to have your material considered for publication in the 1994 Deer Hunters' Almanac, contact editor Patrick Durkin, 700 E. State St., Iola, WI 54990.

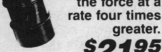

STUMP SITTING TIME

It's stump sitting time once again.

To hurried, pressured, tired men stump sitting time is by far the most meaningful and significant time of all. And it comes just once a year; in autumn. Somehow there just couldn't be a stump sitting time in fresh spring, in hot summer or in cold winter. The air must be crisp for good stump sitting. There must be that thin haze; that hint of smoke. The oaks must be bronze, the aspen yellow and the maples red. Corn stalks too, are important if only as distant background.

Perhaps most essential to productive stump sitting are certain devices which the stump sitter uses to prevent irritants to his conscience. Without these devices he would be most uncomfortable. In fact, without them chances are he would do no stump sitting at all. He would be too ill at ease, too restless.

One of these is a hunting license. So too, is a shotgun. A companionable bird dog is recommended by some, although this is not considered a necessity. An increasing number of stump sitters rely on bows and arrows.

With these necessary accouterments and a typical autumn day at hand the stump sitter is ready to enjoy his great diversion. In no time at all things in his life, yes, even life itself, begin to take their proper places and perspectives. Big things become little; little things become big. It isn't too necessary that game be taken or that all fields in view be searched for birds. The dog can be impatient, the gun primed, the pot waiting at home; but these are the affairs of a different world, a busier place, where stump sitting is unknown.

One danger that has to be faced in such an occupation is the urge to go and do something. It doesn't matter what the something is, whether to hunt or to find the dog or look for companions or go home. Such urges, however, must all be scorned. Ruthlessly. They are only designed to unthrone the stump sitter.

Somehow stump sitting has its own special kind of brain washing; the good, wholesome kind. Trials, tribulations, worries — all are affected by the peculiar cleansing action of stump sitting.

Yes. It's stump sitting time once again. Thank God for that.

Reprinted from Michigan Conservation, Sept./Oct., 1955

CLASSIFICATION AND DISTRIBUTION OF THE WHITE-TAILED DEER

FIGURE 10. Distribution of white-tailed deer (*Odocoileus virginianus*) subspecies in North and Central America

1. *O. v. acadpulcensis*	11. *O. v. mcilhennyi*	21. *O. v. sinaloae*
2. *O. v. borealis*	12. *O. v. mexicanus*	22. *O. v. taurinsulae*
3. *O. v. carminis*	13. *O. v. miquihuanensis*	23. *O. v. texanus*
4. *O. v. chiriquensis*	14. *O. v. nelsoni*	24. *O. v. thomasi*
5. *O. v. clavium*	15. *O. v. nigribarbis*	25. *O. v. toltecus*
6. *O. v. couesi*	16. *O. v. oaxacensis*	26. *O. v. truei*
7. *O. v. dacotensis*	17. *O. v. ochrourus*	27. *O. v. venatorius*
8. *O. v. hiltonensis*	18. *O. v. osceola*	28. *O. v. veraecrucis*
9. *O. v. leucurus*	19. *O. v. rothschildi*	29. *O. v. virginianus*
10. *O. v. macrourus*	20. *O. v. seminolus*	30. *O. v. yucatanensis*

*From **White-tailed Deer: Ecology and Management**, 1984: Courtesy of the Wildlife Management Institute.*

❖ SKELETON ❖

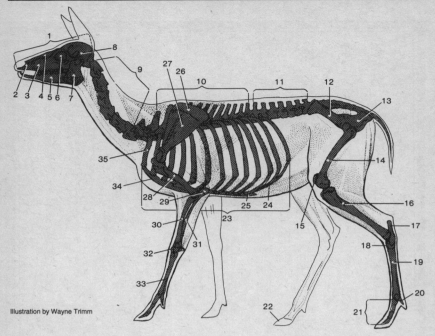

Illustration by Wayne Trimm

1. Skull
2. Os incisivum
3. Maxilla
4. Os nasale
5. Manible
6. Orbita
7. Mandibular condyle
8. Os temporale
9. Cervical vertebrae
10. Thoracic vertebrae
11. Lumbar vertebrae
12. Illium
13. Ischium

14. Femur
15. Patella
16. Tibia
17. Tuper calcis
18. Tarsus
19. Os temporale
20. Dew claw of phalanges
21. Phalanges
22. Hoof
23. Rib cage
24. Rib cartilages
25. Xiphoid cartilage

26. Scapula cartilage
27. Scapula
28. Humerus
29. Olecranon
30. Radius
31. Ulna
32. Carpals
33. Metacarpal
34. Sternum
35. First Rib

*From **White-tailed Deer: Ecology and Management**, 1984: Courtesy of the Wildlife Management Institute.*

❖ MUSCLES ❖

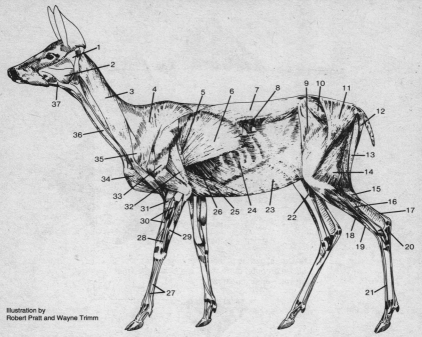

Illustration by
Robert Pratt and Wayne Trimm

1. Arcus zygomaticus
2. Masseter
3. Brachiocephalicus
4. Trapezius
5. Tensor fasciae antebrachii
6. Latissimus dorsi
7. Lumbo-dorsal fascis
8. Serratus ventralis
9. Tensor fasciae externus
10. Gluteus medius vertebrae
11. Trochanter major
12. Semimembranosus
13. Semitendinosus
14. Biceps femoris

15. Gastrocnemius
16. Deep flexor tendon
17. Tendon of Achilles
18. Lateral extensor
19. Long extensor
20. Superficial flexor tendon
21. Anterior tendon
22. Flexor digitorum (pedislongus)
23. Aponeurosis
24. Obliquus abdominals exterrnus
25. Deep pectoral
26. Serratis ventralis

27. Flexor tendons of metatarsus
28. Tendon of extensor digiti
29. Extensor carpi (ulnaris)
30. Extensor digiti
31. Extensor carpi (radialis)
32. Triceps
33. Deltoid
34. Superficial pectoral (brisket)
35. Shouldler-transverse process Muscle
36. Sternocephalicus
37. Sternomandibularis

From **White-tailed Deer: Ecology and Management**, *1984: Courtesy of the Wildlife Management Institute.*

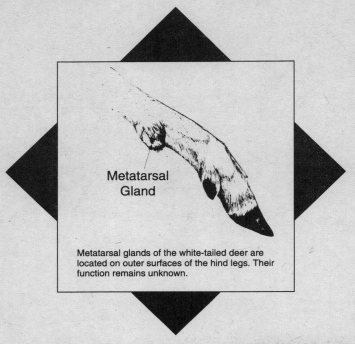

Metatarsal
Gland

Metatarsal glands of the white-tailed deer are located on outer surfaces of the hind legs. Their function remains unknown.

Metatarsal Gland

This gland is not well understood. The metatarsals are located on the outer hind legs between the toes and heel. All deer possess these glands from birth. Many wildlife biologists suggest that gland size, in some cases, can have taxonomic value between species. The mule deer has the largest metatarsal glands, followed by the black-tailed and white-tailed deer. Although smallest in comparison to other deer species, the gland is clearly visible on the whitetail and is noted by a light, tannish-colored circle of hair against the more dominant colors of reddish-brown or gray. The light-colored cluster is actually the hair that surrounds the gland. A closer examination of the gland reveals an area lacking hair, rib-shaped, and not a true external gland. (A true external gland has a surface opening or duct.) The metatarsal glands, actually located below the skin surface, are technically known as sebaceous (sweat) and sudoriferous (scent-producing) glands. This gland secretes very small amounts of scent, but its intended purpose has not been proven. Knowledge of its physiology then is minimal.

Some speculators claim that when a deer lies down the glands rub the ground and leave a scent. Another possibility is that through change and adaptation, the metatarsal gland could be a rudimentary vestigial gland that had a more significant purpose at one time in the evolution of deer. We see this fact evident concerning dewclaws. Dewclaws are remnants of what used to be functional toes.

Tarsal Gland

Tarsal glands on the inner surface of the hind legs of white-tailed deer produce a scent unique to individual deer and are involved in rub-urination and marking behavior.

Tarsal Gland

This is a true external gland located inside both hind legs at the foot/heel junction and is present in both sexes at birth. We know more about this external gland than any other. Clearly visible on all three deer species, the tarsal gland plays an important role in reproductive activities as well as social dominance and communication.

Through years of research, biologists discovered many relevant facts concerning this gland. They know the tarsals are a deer's most important scent gland. Tarsal glands are concealed in hair and measure about four inches in diameter. The hairs associated with the gland have the ability to stand on end or flair out should an unusual or excitable situation arise, putting the deer "on guard." In the excited state, the hairs can be seen at fairly long distances and at this time the gland releases scent that clings to the hairs and acts partly as a warning signal to nearby deer. Wildlife biologist D. Mueller Schwarze states that the active olfactory components in the tarsal gland are lactones. He mentions that lactones are both age and sex specific and that the hairs used to deposit the urine and scent (pheromone) mixture are termed "osmetrichia." These lipid-covered hairs are specialized scent hairs. It can be assumed then that one function of the tarsal glands is that of survival behavior.

During the mating season males, females, and fawns rub-urinate on their tarsals for several reasons. Bucks do it as a means of displaying social dominance. Males smell each other's tarsal glands in determining dominance ranking. Females rub for self-identification. Fawns depend partly on this when they become separated from the does. Fawns also rub-urinate, possibly for identification purposes. L.W. Bouckhout revealed that the more socially dominant males rub-urinate more frequently than do males of lesser dominance. K. Ralls, C.C. Shank, and C. Barrette state that the odor of tarsal glands is stronger in dominant males due to the frequency of urination. Young males and females have been know to lick their tarsal glands after rub-urination more so than older males. This act would seem to remove scent, as an expression of lesser dominance perhaps.

Deer hunters should know that the tarsal gland is associated only externally with deer. The need to remove the gland prior to field dressing or meat cutting is necessary only if a hunter feels he will come in contact with the glands. If contact isn't made, the gland will not spoil or ruin the flavor of the meat.

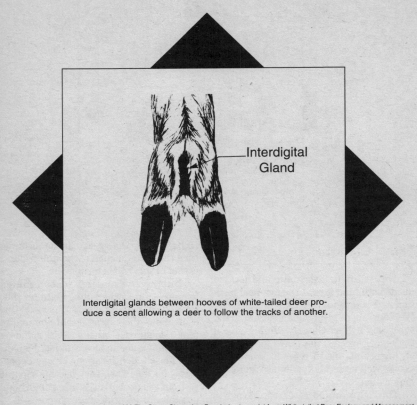

Interdigital glands between hooves of white-tailed deer produce a scent allowing a deer to follow the tracks of another.

Interdigital Gland

Interdigital glands are located between the toes of each foot on both sexes. These glands, functional from birth, are used by deer to track one another. Each deer carries a specific odor from the gland. The interdigital gland is covered with hair and not readily seen with the naked eye. Close examination reveals a duct or opening between the toes, visible only when the toes are spread and the hair parted. The largest interdigital glands are found on white-tailed deer.

An active gland, the interdigital emits scent each time a deer takes a step. Use of the scent differs between sexes. Females rely on the scent to track their young, while males use it to track females during the rut.

An amazing aspect of wildlife ecology is an animal's ability to follow only one particular scent. Many kinds of wildlife, especially the female and her offspring, can distinguish an individual's scent no matter how many animals are in an area or how many scents there are to differentiate. Since deer rely primarily on scent for positive identification, this gland seems especially important.

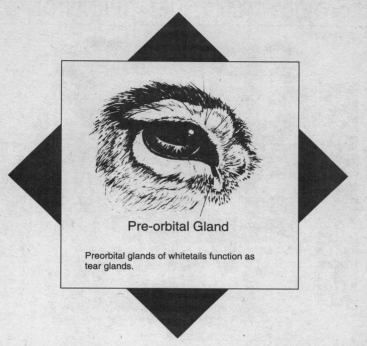

Pre-orbital Gland

Preorbital glands of whitetails function as tear glands.

Pre-orbital Gland

Located below the eyes on all deer, the preorbital gland is not well understood. Characteristics of the gland include a small canal or duct by which small amounts of scent trickle. Easily visible and largest in mule deer, the purpose of the glands is believed to be that of a scent marker.

One theory claims that habitats reflect use of the gland. White-tailed and black-tailed deer would probably make best use of this gland since they inhabit areas of more dense vegetation, whereas mule deer inhabit open plains having little vegetation upon which to rub the gland. It seems unusual that a marking gland would be so near the eye since it is so vulnerable. Sharp twigs and forest debris could impair vision should the animal unknowingly rub near sharp objects.

Another possibility is that through doe/fawn contact the doe smears some of her own scent on her young through nuzzling. This may be beneficial when the fawn wanders out of the doe's sight.

Conclusion

Presented here are some facts as well as assumptions. Each year new information is published concerning glandular activity among deer. We will probably never know all the reasons deer do what they do, but through future studies and new findings, we may see the gap of the unknown slowly close.

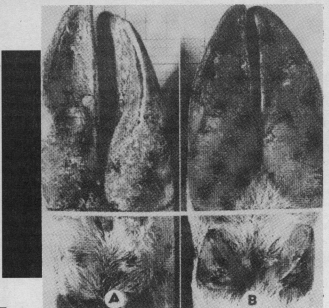

Dr. Frederick Weston

Experts often disagree whether it's possible to positively identify a deer's sex by the tracks it leaves. Leonard Lee Rue III, for example, believes most people who say they can make a positive ID would stop making the claims if they ever saw many of the deer that made the tracks.

That being said, other experienced hunters believe it's sometimes possible to tell a deer's sex by its tracks. Myles Keller, for example, says tracks measuring 3 to 3.25 inches were likely made by a trophy buck. Keller also says a mature buck's rear hooves will usually land short of imprints made by their front hooves (Figure 1).

Here are some other indicators:

• A doe's track usually meanders while bucks maintain a purposeful, fairly straight line. Because of a doe's pelvic structure, her hind hooves will overlap nd land outside the front imprints.

• All deer make drag marks in deep snow, but only bucks drag their hooves in leaves or light snow. During the rut, drag marks reach their maximum lengths.

• Heavy-bodied bucks with swollen necks and large antlers tend to walk with their front hooves more splayed, turned out and wider apart than does and yearling bucks. This puts more pressure on the tips of their hooves, which causes them to dig in and become rounded.

Most bucks, however, are shot as yearlings in much of the country. Therefore, few live long enough to display those tendencies. Also, hard or rocky ground tends to round off the hooves (Figure 2).

Like the fingerprints of man, deer hooves have individual characteristics that can distinguish one deer from another. For instance, the hoof on the left is concave and has a partial break

14

The tracks of a walking doe usually appear along an imaginary straight line with the tracks of the hind hooves ahead of the front hooves.

The tracks above indicate a mature buck in good condition. Note that the toes turn out from the center line rather than follow a straight line and that the tracks of the hind hooves appear behind the tracks of the front hooves.

Figure 1

Experts disagree whether it's possible to positively identify a deer's sex by the tracks it leaves.

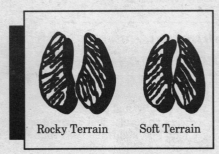

Rocky Terrain   Soft Terrain

Figure 2

in one toe.

• Does hunch back and urinate in their tracks, often with a wide and irregular spray. A buck's urine typically comes straight down and perforates unbroken snow. Also, bucks often dribble urine while walking, while does do not.

Illustration: Buck tracks during the rut

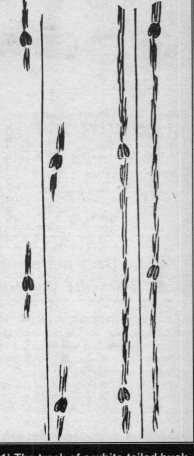

(1) The track of a white-tailed buck before and after the rut. Notice how the toes pointing outward from the center line.
(2) During the rut the drag mark almost extends from step to step.
— Josef Bunner,
    1909 *Tracks and Tracking*

❖ THE DOPE ON DEER DROPPINGS ❖

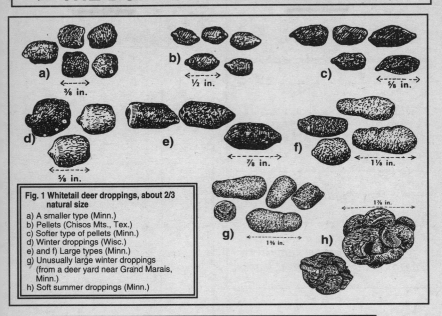

a) ← - - - → ⅜ in.

b) ← - - - → ½ in.

c) ← - - - - → ⅝ in.

d) ← - - - → ⅝ in.

e) ← - - - - → ⅞ in.

f) ← - - - - → 1⅛ in.

g) ← - - → 1⅜ in.

h) 1⅜ in.

Fig. 1 Whitetail deer droppings, about 2/3 natural size
a) A smaller type (Minn.)
b) Pellets (Chisos Mts., Tex.)
c) Softer type of pellets (Minn.)
d) Winter droppings (Wisc.)
e) and f) Large types (Minn.)
g) Unusually large winter droppings (from a deer yard near Grand Marais, Minn.)
h) Soft summer droppings (Minn.)

Deer pellets might be the best scouting tool the hunter can find.

Deer pellets might be the best scouting tool the hunter can find. They help indicate bedding and feeding areas, forage preferences, and the deer's movements and whereabouts.

In addition, pellets give a general idea of how many deer are present in your area and whether they've been there recently. Just be sure not to base your evaluation on areas where deer yard in winter.

Deer droppings vary greatly in shape, color and form at various times of the year and under different food conditions. In winter, when deer feed on browse, the pellets are hard and become harder as the winter progresses. Their color is various shades of brown, and they're about three-fourths of an inch long. In summer, when deer feed on soft vegetation, their droppings form into soft clumps.

Sometimes, however, summer droppings consist of individual pellets.

Research verifies that more droppings are found by nighttime beds than daytime beds. Unlike urination, deer defecate while going about their daily routines. Rarely do they interrupt what they're doing while dropping their pellets. Deer also defecate the most shortly after rising from their bed. On average, they defecate about 13 times a day, with the number of pellets per defecation varying from 42 to 320. The frequency of defecation depends on the quantity and succulence of the forage.

While you generally can get some feel for the deer's size by the size of its pellet, this isn't always true. The type of food ingested may play a larger role than the animal's size or age.

Seasonal Changes

Figure 1. Sequence of velvet loss among males by number of antler points as observed by David H. Hirth of the Welder Wildlife Refuge. N is the number of males of each antler class examined during the shedding season. Vertical lines indicate range of velvet loss dates and the horizontal bars show the mean velvet loss dates. (From *The Southwestern Naturalist*, 1977)

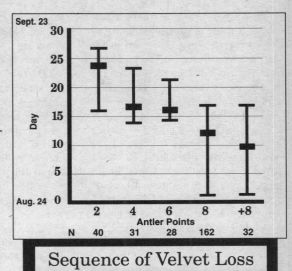

Sequence of Velvet Loss

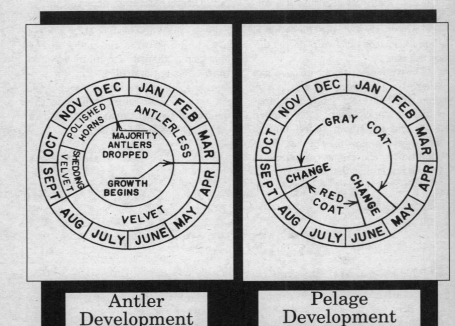

Antler Development

Pelage Development

❖ PEELING VELVET ❖

In August, in our northern areas, antler growth is completed, and the velvet-covered skin which nourished it now becomes shriveled. The buck presents a ludicrous picture when the peeling velvet sometimes hangs in fluttering ribbons from the rack.

The velvet from antlers is not always shed bit by bit in a slow peeling and drawing process. On this I have some first-hand information, for once I found the complete velvet case from a single antler of an eight-point buck. It was during the middle of August, and I happened across the strange object which looked like a piece of dark suede leather. The soft velvet was shed in one entire piece, and it split along the outside length of the beam to free itself from the prongs. The fuzzy growth was about an eighth of an inch thick and was substantial enough in body so that the projections covering the points of the antler stood out firmly on the discarded casing.

The curio was found in an open spot where the pasture grass was closely cropped. There was nothing nearby which the buck might have rubbed against in an attempt to free himself from this skin growth. The soft, damp condition of the casing caused me to believe it was shed that very day.

I brought it home in some sort of triumph, but the next day it was already beginning to shrivel and dry, and in a few days it lost its shape and the mummy-like skin was reduced to something that looked like a withered and twisted leaf. In this aged condition, it might not have caught my attention had I passed over it and only the eyes of a naturalist could have identified it when found. I would guess that at least some velvet shedding takes place in this manner. Most bucks seen at this time are either in or out of velvet, and only in the few is there an indication of a gradual peeling off of the velvet.

There has always been considerable controversy over the manner in which the buck rids himself of the peeling skin, yet there need be no argument. Buck rubs do not normally occur in the northern states until October, at a time when the antlers have been free of velvet for a month or more. In short, the bush fighting is a sex urge building up in the males at the approach of the rut, and if any velvet is worn off or antlers polished in this process, it is an incidental occurrence at best. Anyone in deer country during the months of September and October can make this simple observation.

— George Mattis

❖ HOW DEER REACT TO HUNTING PRESSURE ❖

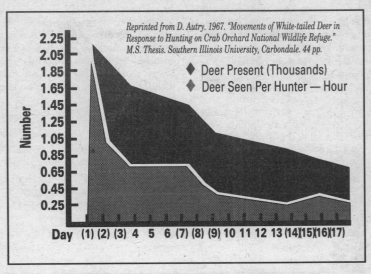

Numbers in parentheses indicate the days of the hunt. The gradual increase in deer seen during the closing days of the hunt occurred as a result of several supervised deer drives.

In most studies of deer tracked by radio telemetry, deer seldom leave their home range, preferring instead to sit tight in heavy cover. A deer's knowledge and familiarity with its home range enable it to survive hunting pressure. This is especially true of mature bucks.

Most studies found that hunting pressure caused yearling bucks to move significantly farther than mature bucks, probably making them more vulnerable to hunters. Bucks that remained in their beds, moving only when flushed at extremely short distances, tended to survive.

After the initial surprise of opening day, mature deer adjust their feeding activities, avoiding open areas, and sitting tight until darkness. The impression that bucks move great distances to sanctuaries or remote regions was usually not confirmed by the studies. After the season's first day, the deer's wariness doubled or quadrupled, and remained at this heightened state the rest of the season.

Deer tend to elude hunters by circling and seeking patches of heavy cover within their home range. Their escape is often triggered not by a hunter's appearance, but rather his disappearance. They allow a hunter to walk by, and then sneak out behind with great evasive maneuvers.

Some researchers have also found that deer in areas open to public hunting are more skilled at eluding hunters than those in areas where hunting pressure is controlled.

❖ PLANT & BROWSE PREFERENCES ❖

Most hunters know that agricultural crops like rye, corn, alfalfa, soybeans and other legumes are high on a whitetail's menu. What about natural browse? Which wild-growing foods do white-tailed deer prefer?

The accompanying charts show some of the more common deer forage that's found in woods or clearings. Remember, though, that a plant's availability varies by region. Not all of these will be found in your area.

And don't forget hard and soft mast such as acorns, apples and persimmons. In addition, look for freshly fallen trees or branches, such as maples or white cedars. Large windfalls become deer magnets with their bountiful supply of buds or succulent leaves. Deer will also munch on lichens, so take note of recently fallen dead trees.

Woody Plants		
White cedar	Red Osier (Dogwood)	Sweetbay
Hemlock	Jack Pine	Poison sumac
Maples	White Pine	Aquatic plants
Poplar	Black Spruce	Berry bushes
Birch	Vines	Ferns
Sumac	Honeysuckle	Cypress
Viburnums	Wax myrtle	
Willows	Bay	

Herbaceous Plants — Species		
Joe-pye weed	Sheep sorrel	Bedstraw
Early goldenrod	Hop clover	St. John's wort
Spotted jewelweed	Bluegrass	Panic grass
Woodland goldenrod	Butter-and-eggs	Pearly everlasting
White wood aster	Grassleaf goldenrod	Field horsetail
Giant goldenrod	Wild geranium	Blueflag iris
Elecampane	Canada bluegrass	Liveforever
Sensitive fern	Clover	Wood sorrel
Virgin's bower	Wild oat grass	Yarrow
Bracken fern	Sweet vernalgrass	White snakeroot
Whorled loosestrife	Strawberry	Ragweed
Goldenrod	Common wintercress	Indian Jack-in-the-pulpit
Water averns	Wild carrot	Thistle
Timothy	Common St. John's-wort	Small purple
Oxeye daisy	Oldfield cinquefoil	fringed orchid
Wrinkled goldenrod	Pussytoes	Rush
Redtop grass	Vetch	Indian tobacco
Hawkweed	Speedwell	Bugleweed
Buckhorn plantain	Common plaintain	Blackseed plantain
Buttercup	Fowl mannagrass	Purple milkwort
Fleabane	Sedge	Arrow leaved tearthumb
Argrimony	Avens	Dock
Selfheal	Virginia bugleweed	Silver goldenrod
Aster	Bulrush	
Red clover	White wood sorrel	

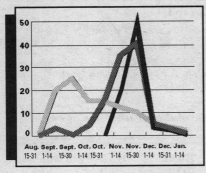

Breeding
Scrapes
Rubs

Rubs, Scrapes and Breeding Chart

The frequency of rubbing, scraping and breeding activity of white-tailed deer in the Georgia Piedmont during two-week periods.

Reprinted from T.L. Kile and R. L. Marchinton, 1977. "White-tailed Deer Rubs and Scrapes: Spatial, Temporal and Physical Characteristics and Social Rule." American Midland Naturalist, 97(2):263.

Rubs and scrapes provide vital clues to a buck's home range. Contrary to popular belief, bucks usually don't start rubbing until weeks after their velvet drops off. Rubbing peaks shortly before the actual breeding season. Fewer rubs are made as the rut progresses and deer open and maintain scrapes.

Rubs tend to be found in clusters and often occur near scrapes. Myles Keller, a well-known bow hunter from Minnesota, believes a high density of rubs indicates the buck's bedding area is nearby. Keller thinks that if a buck beds in a relatively small area, he needs frequent exercise to tone his muscles. He gets this by vigorously rubbing trees.

Georgia researchers offer an additional thought: On several occasions they saw dominant bucks make rubs when encountering other bucks. Because the bucks also snorted and took intimidating stances, the researchers concluded that rubs play a major role in marking a buck's territory and maintaining his social rank.

Bucks prefer to rub smooth-barked trees with few low branches. Most prefer pines or other resinous, aromatic trees. Scientists generally agree that bucks deliberately rub their foreheads on debarked trees to leave their scent, which lasts several days. Because does also sniff, lick and even mark buck rubs with their foreheads, rubs appear to be a form of communication between the sexes.

However, in heavily hunted areas where the herd has a high percentage of does and a young-buck age structure, the role of rubs and scrapes diminishes.

Research shows that even though does participate in scraping, bucks carry out more activities at the scrape. One study showed that the average number of different types of behavior performed per visit for each age class was 2.4 for bucks, 2 for juveniles and 1.8 for does.

Recent evidence indicates scrapes aren't territorial markers. For one thing, various deer of all ages and both sexes repeatedly use the limb overhanging the same scrape. Secondly, all ages of bucks have been observed at the same scrape, and even at the same time.

Researchers also have found that the amount of mutilation on the overhanging limb is a better indicator of visitation frequency than the scrape's size. In many cases, smaller scrapes get the most attention.

❖ RUT SEASON ❖

A PHEROMONE IS — a chemical or a mixture of chemicals which is released to the exterior by an organism and which, upon reception by another individual of the same species, stimulates one or more specific reactions.
— H.H. Shorey, "Pheronomes." 1977 In *How Animals Communicate* (Indiana University Press) edited by Thomas A. Sebeok.

Types of behaviorial events observed and number of each.

Behavior	Total (63)	Bucks (18)	Does (36)	Juveniles (9)
Limb Events				
Smell Limb	40	10	24	6
Lick Limb	23	4	16	0
Rub Preorbital on Limb	2	2	0	0
Rub Forehead on Limb	1	1	0	0
Totals - Limb	**66**	**17**	**40**	**9**
Ground Events				
Smell Scrape	41	13	22	6
Paw Scrape	9	5	2	2
Urinate in Scrape	8	6	1	1
Auto-erotic Behavior	2	2	0	0
Totals - Ground	**60**	**26**	**25**	**9**
Totals	**126**	**43**	**65**	**18**
Average No. of Events/Visit	**2.0**	**2.4**	**1.8**	**2.0**

Michael E. Graham

Find an intensely used overhanging branch for rubbing and licking in July and/or August and you will have found a major dominance area. Sit tight. During the summer months you will be able to view firsthand the expression of dominance — the establishment of a dominance hierarchy via rubbing, sniffing, and licking the overhanging branch. Many deer hunters overlook this pre-season scouting tool.

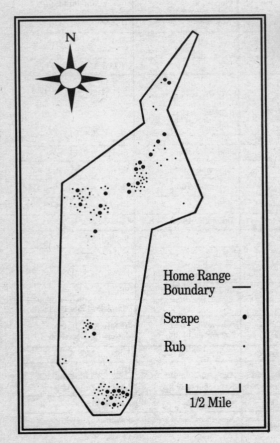

N

Home Range Boundary ——

Scrape •

Rub ·

1/2 Mile

Reprinted from W.G. Moore and R. L. Marchinton. 1974. "Marking Behavior and its Social Function in White-tailed Deer." Page 452 in The Behavior of Ungulates and its Relation to Management. IUCNN, Morges. Switzerland.

HOME RANGE ACTIVITY MAP

FIGURE 1. The distribution of rubs and scrapes made by one Georgia white-tailed buck between Oct. 14 and Dec. 5. Note the clumped distribution or centers of rubs.

In populations with a high percentage of does and a young age-structure among bucks (typical of many heavily hunted populations), the communicative role of rubs and scrapes may be less signigicant. In open habitat, direct visual cues have relatively greater importance than signpost communication. The function of rubbing and scraping in white-tailed deer social behavior is not fully understood. This is highlighted by the recent discovery that does also make scrapes on occasion, and that this behavior among does is not limited to the breeding season.
— *Larry Marchinton and David Hirth, White-tailed Deer: Ecology and Management, 1984*

REPORTED BREEDING SEASONS OF WHITE-TAILED DEER

STATE	BREEDING DATES	PEAK OF THE RUT	SOURCE, YEAR
Alabama Northeast	Mid-Nov. to Late March Late Nov. to Early Jan.	Varies by Region	Lueth, 1967 Adams, 1960
Arizona		Early to Mid-Feb. Feb. to Mid-March	Nichol, 1938 O'Connor, 1945
Arkansas	Early Oct. to Mid.-Jan.		Donaldson & Holder, 1951
Colorado	Oct. to Mid-Dec.		Warren, 1942
Connecticut	Late Sept. to Early Jan.		McDowell, 1966
Florida	Varies by Region		Harlow & Jones, 1965
Georgia	Varies by Region Mid-Oct. to Mid-Dec.	Nov. 15-30	Downing & Whittington, 1964 Kile & Marchinton, 1977
Iowa		November	Haugen, 1958
Kansas	Nov. 8 to Dec. 20 Sept. 6 to March 8		Anderson, 1964 Queal, 1964
Kentucky	October to January		Gale & Meyers, 1954

Louisiana
  Avery Island
  Delta Refuge
  Evangeline GMA
  Jackson-Bienville GMA
  Red Dirt GMA
  Tensas Parish
  West Bay GMA
	Sept. 26 to Dec. 9
	Nov. 15 to Jan. 18
	Oct. 18 to Oct. 31
	Dec. 2 to Jan. 26
	Oct. 22 to Jan. 25
	Dec. 10 to Feb. 26
	Sept. 27 to Dec. 9
		October 1-31
		December 14-29
		October 18-31
		December 1-15
		November 1-15
		January 1-15
		October 16-31
			Robertson & Dennet, 1966

Maine	Oct. 20 to Dec. 28	Mid-November	Banasiak, 1961
Massachusetts	Oct. 31 to Jan. 29	November 10-25	Shaw & McLaughlin, 1951
Michigan	Oct. 9 to Dec. 5	November 16-22	Haugen & Davenport, 1950
Minnesota	Mid-Sept. into Feb.		Erickson et al., 1961
Mississippi	Dec. 5 to Feb. 24	December 18-31	Noble, 1960
Missouri	Oct. to Early Dec.		Robb, 1951
Montana	Nov. 7 to Dec. 10		Allen, 1965
Nebraska	Oct. 21 to Mar. 1		Havel, 1963, 1964
New Hampshire		Mid-November	Silver, 1957
New Jersey	Late Oct. to Jan.		Mangold, 1958, 1963
New York	Sept. 22 to Feb. 22 Oct. 28 to Dec. 28	November 10-23 November 10-30	Cheatum & Morton, 1946 Jackson & Hesselton, 1973
North Carolina	Early Oct. to Early Nov.		Weber, 1966
Ohio	Oct. 22 to Dec. 9		Gilfillan, 1952
Oklahoma		November 2-26	Lindzey, ?
Pennsylvania	Late Oct. to Mid-Dec.	Mid-November	Lang et al., 1971
South Carolina		Nov. 17 to Dec. 13	Payne et al., 1966
Tennessee	Oct. 29 to Feb. 9		Lewis, 1972
Texas		December 15-24	Illige, 1951
Vermont	Early Nov. to Mid-Dec.		Day, 1964
Virginia	Oct. 1 to Late Nov.		Anon., 1948
West Virginia	Oct. 13 to Jan. 11		Chadwick, 1963
Wisconsin	Oct. 1 to Jan. 8	November 10-29	Dahlberg & Guettinger, 1956

24

AGGRESSIVE
Behavior of Deer

Aggressive Behavior:
Bucks and Does

Walk Toward
Aggressor walks toward another deer. Lowest intensity aggressive pattern exhibited by deer.

Ear Drop
Deer presses ears back alongside neck with the orifices directed away from the neck. Low intensity, frequently used aggressive pattern.

Head High Threat
Deer stands erect, holds head high, tilts nose upward, and lays back ears. A seldom used threat.

Head Low Threat
The aggressor lowers the head and extends the neck toward the aggressee with the ears laid back along the neck. Sometimes termed "Hard Look."

Lunge
The deer abruptly jerks its head forward toward the recipient and back without contact.

Head Raise
The head, oriented toward the recipient, is quickly snapped up and backward, then brought back to a resting posture while the ears are held out horizontally.

Front Leg Kick
Dominant deer strikes out at subordinate with a forefoot one or more times. Forefoot does not necessarily make contact with subordinate. Also termed "Strike."

Charge
Deer runs rapidly at another from a distance of three to fifteen feet, but stops before making contact. Deer usually performs another threat at the end of charge.

Chase
Subordinates that do not respond to lower level aggressive displays are sometimes chased by the dominant. Head low threat posture frequently used during the chase.

Rake
Used by dominant deer to displace subordinate from bed. Deer lifts a foreleg about eighteen inches above the ground and scrapes foot across back of the bedded deer.

Poke
One deer contacts another with its nose. Commonly used to direct group movement or supplant another deer.

Head Shake
The deer lowers its head and separates stiff forelegs to lower the anterior portion of the body while shaking the head from side to side with ears relaxed. A high intensity threat performed at a distance from the recipient.

Body Push

The aggressor approaches from the rear and pushes its front shoulder against the flank of the recipient while laying its throat on the back.

Sidle

Sidling deer stand with broadsides toward each other in head high threat posture and move slowly together. A buck usually turns head and body approxi-

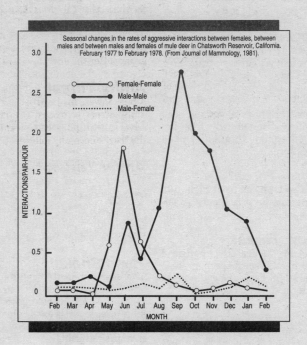

Seasonal changes in the rates of aggressive interactions between females, between males and between males and females of mule deer in Chatsworth Reservoir, California. February 1977 to February 1978. (From Journal of Mammology, 1981).

Aggressive Interactions For White-tailed Deer at Winter Cuttings

INTERACTION	TOTAL NUMBER	Ear Drop/ Hard Look	Strike	Rush	Sidle	Snort	Flail
				TERMINATING AGGRESSIVE ACTION (percent frequency)			
Buck over Buck	39	28	18	36	5	3	10
Buck over Doe	84	32	33	22	1	7	5
Buck over Fawn	59	41	41	12	0	6	0
Doe over Buck	20	15	35	40	0	10	0
Doe over Doe	98	21	40	26	1	7	5
Doe over Fawn	85	21	47	24	0	8	0
Fawn over Fawn	28	15	46	32	0	0	7
Fawn over Doe	4	0	75	0	0	0	25
Total	417						

mately thirty degrees from his adversary. If neither deer retreats, sidling usually followed by flailing or a rush.

Rear Up

A deer rears up on its hind legs into a vertical position. Usually preceded by a head high threat.

Flail

Adversaries stand on their hind legs and strike out at each other with both front feet. Flailing continues until one deer submits to the other. Most intense form of aggressive behavior exhibited by does and bucks without polished antlers.

Aggressive Behavior:
Bucks Only

Nose Licking

The buck constantly licks his nose. He protrudes the tongue alternately from each side of the mouth and flicks it quickly upward.

Crouch

The buck lowers his head and tilts antlers toward opponent. Involves a hunched posture; hind legs partially flexed, shoulder and elbow joints also partially flexed with the combined effect of lowering the height of the buck. Erector pili effect frequently used. The walk is slow, stiff and stilted. The crouch is a dominance display performed only during the breeding season by high-ranking bucks.

Circling

The aggressive male slowly circles his opponent while assuming the crouch position.

Rut-Snort

Mule-deer: Snort occurs while buck circles in crouch position. Buck extends neck almost parallel with ground. The upper lip is raised upwards at each side beneath the nostrils. Nostrils held tightly closed.

Snort is five to ten second expulsion of air through nostrils, causing them to vibrate. Neck muscles bulge, back may arch slightly, hairs stand erect over entire body, and the tail is held outwards or upwards stiffly with the tip turned down. White-tailed deer; Rut-snort not as loud as that of mule deer and performed rarely.
Black-tailed deer: Rut-snort more loudly than mule deer and add series of loud grunts after the snort.

Antler Threat

A buck lowers his head so that the antlers point directly toward the rival. If the adversary duplicates the antler threat, the "rush" normally follows.

Antler Thrust

The buck rapidly lowers his head so that the antlers point toward the rump or side of the opponent then abruptly raises the head. Directed toward males and females. Does not always result in contact.

Sparring

Two bucks engage antlers and push and/or twist their heads back and forth. Relatively non-violent contests. Bucks of all antler sizes participate. Bucks frequently remain in close proximity after sparring.

Rush

This rare form of aggressive behavior involves hostile combat between two, usually large, males. Both bucks lunge at each other in a violent antler clash from a distance of about six feet. Buck may attempt to pull opponent backwards or swing him sideways. Erector pili effect frequently present. Usually of short duration, the rush terminates when one buck turns and bolts. No major differences observed in rushing behavior of white-tailed, mule or black-tailed deer.

❖ DEER AND THE WIND ❖

Generally speaking, deer activity decreases as wind speed increases. Calm and light winds produce more deer sightings while moderate and gusty winds reduce them. The dividing line seems to be somewhere around 15 mph.

However, some researchers and hunters have documented an increase in buck activity during strong winds and less buck activity during calm winds.

Deer tend to group up and become excitable in high winds. During cold months, high winds cause deer to seek shelter on the lee slopes of hills and in dense coniferous woodlands. Conifer stands reduce wind speeds by up to 50 to 75 percent.

Research proves that even though deer will move in all directions in rela-tion to the wind, they'll move directly into the wind whenever possible. Deer trails closely match the prevailing wind direction and traditional wind changes. Wind fits two basic patterns:

Pattern A — Occurs during stable, high-pressure weather systems with clear or partly cloudy skies. This pattern brings little or no wind at sunrise and sunset, and maximum wind speeds in mid to late afternoon.

Pattern B — Occurs during changing weather conditions. This pattern brings constant wind speeds throughout the day with frequent gusts reflecting atmospheric turbulence.

Thermal winds — Thermal currents move uphill as the air temperature increases in the morning. Thermals move downhill as air cools toward evening.

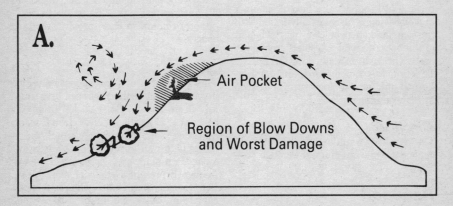

A.

Air Pocket

Region of Blow Downs
and Worst Damage

Gale winds force deer to pick sheltered bedding sites in the air pockets on the lee side of slopes and ridges approximately one-third of the way down from the crest.

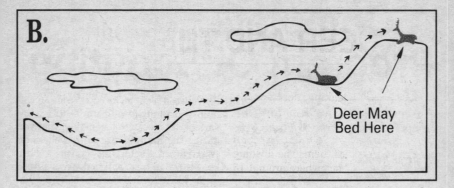

B.

Deer May
Bed Here

Whitetails prefer to bed on slightly higher ground when the terrain permits.Consequently, when they move down-slope toward their feeding area in the afternoon, they experience ideal wind coverage on their trails with the thermal air currents still moving upslope.

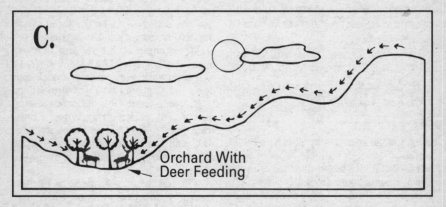

C.

Orchard With
Deer Feeding

When returning to their bedding areas in the morning, whitetails take advantage of ideal wind coverage with the downwind thermal air currents still holding from the higher elevations to the lower ground.

Tips for Judging Wind Speeds:

* **Calm, less than 1 mph** — Smoke rises vertically, leaves on tree remain motionless.
* **1 to 3 mph** — Smoke drifts but wind vanes stay motionless.
* **7 to 10 mph** — Flags extend and leaves are in constant motion.
* **11 to 16 mph** — Small branches move, dust blows and loose paper flies.
* **17 to 21 mph** — Noticeable motion in tall tree tops, and small trees with leaves sway.
* **22 to 27 mph** — Large branches in motion, whistling in wires.
* **28 to 47 mph** — Tar paper pulls off your shack's roof, and whole trees are in motion.

A Complete Program Of Scouting

For some people, deer hunting brings enjoyment throughout the year, not just during the archery and firearms hunts.

In summer, hunters keep tabs on the locations and types of foods that will attract deer during the hunting seasons. In the pre-season, they scout their prime areas, trying to pinpoint where deer will be in a few short days.

If they aren't successful early in the hunt, they continue scouting, knowing that good hunters adapt to changes in deer patterns.

After the season, successful or not, these hunters are back in the woods, piecing together the puzzle that will form next year's hunt.

Although secretive by nature, all wild animals leave identifiable signs of their presence. White-tailed deer leave many types of sign: some dramatic, some more subtle. By finding and understanding deer sign, you can determine patterns to deer activity and plan your hunting strategy accordingly. Deer tell stories with the sign they leave, and it's satisfying to read these stories.

Of course, deer leave sign year round, and the most successful hunters study this sign year round. Scouting trips in winter and spring, for example, enable a hunter to choose his future stand sites with confidence.

In-season scouting remains just as important. Scrapes, rubs, deer droppings and new trails will help you hone in on certain deer, perhaps that trophy buck you saw feeding in alfalfa fields on late summer evenings.

This complete program of scouting will help you identify and understand the various types of deer sign that you find during the hunting season as well as on year-round scouting trips. This knowledge, in turn, will make your future visits to the deer forest more enjoyable and productive.

DEER TRACKS

Deer tracks tell stories. The observant hunter learns to read and interpret these stories as nature's sign language.

Few subjects stir as much debate among hunters as does the study of deer tracks and its bearing on the sex of a deer who left those tracks in the woodland.

While some scientists and hunters point to studies that demonstrate conclusive differences between buck and doe tracks, others do not believe deer tracks alone are reliable indicators of sex.

The only positive way to tell a buck track from a doe track is to see the deer who made it. However, there are other clues to help you make a reasonable guess.

The actual size and shape of deer tracks taken in conjunction with other trail sign aids in determining sex of deer.

Drag Marks — How Reliable Are They?

Bucks typically do not raise their feet as far above the ground as does when walking. As a result, drag marks frequently accompany the tracks of bucks when there is a light covering of snow — less than two inches. In deep snow, however, all deer tracks show drag marks, and therefore, the drag marks no longer provide a clue as to the deer's sex. Sick, weak and wounded animals also leave drag marks. Through experience, you learn to detect disturbances in leaf litter.

Depth of Hoof Prints

Because mature bucks carry the weight of their antlers and a swollen neck during the rut, they place more weight on their front hooves than does. As a result, their front hooves spread more and show more wear than the front hooves of does. Heavy bucks therefore make deeper impressions with the tips of the toes. But also remember that in most areas of the country, most bucks are shot as yearlings. Few bucks grow old enough and large enough to leave these distinctive tracks. There are probably more big does than big bucks where most of us hunt. So the larger tracks may very well belong to does!

What Is A Deer Hoof?

Deer actually walk on their toenails. On a single hoof, the two larger halves represent the third and fourth toenails, which have slowly enlarged to their present size through the process of evolution. Most hunters will refer to these as "toes." The dewclaws represent the second and fifth toes, which over time shrank in size and assumed a position to the rear. Dewclaws are auxiliary weight-bearing units that aid the animal when running at a rapid gait. They show up in the tracks of heavy deer when walking on soft ground or snow and are almost always present in the tracks of running deer. A spread toe print means a heavy deer, not necessarily a buck. Shape of the hoof itself does not always have definite bearing on the sex of the deer, as deer hooves have individual characteristics just like the fingerprints of man.

Hard, rocky ground contributes to wearing off of the toe. Swamp areas allow the hoof to remain more pointed. White-tailed deer living on softer soils, in clay and sand, exhibit longer and more pointed hooves. Generally, the more rounded the toe, the older the deer.

Differences in tracks between the sexes are slight when young and become more definite with age. As a rule, the tracks of a male are one-fifth larger than those of a mature female of the same species. Thus, buck tracks are 1) longer, 2) deeper, and 3) broader in proportion than the tracks of does.

The prints of an exceptional buck are prominently longer and deeper than the tracks of a typical doe. Likewise, the prints of a very large doe are generally larger than the tracks of an average buck.

Deer Numbers By Tracks

Can total deer numbers be estimated by total numbers of deer tracks? Most scientists agree that many factors — including weather patterns, food availability and actual number of deer — contribute to the number and distribution of deer tracks made in an area. Therefore, a hard and fast correlation is not generally possible.

RUTTING SIGNPOSTS

When deer hunting season opens in early fall, you can hunt deer successfully by paying attention to natural patterns of movement between food sources and bedding areas. As the fall progresses and bucks start to prepare for the breeding season, deer activity becomes less predictable — though also more dramatic.

Many hunters concentrate their hardest efforts during the rut, when the biggest bucks seem to "come out of the woodwork."

Big bucks are more active during the rut than any other time of year: however, they don't throw all caution to the wind. Large bucks still pay attention to survival skills during the rut, and in heavily-hunted areas most rutting activity still occurs during the night.

The "peak" of the rut coincides with the period of actual breeding. Regional differences occur in timing of the peak. the peak can also vary within a state. East Texas deer breed about the second week of November; south Texas deer breed at the end of December. In parts of Georgia stocked originally with deer from Wisconsin, breeding occurs the second

Scouting

week in November. One state to the east, Alabama, deer breed the first week of January.

The actual breeding season of the whitetail may last for several months, depending on how many times the does come into estrus before they are bred. Generally, the months of November and December are when the majority of the breeding takes place, although females that become sexually mature while still fawns may be bred in January or February.

The beginning of the rut coincides with the shedding of velvet, as bucks are then capable of breeding. In general, the breeding season is known as "the" rut, while the term "in rut" is commonly applied to the male of the deer species. The reason for this is simple. Up until the time the does are ready to breed, they pretty much go about their normal routines. Bucks, on the other hand, seem impatient as they wait for the does to come into heat.

As the testosterone level in bucks increases, bucks become less tolerant of each other and the bachelor groups of summer begin to break up. Bucks become solitary travelers, wandering the limits of their range, investing more of their energy in preparation for the breeding season. The bucks become more and more aggressive, attacking small trees and saplings with their antlers, leaving visual signs and chemical messages of their dominance.

Two of the most visual signs of bucks in rut are rubs and scrapes. Finding this kind of sign is exciting. It tells you that bucks exist in an area, and it provides a clue as to where you'll likely see them.

Scrapes

A typical scrape is an area two to three feet in diameter where a buck has pawed away surface leaf litter to expose bare soil, which he then urinates on.

You can find fresh scrapes nearly year round, but the majority of scrapes occur as the breeding season of the white-tailed deer begins. As bucks become solitary travelers, scraping activity increases greatly. This occurs a few weeks before the first females breed.

A combination of factors causes this increased scraping, including increased testosterone production in the males, which is probably tied to seasonal changes in female scent as well as decreasing amount of daylight.

The primary purpose of the scrape is to attract breeding females. Does tend to travel in doe groups. The solitary breeding buck moves from one doe group to the next in search of receptive females, who are ready to breed. A buck leaves his calling card in the form of a scrape.

Most scrapes occur in a woods with an open understory, in contrast to rubs which are found in dense sapling growth. Bucks seem to cluster their scrapes in key areas, on the perimeters of or in corners of woods, where they draw the greatest attention from neighboring deer. Sometimes "lines" of scrapes occur along a buck's route of travel.

While pawing the scrape, the buck deposits scent from the interdigital glands between his toes. Usually bucks urinate on their scrapes, allowing the urine to flow over the tarsal glands located on the inside surface of his hind legs. This produces a pungent, musky odor that even humans can detect at considerable distances. In this way, does that visit the scrape learn the maker's identity and breeding readiness.

The "Licking Branch"

A "licking branch" accompanies virtually every scrape. Either a single branch or a clump of multi-branched stems, the licking branch extends directly above the pawed scrape. Bucks almost always break off the tip of the branch, sometimes leaving a dangling stem. As the broken branch dries out, it presumably holds scent better.

White-tailed bucks nibble, chew, lick,

sniff and thrash the overhanging branch above the scrape. They grasp it with their teeth and pull it down. They twist it and rake their antlers through it. They rub their forehead scent glands on it. The process is careful and deliberate — bordering on pure ecstasy. By licking their tarsal glands, on which they have urinated, bucks may transfer even more scent to the overhanding branches.

Does sometimes spray or scent mark the ground portion of the scrape, but it seems does are more active in depositing or detecting pheromones on the overhanging limbs. A pheromone is a chemical substance produced by a gland which serves as a stimulus for one or more behavioral responses within a given species.

It remains difficult to say which is more important, the scrape or the overhanging branch. From the amount of time deer spend working it, the overhanging branch may well be the more important component.

At any rate, the overhanding limb appears to be the most sensitive part of the scrape, serving as a focal point of communication for the whole herd rather than a territorial marker for just one buck. Further, the overhanging limb is actively used for a longer period of the year than the ground portion of the scrape. This activity may continue throughout the year.

The preorbital glands of a whitetailed deer, which have ducts at the corner of each eye, have received a lot of attention. For many years scientists and hunters thought these glands were the primary scent producers for marking overhead branches at scrapes. Currently we believe the preorbital gland serves as a tear duct.

Many hunters, as well as some deer researchers believe that scrapes also define the territory of a certain buck. Current research, however, points to more evidence that refutes this theory. Subordinate bucks, for example, will freshen the scrapes of a dominant buck, and several prime age bucks may also "share" a scrape, each visiting it at different times.

During one study in Missouri, bucks of different size or age classes were observed in a scrape together, performing one or more scrape-associated behaviors. No aggression or submissive posturing was observed, thus suggesting that deer are *not* territorial animals.

Some hunters and researchers believe that does attracted to a scrape will urinate in or near it, making sure to step in the deposited urine before leaving. Supposedly, when the buck revisits his scrape, he can tell through the urine's odor if the doe is in estrus and then scent-trail her. Solid scientific documentation of this behavior does not exist.

The fact remains, however, that bucks find out which does are in estrus by their visits to scrapes, and does remain in the vicinity of the scrapes so that a buck will be able to find them.

Therefore, hunting near active scrapes usually produces buck sightings.

BUCK RUBS

Buck rubs are not the result of velvet shedding, nor are they made because bucks are deliberately trying to polish their antlers. It's true that during the process of removing velvet, bucks do some rubbing on trees and saplings, but they usually complete this whole process within twenty-four hours.

Rising testosterone levels cause bucks to become more aggressive, which drives them to advertise themselves through scent marking. Essentially, this is the purpose of rubbing. In a strict sense, white-tailed deer are not territorial; however, rubs do serve to inform deer of the social hierarchy within a given area.

Buck rubs are part of the communication system of deer. We detect rubs — the white scars of the deer forest — by sight. More likely deer detect them by smell. When a buck rubs a sapling, he deposits scent from glands in the forehead, and he will also pause to actually lick the rubbed tree or sapling.

Scouting

Other bucks visit that rub to detect these pheromones, or chemical messages.

Bucks do not make rubs with their antler tines, but rather with the ridges on the base and burr of their antlers. As if using a vegetable shredder, the buck grates the bark from the tree into long strings, which he frequently eats.

When locating buck rubs while scouting, an important clue remains the diameter of the tree. It's true that large bucks will rub small trees, but rarely do small bucks rub large trees. So when you find a rub that stands out in terms of tree size, you can be pretty certain it was made by a big buck. Also keep in mind that the scrapes of a buck will generally be found within 100 to 200 yards of his rubs.

Generally, small bucks do not make many rubs. Large bucks prevent small bucks from breeding, so small bucks have little need to advertise their presence. The more dominant a buck, the more active his forehead scent glands and the more rubs he makes.

The rubs of a dominant buck serve as signposts to inform other bucks of who is "the boss" in a certain area. The companions of the dominant buck will freely travel the same range; however, they heed the warnings the lead male posts and act submissively whenever he's in the immediate vicinity.

Studies show that an individual buck may make 500 or more rubs in a single season. The 100 to 300 figure, however, is probably more common. Still, this amounts to at least one or more rubs per day over a four month period for the average buck. It is not unusual to see forty or fifty buck rubs in a small area, in a stand of young, even-aged timber such as aspen.

Regardless of where you find the white-tailed deer, bucks seem to prefer saplings with a strong resinous sap above all others. Pine remains a favorite softwood species for rubbing as well as cedar, tamarack and balsam. In hardwoods, black cherry and apple are common targets for rubs. Bucks also rub wooden fence posts and power line poles.

Bucks often return to the same tree for rubbing, and the same tree may be rubbed several times over a period of years. Some of the smaller saplings die after the first rubbing, but many trees survive the first and subsequent wounds.

Breeding rubs differ entirely in their appearance from rubs made in early fall. These savage rubs, the white scars of the deer forest, frequently damage or kill bushes, branches and roots in and around the main target.

Look for an area with a high density of breeding rubs, for being in an area with big rubs results in seeing big bucks. Watch particularly for areas that exhibit vigorous rubbing activity over a period of many years in the same small spots.

DEER TRAILS

Deer biologists generally define deer trails as distinct and pronounced paths or runways in the low-lying vegetation caused by repeated use. Deer hunters often use the words "runway" and "crossings" interchangeably, but they are not quite the same thing.

A runway is a well-defined path: a crossing a limited area through which deer are likely to pass through. Another term for crossing is "funnel" or "bottleneck." Natural features in the landscape, such as a steep ravine, as well as man-made features (a road, gravel pit, fence or farm field) that impede free movement of deer create funnels.

Deer typically move into the wind;

Duration of Various Activities		
	Spring/Summer	Autumn/Winter
Feeding	6 Hours	7 Hours
Cudding	6 Hours	7 Hours
Bedding	6 Hours	5 Hours
Sleeping	4 Hours	2 Hours
Movement	2 Hours	3 Hours

Reprinted from Richard Prior, **The Roe Deer of Cranborne Chase** (London, 1968)

therefore, most trails are used one-way. When the wind shifts, deer use different trails.

Deer generally follow the path of least resistance, and a route free from obstruction improves efficiency. Deer trails cross through heavy and inaccessible terrain at the most convenient places. Often a hunter trying to find a way through thick brush or up steep terrain unconsciously finds himself traveling a deer trail.

With the exception of the rut, most major deer trails contain the movement pattern of does, fawns and yearling bucks. Adult bucks avoid these trails most of the year. Their trails often parallel the distinct, major trails, twenty to thirty yards away.

A study in the spring of 1977 conducted by *Deer & Deer Hunting* magazine produced some interesting results pertaining to deer trails. The study involved electronic monitoring of deer trails as well as actual field observations. The following ten general rules emerged:

1. Some trails are one-way; others employ two-way traffic.

2. Deer use major trails throughout the year while using minor trails at varying times of the year, depending on the availability of food.

3. Deer commonly use one trail to a feeding area and a second trail when leaving.

4. Deer generally use certain trails only at specific times of day.

5. Few deer trails are used at the same time of day throughout the year.

6. Trails being used regularly in late summer may see very little use as fall begins and food supplies change.

7. There are distinct morning trails and evening trails.

8. There are generally four basic types of trails that exist in all hunting terrain: highway trails, feeding trails, bedding trails, and escape trails.

9. Deer trails remain a primary consideration regardless of your method of hunting (stand hunting, still hunting, or driving).

10. Always ask yourself these questions about trails: Why are they being used? When are they being used? How often are they being used?

Locating Deer Trails

Spring scouting provides a good time to locate deer trails. The deer trail meltdown in spring results in the unique opportunity for you to distinctly see, for a very short time, white, ice-packed trails in sharp contrast against the rest of the mud-covered forest floor.

When you find a well-worn deer trail, study the relationship between the trail and nearest bedding locations and food sources. Generally, the closer you can approach the bedding area, the better for stand placement.

In areas of heavy grass where you cannot find trails worn into the ground, you can often find body-width trails where the deer have broken down foliage such as goldenrod or ferns.

In more open country, or on harder ground where deer trails are not easily discernible, wide saddles on a ridge top often emerge as major runways. Even in perfectly "flat" country, contours exist that the deer cross or follow.

In the bottomlands of the east Texas piney woods, for example, a three- or four-foot difference in elevation constitutes a "ridge." The deer may use trails that flank these ridges or cross them as a site where there are preferred foods, such as a grove of acorn-producing white or post oak.

A very good way to locate deer trails is to follow a barbed-wire fence. Look for places where deer have been crossing it. Often, deer leave clumps of hair on the barbs at these crossings.

Look for places in the fence where the middle or top strand of wire is down or missing. A hunter would naturally cross a fence at these places, and deer also choose this same path of least resistance. From a crossing, follow the trail in either direction. Or simply begin hunting close to where the deer have crossed the fence line, for that location serves as a "funnel."

Apparently, fence posts and lines serve as natural routes of travel for deer, as deer trails often run parallel to fences for great distances at a time. This explains why we frequently find shed antlers along fence lines and why we recover wounded deer along fence lines as well. Trophy bucks will also use wooded fence posts for rubs. Evidently a stout post provides the resistance a big buck requires.

Eight Ways to Distinguish a Buck Trail from a Doe Trail.

1) Presence of rubs near the trail.

2) Presence of scrapes on or near the trail.

3) Distance of tracks from the centerline. Heavy-bodied bucks show a marked tendency to walk with their front hooves wider apart than yearling bucks and does.

4) Pointing outward of toes from centerline of tracks. Bucks show an inclination to "toe out" with their front hooves as their toes turn out from centerline; does keep their toes pointed more in the line of travel.

5) The lagging back of the hind hoof, in contrast to the superimposing of the hind hoof over the track the front hoof left.

6) Drag marks in leaf litter or light snow. All deer leave drag marks in deep snow.

7) The tendency of bucks to stay in heavy cover.

8) The tendency of a buck movement to be more purposeful and more direct. Bucks walk in a straight line; does meander.

DEER BEDS

Deer beds are oval-shaped depressions in grass, leaves, soft dirt or snow and are easy to recognize. Many beds are only used once, though beds in the prime, most concealed locations probably see intermittent use. Usually, whitetails return to the same general bedding area,

even if they shift their actual beds around.

It is not known how long deer actually sleep or whether deer sleep at all. Deer sometimes will lay their heads back on a flank or hind leg, their eye lids will droop and total alertness will be lost. For practical purposes, this is sleep. But there are other reasons why deer lie down, other than to sleep.

Cud chewing represents one basic reason why deer bed down. They also bed down to conserve energy.

Deer are herbivorous cud-chewing animals related to cattle and sheep. They need to eat large amounts of food as quickly as possible so that they can return to the safety of thick cover. Once in their beds, deer are able to regurgitate small packages of food, re-chew it and then swallow and digest it in a leisurely manner. Deer spend from six to seven hours a day chewing their cud, although they rarely spend more than twenty minutes consecutively in the cud-chewing process.

Deer that bed down in a snow storm will likely remain bedded, if undisturbed, until the storm passes, even if the storm lasts for several days. Snow can literally bury them, yet deer remain perfectly warm. The insulating qualities of their coats prevents snow that falls on them from melting, and the covering of snow acts as additional insulation.

Deer bed down for as long as an hour and a half at a time. Few systematic observations exist on the actual proportions of the day in which deer spend bedding. The more time deer have to spend traveling from a food source to a bedding ground will influence how long they bed. Undisturbed deer frequently bed near their food supply, such as in oak woods producing acorns, or in cornfields. Deer that are pushed seek more secluded spots and may spend more time in transit.

When preparing to lie down, deer frequently circle and often scrape with the forefoot on the selected spot. In winter, deer often try to scrape away snow to get down to leaves or grass.

Weather and terrain greatly influence a deer's selection of a bedding place. During summer months, deer seek protection from extreme heat and pesky insects by lying in water. During the winter, whitetails seek shelter from cold winds in swamps and low-lying thickets. In the fall, standing cornfields provide excellent concealment for bedded whitetails.

In general, whitetails prefer high ground, such as knolls and ridges, where they can be sure of detecting the approach of danger well in advance of its arrival. They also frequently bed just under the crest of a hill rather than on top, where the wind is less steady. They rely heavily on sound and smell, rather than sight, to herald the approach of a hunter. Actually, they use their bedding cover as a blind to slip out of existence.

Family groups tend to have their own special places for bedding. Does, yearlings, and fawns will bed within a few feet of each other. Mature bucks frequently bed in small patches of cover, little hideouts that are overlooked by many deer hunters. A big old buck can live to old age by bedding in cover that looks less than ideal.

Generalizations About Deer Beds

1) Bed counts fail as a method for measuring deer populations.

2) While deer do not necessarily use the same bed twice, they do tend to bed down in the same area. The area varies with the seasons.

3) Adult bucks are frequently the first to bed down in the morning, but mature bucks are the least likely to establish patterns to their bedding.

4) The pattern formed by a group of deer when bedding is random.

5) Deer examine a site thoroughly before bedding down.

6) Deer seek sunny spots and change beds to stay in the sun.

7) Deer seek sheltered bedding sites in strong winds.

8) Deer maintain a major rest period during the middle of the day.

9) Bucks apparently urinate in their beds immediately after rising.

10) Deer normally defecate shortly after rising from their beds. Droppings can be found in the beds and on the edges.

11) Deer commonly change their positions at least once in a three or four-hour rest period.

12) Bedding activity increases during the winter months and occurs during the greater part of the night. Three long bedding periods interspersed with shorter feeding periods frequently characterize nighttime activity during the winter months. The first period is generally longer than the other two.

13) Bedding habits are not uniformly regular.

DEER DROPPINGS

Deer droppings frequently represent the only or principal sign indicating the presence of deer. Aside from seeing the deer itself deer droppings afford us the most definitive information of the deer's habitats, food and whereabouts.

The deer bean might just be the best scouting tool the hunter has, being especially useful for spring scouting because pellets deposited since leaf-fall can be identified as such. They verify whether a bedding area is being used. They make tracks easier to follow.

Deer droppings give you an idea of the activity of the maker. When an animal stands still, his pellets will be found in piles; when deer move, the pellets will be strung out. If you find fresh, but cold pellets in the morning, you can assume the deer fed at night. If they are warm, the maker is probably not far from you.

Whitetails defecate approximately twenty-five times a day, according to new research presented at the Twelfth Annual Meeting of the Southeast Deer Study Group in February 1989.

The number of pellets per defecation varies from forty to more than 300. If you locate pellets, there are deer in the area.

Although some deer trails will cross sections of bare earth, leaving tracks for you to study, one of the best signs of deer usage revolves around an abundance of fresh droppings.

Deer droppings vary a great deal in shape, color and form at different times of the year. During the winter months, when deer feed or browse, the pellets are hard and become harder as the winter advances; they are various shades of brown and about three-quarters of an inch long.

During the summer months, when deer feed on soft vegetation, the droppings consist of clusters of pellets that are more or less stuck together in one mass — linked one to another in bead fashion, although they occasionally remain separate at this time of the year as well. Fresh pellets during the summer acquire a greenish hue; they tend to glisten and are quite soft inside.

In other words, the form of deer dung depends upon the relative succulence of the seasonal food: when deer are on green succulent feed, the pellets are shapeless and often congealed; on winter dry feed, they are dark, hard and oblong. The form also depends upon the length of time the material remains in the colon. The longer it is held there, the more consolidated and elongated the pellet.

Bedding areas contain a high concentration of deer droppings, for most defecation occurs shortly after a deer rises from its bed. If undisturbed, deer take plenty of time to get up and stretch before leaving their beds, so many pellets are left in or very near the edge of the bed. More droppings accompany nighttime beds than daytime beds. In contrast, a clean bed, especially if it's still warm, may indicate that you jumped a deer.

At least one well-know naturalist, Olaus Murie, believed that we could determine the sex of the deer from the shape of the pellet. he hinted at this in an illustration of mule deer droppings in his excellent book, *A Field Guide to Animal Tracks.*

Some hunters also believe that deer droppings increase in size with the age of the animal. There is no consensus of scientific information, however, on this subject.

Further, physical appearance in itself is not an accurate way to determine their origin. In areas where several species of deer and other ruminants overlap, biologists determine which species droppings come from through pH analysis. Not too many hunters, however, are going to carry a pH kit in their day pack!

Are the Droppings Fresh?

It is fairly easy to determine if droppings are fresh, and this is an important skill to learn.

Fresh pellets take on a bronze hue, a moist varnished appearance, and they mash easily. When you find them squeeze them!

Old pellets lose this luster and mash with more difficulty. The pellets dry from the outside in; thus the thicker the outside dry layer, the older the pellet. Consider the effect of weather on droppings. Immediately after a rain, all droppings appear fresh at first glance, but many are not.

Pellets deposited under dry conditions harden and persist in an unchanged condition for as long as two to five years. Two year old pellets tend to crack and have a rough outer surface; they appear dull and lusterless. One year old pellets on the other hand, exhibit a smooth shiny outer surface. They are brown to black in color and are not embedded in the soil. Older pellets tend to embed in the soil.

The dung beetle probably assumes final responsibility for destroying droppings, although one deer biologist in New Zealand reports that mountain parrots eat deer droppings as well. Pick up a few droppings and put them in your scent box, to help mask human odor on your clothing and hunting equipment.

❖ SHOT PLACEMENT ❖

The Broadside Shot

The Straight-On Shot

The Angling-Away Shot

> *Making quick, certain kills should be the top priority once a hunter decides to shoot a deer.*

Making quick, certain kills should be the top priority once a hunter decides to shoot a deer. Consistent one-shot kills require marksmanship, knowledge of deer anatomy, and a true-shooting rifle or bow.

The best shot for archers and firearms hunters is one that angles forward through the deer's chest cavity. These shots leave the most room for error. Broadside shots through the chest are equally deadly, but the target area is smaller than quartering-away shots.

Whatever the weapon, deer shot through the heart or lungs drop fairly quickly. This results in a well-bled carcass and a minimum of ruined meat.

To kill a deer almost instantly, however, firearms hunters should aim for the shoulder blade unless they're using light bullets and small-caliber rifles. A bullet through the middle of the shoulder blade will almost certainly break the spine, causing instant unconsciousness and paralysis. The deer drops in its tracks and expires quickly, unable to breathe or move its legs.

The shoulder-blade shot results in a modest loss of meat, but this must be weighed against the likelihood of losing the entire animal because of poor tracking conditions, darkness or other factors.

A GOOD DEER WATCHER

By Richard Prior

Deer study, no matter what your particular field may be, becomes more and more fascinating as experience builds up. If by degrees you find that you can think like the deer, anticipating their movements and trying to understand their way of life, it will become a challenging battle of wits — human brains matched against their finer senses. Never forget the consideration which these lovely animals are due. To us it is just a hobby — to them a life or death struggle for survival in a very hostile world. Much of their ability to survive stems from their ability to watch us without our being aware, and to act accordingly. A good deer watcher should always try to do the same.

WEATHER & DEER

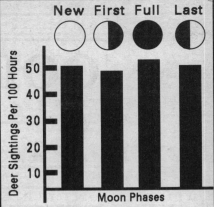

In The Moonlight

Deer Sightings Vs. Places Of The Moon
Al Hofacker. 1981. *"The Lunar Cycle and Deer Activity."* Deer & Deer Hunting 4(6):4.

Comparison of daily deer activity during the light and dark phases of the moon as indicated by the average movement of seven deer within two-hour intervals from July to December 1973

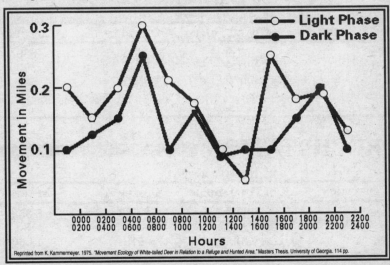

Reprinted from K. Kammermeyer. 1975. "Movement Ecology of White-tailed Deer in Relation to a Refuge and Hunted Area." Masters Thesis. University of Georgia. 114 pp.

WIND

Observed and expected deer for differing wind velocity.

Wind Velocity	% of Total Hours	Observed	Expected*
Calm	8.2	877	810
Light	44.9	4,943	4,437
Moderate	28.1	2,548	2,777
Gusty	12.2	977	1,206
Strong	6.6	537	537

*Expected Values = % of Total Hours x Total Deer Observed

Observed and expected bucks for differing wind velocity.

Wind Velocity	% of Total Hours	Observed	Expected*
Calm	8.2	105	120
Light	44.9	769	658
Moderate	28.1	361	412
Gusty	12.2	128	179
Strong	6.6	103	97

*Expected Values = % of Total Hours x Total Bucks Observed

CLOUD COVER

Observed and expected deer for varying cloud cover.

Cloud Cover	% of Total Hours	Observed	Expected*
Clear	41.9	4,541	4,217
Partly Cloudy	21.9	2,112	2,204
Overcast	36.2	3,411	3,643

*Expected Values = % of Total Hours x Total Deer Observed

Observed and expected bucks for varying cloud cover.

Cloud Cover	% of Total Hours	Observed	Expected*
Clear	41.9	665	630
Partly	21.9	324	330
Cloudy	36.2	525	544
Overcast			

*Expected Values = % of Total Hours x Total Bucks Observed

PRECIPITATION

Observed and expected deer for precipitation.

Precipitation	% of Total Hours	Observed	Expected*
None	82.6	8,588	8,358
Fog	1.8	99	180
Rain	10.5	919	1,060
Snow**	5.2	515	523

*Expected Values = % of Total Hours x Total Deer Observed
**Snow includes snow (4.9%), sleet (0.2%), and hail (0.1%)

Observed and expected bucks for precipitation.

Wind Velocity	% of Total Hours	Observed	Expected*
None	82.6	1,265	1,246
Fog	1.8	16	27
Rain	10.5	159	158
Snow**	5.2	69	78

*Expected Values = % of Total Hours x Total Bucks Observed
**Snow includes snow (4.9%), sleet (0.2%), and hail (0.1%)

THE WIND CHILL FACTOR

ACTUAL THERMOMETER READING (F°)

| 50 | 40 | 30 | 20 | 10 | 0 | -10 | -20 | -30 | -40 |

EQUIVALENT TEMPERATURE (F°)

	50	40	30	20	10	0	-10	-20	-30	-40
Calm	50	40	30	20	10	0	-10	-20	-30	-40
5	48	37	27	16	6	-5	-15	-26	-36	-47
10	40	28	16	4	-9	-21	-33	-46	-58	-70
15	36	22	9	-5	-18	-36	-45	-58	-72	-85
20	32	18	4	-10	-25	-39	-53	-67	-82	-96
25	30	16	0	-15	-29	-44	-59	-74	-88	-104
30	28	13	-2	-18	-33	-44	-63	-79	-94	-109
35	27	11	-4	-20	-35	-49	-67	-82	-98	-113
40	26	10	-6	-21	-37	-53	-69	-85	-100	-116

Over 40 MPH (little added effect)	LITTLE DANGER (for properly clothed person)	INCREASING DANGER	GREAT DANGER
		(Danger from freezing of exposed flesh)	

CELSIUS CONVERSION CHART

°C (Celsius)	°F (Fahrenheit)	K(Kelvin)
-40	-40	233
-35	-31	238
-30	-22	243
-25	-13	248
-20	- 4	253
-15	+ 5	258
-10	14	263
- 5	23	268
0	32	273
5	41	278
10	50	283
15	59	288
20	68	293
25	77	298
30	86	303
35	95	308
40	104	313
45	113	318
50	122	323

❖ AFTER THE SHOT ❖

A. Broken Fore Leg

B. Broken Hind Leg

The tracks left by wounded deer offer clues to the wound's location.

Deer with a broken foreleg (**A**) or a broken hind leg (**B**) will leave drag marks. The lower a leg is broken, the more pronounced the drag mark.

Deer shot through the intestines, liver (**C**) or lungs will often leave tracks that are bunched in twos.

A cross jump track (**D**) results from a bullet through the intestines or liver with the animal standing broadside to the shooter.

C. Bullet through Lungs, Liver or Intestines

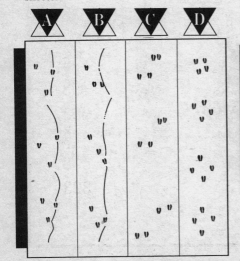

D. Bullet through Intestines or Liver

❖ DEER HAIR ❖ IDENTIFICATION

Most color differences in hair are found near the tips. Other noteworthy differences are thickness, straightness and length. Remember that hair you examine may have been cut short by a bullet or broadhead.

Heart: The heart is covered by long, fine hairs 3.5 to 4 inches long with fine black tips leading to tan or brown for a half-inch or more, with the rest gray.

Front leg, outside: Hairs will be fine and 1.5 inches long, with black-brown color and black tips. Neck hairs are similar except base will be more gray with leg hairs slightly lighter. Neck hairs will be 1.75 inches long.

Shoulder: Shoulder hairs are about 2.5 inches long with black tips and band of brown below, followed by a band of black and continuing with gray the rest of the length.

Paunch: Hairs are 2.5 to 2.75 inches long. Most of the coloring is whitish-gray rather than gray. Hair will have black tips with a band of brown below.

Chest: Chest hairs are fine and about 2.25 inches long with black and tan tips with the rest whitish gray. They're similar to lower side hairs except they're longer and not as fine.

Brisket: Wavy hair 1.5 to 2 inches long with black tips. The rest are whitish-gray.

Hind leg, upper ham: Wavy, hollow hairs 1.75 to 2 inches long, black and brown at the tip, changing to gray and whitish-gray at the base.

Neck (side): Short fine hairs 1.75 inches long, similar to those on the outside of the front legs. Black-brown with black tips and gray base. Front leg hairs will have a lighter colored base.

TRACKING GUIDE

The myth of the waiting game.

REASONS FOR WAITING

1. Deer will lie down and "stiffen up."

2. Hunter needs pipeful of tobacco.

3. Deer will get the "blind staggers."

REASONS FOR NOT WAITING

1. It's snowing.
2. It's raining.
3. You're in an area of high hunter density.
4. Darkness is approaching and you can't hunt in the morning.
5. Tracking takes place freely in warm weather.
6. Deer bleed freely in warm weather.
7. Trailing wounded deer with dogs permitted in the area you hunt.
8. Rigor mortis does not occur until three to six hours after death.
9. A running deer has three times the heart rate of a bedded deer.
10. Movement creates greater and more rapid blood loss, thus inhibiting coagulation.

❖ HOW FAR WILL A DEER TRAVEL ❖ WHEN HIT THROUGH THE HEART?

Every fall around the evening fires in the deer camps the old question has come up as to how it is possible for a deer to run from fifty to 200 yards after his heart had been perforated by a bullet. We all know he does this but to date no answer has really explained how. We usually wound up the evening in agreement on but two points: 1) The deer should drop when circulation ceases and the brain "suffocates." This should happen almost immediately after the heart is perforated, for, of course, it is taken for granted the heart stops instantly. 2) As we know deer have run 200 yards after a heart shot, this explanation cannot be true and there is something phony about it somewhere. So the question has never been logically answered as far as the deer hunters are concerned.

Then, on October 31, 1928, murderer John W. Deering was placed before a stone wall in Utah State Prison with an electro cardiograph attached to his person. He was outwardly calm. The prison doctor placed a target over his heart. Five picked riflemen fired at that target at short range and four bullets simultaneously pierced his heart. Yet Deering's heart did not stop when pierced by four bullets but continued to beat for 15.6 seconds thereafter. The cardiograph record also showed that a few moments before the shots were fired, through fear, Deering's heart beats, normally seventy-two per minute, were increased to 180 per minute.

Now I cannot say that the effect of a heart shot on a deer and a man are in any way similar. But let us see what would happen if we suppose this might have a bearing on the deer question. If the deer is frightened before the shot, his heart beats would increase tremendously, also increasing circulation of blood to the brain and muscles. And how far would he run in the 15.6 seconds before his heart stopped? At Anticosti Island I timed a mature white-tailed deer over a measured course with a stopwatch. It was shot at but purposely missed. Its speed was eighteen miles per hour. The highest speed when another deer was fully extended and had to run, was about thirty miles per hour. At eighteen miles per hour, the deer could travel 137 yards in 15.6 seconds. At twenty-five miles per hour the deer could travel about 152 yards. At thirty miles per hour the deer could travel about 229 yards. Doesn't it sound to you a little bit as if John Deering may have solved the riddle and that the deer's heart does not stop when perforated?

— *William Monypeny Newsom*

Maps of wounded deer behavior

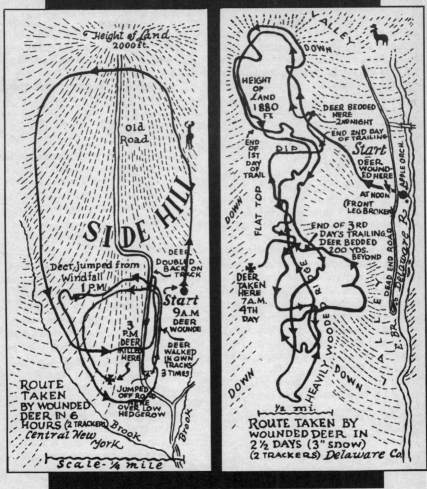

These maps of wounded deer behavior indicate the complex nature of the problem: **(1)** Deer will often double back and backtrack. **(2)** They will walk in their own tracks for considerable distances. **(3)** They will travel in a circular direction, frequently crossing their own trails. These examples also suggest that wounded deer will stay in their home range unless pushed terribly hard. Note that in both cases the trackers retrieved the deer quite close to where the animals were shot.

Tracking

Responsibilities

Anyone who hunts has a responsibility to the game pursued, to the person or persons who own the land, to other hunters and to him or herself. A good hunter tries to learn all that is possible about the species hunted. Shots should be planned and carefully taken and if a hit is made the game should be trailed until found or until it is reasonable to believe it was not vitality hit. Once the game is found it should be properly handled so it will not be wasted. This ranges from correct field dressing to preparation of the meat and/or the trophy.

Hunters should consider the landowner by treating the landowner as a friend, and the land as if it were their own home. Mutual consideration between hunters and landowners can do much to keep hunting available.

Hunters are conspicuous because of their clothes, hunting devices, and other features. For this reason it is important to realize that the behavior of one hunter will be identified with all hunters. Good field behavior and courtesy will reflect well on the whole sport. Discourteous, illegal and irresponsible behavior of one or a few individuals can prejudice people against all hunters. Realize that hunters are in the minority in this country and that many people who are not hunters are watching. The future laws on hunting and hunting devices may depend on these people. Act accordingly.

There are several procedures recommended when a hit is made on a big game animal.

❖ After a shot, stay put and try to remember where the hit was made on the animal. Wounded deer usually run with their tail down.

❖ Take compass readings on the last sighting and/or sound of the game. If no compass is available, carefully note direction the animal traveled.

❖ With binoculars check the details of the place where the game was last seen. Try to identify some land mark to aid in locating correct trail.

❖ Wait for at least an hour before starting to trail. Wait at least six hours before starting to trail an animal hit in the guts, weather and circumstances permitting. Gut-shot animals almost always die from the wound. Gut-shot animals often "hump" their back when hit.

❖ A string tracking device attached to the bow and arrow is sometimes useful in recovering game. However the string does affect the arrow flight on long shots so practice is required.

When the trailing begins:

❖ Move to the place where the animal was standing at the time of the shot and check for blood, arrow, hair or other signs to verify a hit. Trail very quietly. Avoid talking. Use hand signals or soft whistles if with companion.

❖ Even if there is no blood, mark the beginning of the trail with survey-ors tape or other easily visible material, placed high enough to be easily seen from a distance. All tape should be removed once the animal is found or the trail is lost. Some people use colored crepe paper or toilet paper to mark a trail.

❖ Move in the direction the animal travelled checking constantly for blood sign. When first blood is found mark the location with tape. Note location of blood; i.e., in a foot print, on bushes, grasses or other vertical objects, right or left side of trail, etc. See special note on blood sign.

- Look for different or abnormal scuff marks or hoof prints that would identify a wounded animal.

- If trailing alone, mark location of every blood sign until the quantity becomes so great that there is no need for further marking or the sign disappears.

- Be careful not to disturb the trail and sign by staying just to the side.

- If trailing with another person, mark occasional blood sign locations to give direction of travel. The person who locates sign stays put while partner looks for next sign.

- Three people should be the maximum number trailing. Even with this number, trailing should be silent.

- If the blood trail is lost make sure the last blood sign is conspicuously marked. From this point check all main trail lanes or trails for at least half a mile.

- If no more blood sign shows on trails come back to last sign and start walking in concentric circles outward around the last sign. Animals often double back on a trail or stagger off of regular trails shortly before they die.

- Some people have difficulty walking circles, particularly on varying levels of ground. Another method of search is to walk a grid pattern using compass readings: if the grid is tight, 3 to 5 feet in grass and brush, this a good method of searching for more blood signs or a downed animal.

- If no blood or animal can be found but you feel the hit was a lethal one sit down and listen. Often crows, ravens, magpies or jays will be attracted to a downed animal. Listen for their calls.

- Game, after being hit, will often circle back to where it came from. If there is a problem locating a good blood sign, check along the trail on which the animal first appeared.

- Check all major crossing points on human trails, back roads or stream banks for possible sign.

- Vitally hit animals often go down hill rather than climb.

- Be sure to check in streams or swamps for a downed deer if the trail leads in that direction. Gut-shot animals become thirsty and often head towards water.

- Heart-shot animals may travel surprising distances and show little external bleeding.

- Deer, particularly in northern areas, have thick layers of tallow along the back and below the brisket. This can plug wounds preventing a good blood trail. Avoid straight-down shots from tree stands for this reason.

- Do not start to follow big game hit in the gut for six to eight hours if day light permits.

- An exception to the rule about waiting before starting to trail a wounded deer is when the hunter knows the only hit was in the leg. If the animals is kept walking the wound may stay open.

- If there is a threat of rain or snow then it may be necessary to start trailing sooner than preferred. Always trail quietly, even more than when stalking uninjured game.

- In blood trailing sometimes it is necessary to actually rub reddish spots with the fingers to verify that it is not just autumn colors on a leaf. Sometimes getting down to almost ground level will help a hunter spot blood sign that otherwise might be missed.

- When blood trailing, look at specific objects such as stones, twigs and leaves, rather than the whole trail.

Women are often excellent at trailing because they notice detail and fewer are color blind.

❖ Practice blood trailing on a simulated trail with artificial blood.

❖ Near populated areas remove viscera as well as deer from woods. Rotting guts are poor public relations.

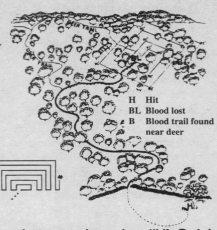

H	Hit
BL	Blood lost
B	Blood trail found near deer

Types of Blood Sign

❖ Blood that is frothy with bubbles usually indicates a lung hit.

❖ Very dark blood may indicate a liver or kidney hit.

❖ Blood mixed with vegetable material often greenish in color indicates a "gut" or viscera shot.

❖ Blood with bubbles may indicate a neck hit where the arrow has cut the neck arteries and windpipe. The arrow may show almost no sign of blood.

❖ Blood in spattered pattern may indicate a rapidly moving animal or one in which major blood vessels have been cut.

❖ Blood on both sides of the trail usually indicates a pass-through wound. In some instances a one-opening wound may produce this sign if the animal doubles back on trail.

❖ The height of blood sign is an indication of wound location.

❖ Blood spatter drops usually point direction of travel of a rapidly moving animal like the fingers of a hand.

❖ No blood sign doesn't always mean a miss. Bleeding may be internal.

Increasing the "L" Grid

❖ Pick a length unit (e.g. 10 paces)

❖ Walk ahead this distance, looking for sign of deer.

❖ Make a right corner turn and search the same distance. This completes the first "L."

❖ Now make another right angle, turn and search two lengths (20 paces).

❖ Turn again (always to the right) and search two lengths again, completing "L" #2.

❖ Turn again to start "L" #3, which will be three lengths (30 paces) on both sides.

❖ Continue making "L", each one unit longer than the last.

❖ Continue enlarging the grid unit the game is found or the trail is definitely lost.

❖ Another effective search pattern, also using the compass, is the U-shape. However this would miss deer that back-track.

- ❖ If a hit is made late in the day, and the weather is cool, wait until morning, unless there are a lot of coyotes, wild dogs, raccoons or bears around that might destroy the game.

- ❖ If a late hit is made and there is a threat of rain or snow get good lights, gas or kerosene lantern, leave the bows or guns in camp or vehicle and trail the game. Sometimes it is even easier to trail at night. Be sure to mark trail for two reasons. If the blood trail is lost, there's a better chance of locating it again if tape is tied in conspicuous spots. Also it is very easy to get lost at night while trailing. A well-marked trail will at least get the hunter back to where the trailing started. Reflector tape is a good addition for night trailing.

- ❖ If there is no blood, look for compressed or disturbed leaves or vegetation.

- ❖ Look for flattened plants with leading edge disturbed. Deer prints are usually narrow and tapered, even in leaves and grass. A running deer tends to scatter leaves to the side of the trail.

Approaching Down Game

When game is found approach cautiously and quietly and, if possible, from the back of the animal. Sometimes a wounded animal will suddenly spring to its feet and run. Try to watch the eyes. If they are glazed or unblinking the animal is safe to approach. If the animal is down but still obviously alive try to get close enough for another shot. Bowhunters should try to place a shot in the rib cage then either quietly back off and wait at a distance or wait silently in place so as not to further "spook" the animal. It's better to have an extra hole in a skin than lose a wounded animal.

Reprinted from **Big Game Recovery Guide.** Courtesy of National Bowhunter Education Foundation.

❖ DRESSING DEER ❖

Field-Dressing Deer

1) With the deer on its back, carefully open the deer's abdomen.

2) Place a small log under the rump to get it off the ground. Cut deeply around the rectum, being careful not to cut off or puncture the intestine. Pull to make sure the rectum is separated from tissue connecting it to the pelvic canal. Do not split the pelvic bone. Lift the animal's back quarters a bit, reach into the front of the pelvic canal, and pull the intestine and connected rectum into the stomach area.

3) If you want to make a full shoulder mount, do not cut open the chest cavity. Reach into the forward chest, find the esophagus, cut it off as far up as possible, and pull it down through the chest. If the buck won't be mounted, split the chest and sever the esophagus at its lower end. Or, simply cut into the deer's throat patch deeply enough to sever the esophagus. After it's cut, reach into the chest cavity, find the lower end of the esophagus and pull it through.

4) Roll the deer onto one side and cut the diaphragm away from the ribs all the way to the backbone area. Roll the deer onto its other side and finish cutting away the diaphragm.

5) Leaving the deer on its side, grab the esophagus with one hand and the rectum/intestine with the other. Pull hard. The deer's innards will come out in one big package with a minimum of mess.

Caping A Trophy

Caping — the process of skinning out a trophy deer's shoulder and head — is best left to the taxidermist. In a remote setting, however, storage problems may require you to cape a deer if you want to preserve it as a full shoulder mount. Follow the illustration above when making your cuts.

1) With a short, sharp knife, slit the skin from the top of the withers, up the back of the neck to the midpoint between the ears. Now, going back to the withers, circle the body with another cut. This should leave plenty of hide for the taxidermist.

2) Peel the skin forward up to the ears and jaws, exposing the point where you want to cut through the neck. The easiest way to separate the head from the neck is to make an encircling cut through the neck to the atlas joint, the first vertebra under the skull. This is the only joint on the neck that has no interlocking bones.

3) After making this cut, simply grasp the antler bases and twist the head off the neck.

4) Remember, when field-dressing a trophy to be mounted, don't cut into the chest or neck area. If blood gets on the area to be mounted, wash it off with snow or water as soon as possible. Also, when taking the deer out of the woods, place it on a sled or rickshaw. All it takes is one sharply broken branch on a deadfall to damage the hide.

Skinning Your Trophy

Skinning deer does not have to be a long, laborious chore that leaves hair all over the meat and a knife-riddled hide. Take a hint from butchers who winch off the hide. A car, truck or come-along works just as well. With practice, this technique requires about five minutes of work.

1) With the deer hanging by its antlers or neck, slice the hide around the neck as close to the head as possible. (Don't cut into the meat. The neck muscles bear much force later as the hide is pulled off.)

2) Cut down the front of the neck to the opening made during field-dressing.

3) Saw off the legs slightly above the knee joints.

4) Pull the neck hide down until about one foot of it is free. Take a golf-ball sized rock or 1.5-inch section of 2-by-2 and wrap it into the hide's end. Make a tight package and cinch it off with high-quality nylon rope of about three-eighths inch thickness. A double half-hitch works well. Pull hard on the rope to make sure everything is secure.

5) Tie the rope's other end to a car, truck or come-along hook. (A rope 10 to 12 feet long is plenty.) Back up the vehicle until the hide is pulled to the brisket and shoulders. It will bind slightly here. If necessary, have someone work the hide around the brisket. With tension on the rope, the hide will slide over fairly easily.

6) Continue backing until the hide is pulled free of the carcass.

❖ WHITE-TAILED DEER WEIGHT FORMULA ❖

Take measurement of chest around heart, just behind foreleg.
Chest Measurement x 5.6037 - 94.0982 = Live Weight.
Live Weight x .78 = Field Weight. • Field Weight ÷ 2 = Edible Meat.

Chest	Live Weight	Field Weight	Meat	Chest	Live Weight	Field Weight	Meat
25	46	36	18	49	180	141	70
26	52	40	20	50	186	145	73
27	57	45	22	51	192	150	75
28	63	49	24	52	197	154	77
29	68	53	27	53	203	158	79
30	74	58	29	54	209	163	81
31	80	62	31	55	214	167	84
32	85	66	33	56	220	171	86
33	91	71	35	57	225	176	88
34	96	75	38	58	231	180	90
35	102	80	40	59	237	184	92
36	108	84	42	60	242	189	94
37	113	88	44	61	248	193	97
38	119	93	46	62	253	198	99
39	124	97	49	63	259	202	101
40	130	101	51	64	265	206	103
41	136	106	53	65	270	211	105
42	141	110	55	66	276	215	108
43	147	115	57	67	281	219	110
44	152	119	59	68	287	224	112
45	158	123	62	69	293	228	114
46	164	128	64	70	298	233	116
47	169	132	66	71	304	237	118
48	175	136	68	72	309	241	121

❖ Thoughts on Deer ❖

Deer hunting is much more than statistics, success stories and new gadgetry. Deer hunters are linked by the philosophies, experiences and observations of others who preceded them in the woods. In many cases, they never knew their predecessors personally, nor shared a cabin with them in the November woods. Still, they feel a kinship with these deer hunters of bygone days. Much of those feelings are expressed in writing, thereby ensuring they'll be passed on to new generations of hunters. In fact, some of the nation's favorite outdoor literature revolves around deer hunting. Well-known deer hunting tales have come from such writers as Aldo Leopold, Gordon MacQuarrie and William Faulkner. And although entire books have been written on deer hunting, in many cases the writer captured the hunt's mood in a paragraph or two. What follows are some examples of that rare talent of taking a deer hunt and boiling it down to its essence with a few bold strokes of the pen.

IN A DUSTY, RUSTIC, OLD CABIN

We are in a dusty, rustic old cabin up in the brush.
We have porcupines gnawing at the door,
And a den of skunks under the floor.

Some of the boys are cussing about the heat,
Others are, complaining of cold feet.
Some of the boys sleep in pajamas,
Others in their drawers.
All these things don't make any difference
Everybody goes to bed and everybody snores.

Some of the boys are killing deer that's been
Dead for twenty years or more,
Others are still fighting the first World War.

Some of the boys are sitting at the table,
Hollering fifteen-two and fifteen-four,
With part of the cards on the floor.
A few more rounds of Roses Four,
They would still be hollering
Fifteen-two and fifteen-four if
All the cards were on the floor.

There is the good cook standing
By the door, he says, "Boys you have
Time for just one hand more, then
Clear the table and put on the
Plates and get ready for your
T-Bone steaks, some of you like
Them rare, some like them well,
You will eat them the way I
Cook them or go plum to Helena.

Such is life in a dusty, rustic
Old cabin up in the brush.

-Author Unknown

GOING HOME EMPTY-HANDED

It is not essential to the hunt that it be successful. On the contrary, if the hunter's efforts were always and inevitably successful, it would not be the effort we call hunting; it would be something else. Corresponding to the eventuality or chance of the prey's escaping is the eventuality of the hunter's going home empty-handed. The beauty of hunting lies in the fact that it is always problematic.

-Jose Ortegay Gasset,
Meditations On Hunting (1942)

OUT SPRINGS A BUCK

When the tamaracks are smoky gold, it is hard to keep one's mind on grouse, for there are many distractions. I cross a buck track in the sand, and follow in idle curiosity. The track leads straight from one Jersey tea bush to another, with nipped twigs showing why.

This reminds me of my own lunch, but before I get it pulled out of my gamepocket, I see a circling hawk, high skyward, needing identification. I wait till he banks and shows his red tail.

I reach again for the lunch, but my eye catches a peeled popple. Here a buck has rubbed off his itchy velvet. How long ago? The exposed wood is already brown; I conclude that his antlers must therefore be clean by now.

I reach again for the lunch, but am interrupted by an excited yawp from the dog, and a crash of bushes in the swamp. Out springs a buck, flag aloft, antlers shining, his coat a sleek blue. Yes, the popple told the truth.

-Aldo Leopold

ALL IS QUIET

The Old Devil comes out late, and he never stands still, but always moves about as he grazes. The slightest sound, and up comes his head to be turned proudly in the direction of the noise. Obviously he is nibbling grass, but suddenly he will jerk up his muzzle afresh; a few munches, and then down it goes to the food once more. He will carry out the same surprising maneuver two or three times in quick succession ... all is quiet! And so he trips on, munching, nibbling, restless, alert, never turning broadside to the gun. It seems as though he can guess the places where a sportsman may hide and knows that his stem is invulnerable: no one would shoot him from behind.

Svend Fieuron, 1935
Monarch Of The Glen

ANTLERS

Antlers are still an outstanding interest to most people; as a thing of beauty when fully developed, they are well deserved subjects of admiration. When it is learned that they are merely hardy annuals, existing only for a single season completely disappearing every year only to promptly reappear, and then, in certain circumstances in an improved and enlarged form, admiration is exchanged for wonderment.

-A.I. McConnochie
Deer Forest Life, 1932

THINGS PERMANENT AND PRICELESS

We cannot live in close touch with beautiful scenes and stimulating environments without being enriched by them. Is it unlikely that we will forget the way the wilderness appeared on a certain autumn morning when every brilliantly hued leaf was encased in glittering snow-crystals and kindled into prismatic fires by the beams of the rising sun? Do we cease to remember the advent of the Hunter's Moon — a blood-red and fabulous lantern — as it peered at us across the lonely mazes of a black spruce swamp? Do we fail to recollect the spellbound mystery of a secluded lake, girdled by virgin timber, and sleeping like a liquid tourmaline in the shadowland of twilight? These are things permanent and priceless — poems of loveliness and beauty impressed upon the mind by nature in her wild state. These are things that time cannot take from us as long as memory lasts. The deerskin on our study floor, the buck's head over the fireplace, what are these after all but the keys which have unlocked enchanted doors, and granted us not only health and vigor, but a fresh and fairer vision of existence?

-Paul Brandreth
Trails of Enchantment, 1930

THE LOVE OF HUNTING

Golf is a delightful accomplishment, but the love of hunting is almost a psychological characteristic. A man may not care for golf and still be human, but the man who does not like to see, hunt, photograph, or otherwise outwit birds or animals is hardly normal. He is supercivilized, and I for one do not know how to deal with him. Babes do not tremble when they are shown a golf ball, but I should not like to own the boy whose hair does not lift his hat when he sees his first deer.

-Aldo Leopold

THE WHITETAIL DEER

The whitetail deer is now, as it always has been, the most plentiful and most widely distributed of American big game. It holds its own in the land better than any other species, because it is by choice a dweller in the thick forests and swamps, the places around which the tide of civilization flows, leaving them as islets of refuge for the wild creatures which formerly haunted all the country. The range of the whitetail is from the Atlantic to the Pacific, and from the Canadian to the Mexican borders, and somewhat to the north and far to the south of these limits. The animal shows a wide variability, both indiviudally and locally, within these confines.

-Theodore Roosevelt, 1921

HE'S GONE!

'Twas on a clear and frosty morn,
When loudly on the air were borne
Those weird and deeply thrilling sounds,
The clanging tones of clamorous hounds.
"How sweet," said he, "that music floats
And rolls in wild tumultuous notes;
Now ringing up the mountain's side,
Now waxing, waning, like the tide,
Or swinging loud across the dell
Like Pandemonium's carnival."

Hot bounds his blood in swift career,
When bursts the uproar still more near,
And hope and fear alternate play
With bounding joy and dark dismay.

As louder, nearer, bays the pack,
Cold shivers dance along his back;
From tip to toe his nerves all tingle,
His knee-pans seem almost to jingle,
All o'er his skin hot flashes amble,
And on his head each hair doth scramble;
He feels his heart erratic beat,
He nearly melts with inward heat,
And grasps with quivering hand the gun
As nears the pack in rapid run.

And now there comes an ominous sound
Of hoofs that fiercely spurn the ground,
Close followed by a sudden crash,
As through the brush with headlong dash
There bursts in view a lordly buck.
"Ye gods!" he chattered, "oh, what luck!
But oh! ain't he a splendid sight!
Those spirit-eyes! How wildly bright!

What graceful form! What glossy vest!
What massive neck! What brawnly chest!
What proud defiance seem to shed
Those antlers o'er his shapely head!
How in the sun they flash and shine
From rugged base to polished tine!"

"Phew!" said the buck, with lofty bound
That scattered dirt and leaves around;
Then skipped across the field of view,
Waved with his flag a fond adieu
To his admirer's ravished eye,
Just as the hounds came foaming by.

"But where's my gun? He's gone! Oh, thunder!
How could I ever make such blunder!
It looked go fine to see him run
I quite forgot I had a gun."

-T S. Van Dyke, 1882

REFLECTIONS
OF THE DAWN

I know the whitetail he is big and free
and this is his range.
Soon his form will break the stillness
of the dawn.
By his presence, my spirit is feverish.
By this light my bones are cold.
The sun has yet to mount the peak at my back
to warm the air.
But my heart is warm. This is my sunrise, my day.
I am the hunter.
I marvel that I have lived to enjoy this moment
and the freedom of hunting
in a land teeming with wildlife;
A land painted by the Maker's hand.
I cherish this moment, this mountain,
this day and this life.
Where but here can a man know such freedom?

-Anonymous

A FLASH OF OPPORTUNITY

Hunting is not simply casting blows right and left in order to kill animals or to catch them. The hunt is a series of technical operations, and for an activity to become technical it has to matter that it works in one particular way and not in another. Technique pre-supposes that success in reaching a certain goal is difficult and improbable; to compensate for its difficulty and improbability one must exert oneself to invent a special procedure of sufficient effectiveness. If we take one by one the different acts that comprise hunting, starting with the last - killing or capturing the prey - and continuing backward toward the initial operation, we will see that they all presuppose the scarcity of game. The term used in big-game hunting *jugarse el lance* (the opportunity), is very indicative of what I am saying. It is the culminating moment in the hunting process: finally the prey appears at an adequate distance. But an instant later it will have gone, will have disappeared, and, very likely, another will not appear. Anybody who has hunted will recognize that each prey, when it appears, seems as if it is going to be the only one. It is a flash of opportunity that one must take advantage of. Perhaps the occasion will not present itself again all day. Thus the excitement, always new, always fresh, even in the oldest hunter.

- *Jose Ortegay Gasset,*
Meditations on Hunting (1942)

*D*eer Browse

Anyone who spends much time in the woods knows deer are unpredictable. Whether it's their behavior, travel patterns or physical traits, no two deer are exactly alike. As soon as you create labels such as "typical behavior" or "normal pattern," the next deer that comes along will shatter your notions.

Years ago, the editors of *Deer & Deer Hunting* decided the magazine needed a special section devoted to short articles that discuss unusual occurrences. The unique stories contained in "Deer Browse" come from all corners of the United States. Sometimes they're about the deer themselves, and other times they're about newsworthy local events that involve deer. The response to this special section has been phenomenal. Readers stuff the *Deer & Deer Hunting* mailbox with letters, newspaper clips, unique photographs and personal observations that are entertaining and informative. Many of these end up as items in "Deer Browse."

We hope you will enjoy the selections that follow.

Freak & Bizarre Deer Happenings

Text & Photo: Richard Haverlah

■ ALL TIED UP

In November 1989, during the rutting season, I photographed a rather unusual buck in South Texas at Choke Canyon State park, approximately eighty miles south of San Antonio.

For several days prior to photographing this deer, I saw him in the same general area but failed to get a good look. I just assumed he had some vines entangled in his antlers. Each time I saw the buck he was chasing does so I decided to attempt rattling him up for a better look and a possible photograph. Upon rattling, I lured the buck close enough to see that the "vines" were actually a length of rope.

There a number of campsites and a boat launch nearby, I'll never know for certain, but I would guess the deer somehow got the rope entangled in his antlers around the boat launch or one of the campsites.

I observed this buck again in late January and he appeared to be in good health. I suspect this will be one happy buck after he drops his antlers.

■ BAD FIT FOR BUCK

After Fred Stimeling of Richfield, Pa., shot a four-point buck Dec. 1, 1990, during the Pennsylvania firearms season he noticed a plastic cap wedged into one of its hooves. The buck had obviously stepped on this piece of litter, and had been unable to remove it.

Stimeling fared no better when he tried to pull it off. The buck's hoof had either swollen or grown around the cap. To remove it, Stimeling had to cut away part of the hoof.

Stimeling said the buck had adapted to the handicap. It didn't limp, even though it had to be painful.

The message here is obvious but is worth repeating. Don't litter. It not only looks bad on the landscape but can have painful consequences for wildlife.

■ LIGHTNING STRIKES DEER

When Carroll Hanna, Jr., of Appleton, Arkansas went fishing on March 21, finding a dead deer was the farthest thing from his mind. But find one he did. In fact, he found five.

Hanna and a companion spied what looked like several deer bedded down in a small pasture 150 yards from Conway lake. But the animals made no effort to leave.

Hanna though it was strange for deer to be so unconcerned about the presence of humans, so he investigated. He threw rocks and sticks as he approached the animals, but they still didn't move. When he determined the three button bucks and two does were dead, he summoned Arkansas Game and Fish Commission wildlife officer Clayton Rogers.

"At first I figured it was a case of poaching," Rogers said. "But after I arrived at the scene, I couldn't find any bullet holes. They were all laying in an area the size of a carport, and the ground was all torn up around them."

Rogers said an electrical storm passed through the area just before dark the day before. The deer were apparently crossing the small pasture when they were struck by lightning.

The Conway County incident isn't the only recent case of wildlife being killed by lighting. Last summer, research biologist Joe Clark found a black bear that apparently died the same way.

The Commercial Appeal
26 March 1989

Charles J. Alsheimer

■ LARGEST VELVET BUCK EVER?

Down through the years many Boone & Crockett whitetails have been harvested. According to the latest Boone & Crockett record book, more than 125 have exceeded the typical score of 180. However, entry in the record book does not allow for trophies still in velvet. Of course, the taking of a trophy-class buck in velvet is rare today because hunting season throughout the whitetail's range begin after the velvet has been shed from the antlers.

This was not always the case, however. Before the turn of the century and shortly after, white-tailed deer hunting was not restricted to the autumn months in all parts of North America. Even when hunting seasons were set, some states opened their deer season in late summer. From 1900 to 1905, New York State opened its Adirondack deer season on September 1. As a result, many bucks were taken in this region before they shed their velvet.

One such buck was killed during this time by Lyman Avery in Hamilton County, in the heart of the Adirondack Mountains. Though actual details are sketchy, it's believed Avery, who was a well known Adirondack guide, killed the buck around Labor Day in 1900.

The velvet-covered rack is extremely impressive. Though not recognized by Boone & Crockett, the New York State Big Buck Club does acknowledge this trophy. The buck, know as the Avery head, scores 180-3/8 typical and is tied with another buck as the state's third largest of all time. It is also the largest known Adirondack and has an 18-7/8 inch inside spread and 27-3/4 inch long main beams. Its longest tines are 12-5/8 inches long and the beam diameters at the base of the antlers are six inches. Overall, the fifteen-pointer may well be the largest white-tailed buck ever legally killed by a hunter while still in velvet.

Charles J. Alsheimer

Richard P. Smith

■ ANTLER ODDITY

Richard Schenden from Boyne City bagged a Michigan buck that had one of the most unusual set of antlers for 1986. One of the small, three-point antlers was normal, but its mate was still covered with velvet and angled off the the side. The unhardened antler wasn't stationary, though, flopping loosely on the buck's head.

There was an infected wound at the base of the antler where it had been damaged before the beam was fully developed. Schenden doesn't know what was responsible for the damaged antler. He shot the buck on opening day of Michigan's 1986 gun deer season. The accompanying photo shows Schenden's son, Steve, holding the buck's head.

Richard P. Smith

Richard P. Smith

Ray Loehr

■ CURIOSITY KILLS DOE

Curiosity apparently caused the death of an adult doe southeast of the community of Rock in Delta County, Michigan during March.

The deer was found dead on the edge of a cutting with her head stuck in the cavity of a tree. The hole was wide enough for the whitetail to stick her head in while either standing on her hind legs or stepping on a nearby stump with her front feet.

The cavity narrowed toward the bottom, however, and the doe apparently dropped back to ground level before pulling her head out of the hole and it became lodged in the cavity. The deer either died of exposure or choked to death while struggling to free itself.

There was no obvious reason why the doe would have stuck her head in the cavity, other than curiosity. DNR Wildlife Biologist Frank Short from Escanaba said the whitetail had seventy percent fat remaining in her bone marrow, so she was healthy before the mishap.

Richard P. Smith

■ ONE TOUGH BUCK

This 5.5 year-old Illinois buck, brought to a local taxidermist for mounting, survived plenty of hardship in his time. Especially noticeable is the right ear, which the hunter who shot the buck said hung limp and flopped about as the animal moved. The face and head portion of the buck showed that he had apparently been in a number of scraps with other bucks.

The buck's main antlers, which turn downward, still had pieces of velvet on the ends of the tines when the deer was shot. Deep inside the ear and completely encased was what appeared to be the start of another set of antlers.

One of the front legs was much shorter than the other. It had not been shot off, but appeared to be a clubbed-foot with the hoof fully-encased by flesh and hide. Otherwise, the buck seemed normal. It weighed over two hundred pounds (live).

When studying the wounds and deformities of deer, it is hard to imagine how some deer survive. Nevertheless, bow and gun hunters should both pass up low percentage shots that might cripple deer. The animals deserve this respect, and we as hunters will feel much better for it.

Ray Loehr

■ LONG-LIVED BUCK

The accompanying photograph shows a collection of antlers from a single buck who lived nearly eighteen years in captivity. This is relatively old for whitetails, even those in captivity, and the deer probably would have lived another few years if it hadn't been killed prematurely by a couple of roving dogs.

The deer was owned by Ted and Chris Boskovich of Plainfield, Connecticut. Ted has raised deer, with help from local orchards and restaurants, for more than twenty-seven years. The antlers in the photo were from a buck that was born in captivity in the spring of 1970 and killed in December 1987. The deer was in pretty good health at the time.

It is rare to observe such an extensive collection of cast antlers from a single animal, so when Ted called me to tell me of the death of his pet, I came with camera to talk with him for a newspaper article I was planning to do on the deer's story.

The antlers were all tied together in pairs, labeled and stored in a box in the corner of Ted's garage. Over the years, Ted had shown individual sets to friends and interested people, but had never taken the entire set out to view in chronological order. Once laid out in display, the collection was quite impressive. Evenly spaced and paired, the antlers covered a distance of about twenty-five feet.

Spiro T. Deer was quite an animal, spirited like his Vice Presidential namesake, and sported a rack that had spread as much as twenty-five inches with similar beam lengths, a circumference of nearly five inches and eight to twelve tines up to nine inches in length — a fine buck in his prime.

Looking at Spiro's cast antlers, a definite pattern could be observed. The deer's first set of antlers, small spikes, were never recovered in the winter of 1971. His second rack was a fork horn, slightly larger in size than a typical

Bob Sampson, Jr.

Connecticut buck of similar age.

His third rack was an eight-point set that was decent sized but not nearly as large as those that followed. The general configuration of points and beam shape was the same as the general antler pattern that the deer displayed for the rest of its life. One interesting note. That year, Spiro, who was feeling his oats for the first time, was beaten in a fight with his father, a much larger buck at the time. His left antler was broken off at the base. An injury that would show up in antler patterns later in life.

That following year, 1974, the deer's antlers were nearly at their maximum size and thickness. By 1975 through 1980, the antlers were about maximum size, with slight variation in beam, point count and thickness from year to year. Spiro's largest and thickest racks occurred from 1976-79. In 1979, for some reason, he exhibited bifurcated tines (split tines like a mule deer) on the right beam and grew a couple of drop tines on the left beam, bringing his point total to twelve.

From 1979 the rack, though still impressive in size, began to show more twists, more bumps around their base, less thickness and beam width, and more aberrations in point count and configuration. The interesting feature that remained throughout its life is the fact that the left antler (the side that was broken off in its youth) always had a slight asymmetry to it (that was similar each year) and consistently had more and larger droptines and other abnormalities than the right antler. From 1985 to the deer's death, the left antler was severely stunted and deformed in shape.

Obviously, the damage to the deer's pedicel early in its youth affected its antler growth throughout its life, particularly in its twilight years. Something that may account for at least some of the abnormal antler patterns we see each year in the woods.

Bob Sampson, Jr.

■ A THREE- ANTLERED BUCK

During the 1976 deer hunting season, Alan Burlett of Darien Center took a nine-point buck in the Town of Pomfret in Chautauqua County, New York. The ninth point consisted of a prong protruding from the forehead just at the inner edge of the right orbit. Through the kindness of Frederick Namlik of the Adventure Taxidermy Studio in Hamburg, the author was able to

examine, measure, and photograph this anomalous skull.

The supernumerary antler arises from the extreme anterior end of the frontal bone and has no connection with the base of the regular antlers. It measures 123 millimeters (4.8 inches) in length and 23 millimeters (4.8 inches) in diameter at the base. The pedicel is not entirely normal, and it is not clear whether or not the antler would have deciduous. If not, the animal would have borne a remarkable resemblance to the mythical unicorn after its normal antlers had been shed.

While extra prongs are not extremely rare in white-tailed deer, they are usually attached to the pedicel of one of the antlers and simply run under the skin for short distance before emerging. This antler is remarkable in being quite separate and distinct in its origin from the normal antlers.

Allen H. Benton
New York Fish And Game Journal
July 1978

Lawrence K. Rohm

■ AN UNUSUAL BUCK

I noticed your article in the February issue of Deer & Deer Hunting with regard to deer photographs. I have enclosed several prints of a deer which I shot this December in Pennsylvania. I felt your reader might be interested in the deer's unusual rack.

Lawrence K. Rohm
Newark, Delaware

Darell P. Saunders

■ THE STICK DEER

The 1981 Michigan Bowhunting season is rapidly approaching and soon we will be hopefully waiting for the elusive whitetail to make his silent appearance by our hunting stands. Before I take to the woods this fall I felt I should share with other readers the experience which enabled me to use my 1980 bow hunting tag.

Sunday, Dec. 14, 1980 was a calm, clear morning I shared with two fellow bow hunters, Jim Peters of Ann Arbor and Jim Carli of Livonia on private land near Stockbridge, Mich. We hunted from tree stands adjoining a harvested corn field with Jim C. getting two long shots at a deer standing the open area. After finding the two arrows and determining the deer was not hit, both my companions said they had afternoon commitments and left shortly thereafter.

Intending to hunt that evening, I decided to make an early afternoon check of a nearby woodlot. Moving through the woods slowly on a trail, I was startled by several deer exploding out of their mid-

day beds and disappearing from sight quickly, in typical whitetail style. Assuming they would be moving across harvested corn fields towards a swamp in the distance, I followed them hoping to be able to at least count the deer in the open. As I emerged from the woods I noted twelve deer entering the swamp so I started back towards my original hunting area.

Walking along the grassy fenceline and watching the distant woods I almost stepped on what appeared to be a sleeping deer! After recovering from the initial shock and noting the deer did not move, my first thought was that the animal was probably an unfound deer from the gun season which had ended two weeks prior. The deer was laying on its left side and as I touched it I discovered the carcass was still warm. There was a slight bulge under the skin in the rib area on the right side so my next assumption was that some archer had lost his deer. Using my hunting knife, I made a cut in the hide fully expecting to find some kind of broadhead and broken arrow in the deer. To my surprise, I found a piece of tree branch!

I immediately field dressed the young doe and found a ten inch piece of branch within the lung cavity. I concluded the deer was one of the group I had pushed out of the woods earlier. While making her frenzied escape she impaled herself on the dead tree branch and then traveled approximately 300 yards before collapsing. The point of entry was just behind the extended front left leg and the resultant bleeding was all internal. If I had walked down on the other side of the fencerow, I would not have found the deer!

Needless to say, my hunting companions chuckle about my "stick deer," but we have hunted together for years and know that "truth can be stranger than fiction."

Darell P. Saunders
Plymouth, Michigan
23 August 1981

A VIRGINIA DEER WITH FIFTY-FOUR TINES

In November of 1943, a group of railroad section hands discovered the carcass of a white-tailed deer (Odocoileus virginianus) along the right-of-way of the Erie Railroad near Windham Station, Portage County, Ohio. It is believed that the animal was killed by a train. The workmen, noticing the peculiarity of the antlers, cut off the head for preservation. Upon examination it was found that the antlers possess 54 distinct tines over one inch in length and remnants of 6 others that had deteriorated. Normally no more than 10 or 12 points develop. Probably the odd development and configuration of both the beams and the tines of this specimen resulted from repeated physical injury while the antlers were in velvet. The decay of the lower extremities of the antlers would indicate that they may have been rested often on the ground. Published reports show that imperfectly developed antlers on the Virginia deer are more usual than not, but the writer does not know of any record with a rack as grotesque or containing as many tines as the one reported here. The head was mounted and the photograph published through the courtesy of the Kent Canadian Club, Inc., the present owners.

Ralph W. Dexter,
Journal of Mammalogy (1945)

BUCK KILLED BY LIGHTNING SPLINTER

In 1933 lightning struck a black oak in the woodlot of the Lloyd Straus farm 3 miles west of Rockford, Ill.

A splinter of oak 8' long and up to 4" thick was torn off and hurled 40 yards through the woods, where it struck a big whitetail buck and killed him.

On Oct. 13, 1936, I saw the bones and skull of the buck, the splinter nearby, and paced the distance to the tree. The splinter fits the wound on the tree.

Straus found the buck dead and deduced the story from the evidence.

Aldo Leopold
Personal Papers

ANTLERED FAWN

Clinton County - Can a spotted fawn have antlers? Here's one that did. Recently I was called to remove deer from the highway that had met the fate of so many deer. With me at the time was Forest Ranger Clarence Billotte. The deer was a three point buck, in the velvet, but the amazing thing was the fact that its coat was spotted just a like a fawn. I do not infer that it was a 1953 fawn, but it must have been an instance where the last year's fawn broke out in spots again this year. Nice camouflage, but it proved ineffective against one of our modern vehicles.

District Game Protector
Charles F. Keiper
Renovo, Pennsylvania
November, 1953

Roland Nisleit

■ TRAPPED

This unusual photo was taken by my brother, Roland Nisleit. It shows a three-point buck that become trapped among a cluster of trees when he apparently tried to jump through them.

Roland found the deer while on a snowmobile trip in early December 1985. The only noticeable physical damage was on the hindquarter above the tail where a coyote or dog had chewed on him. Having escaped the record deer harvest of 1985, this whitetail met its demise at the hands of Mother Nature.

James Scriven

Richard P. Smith

■ BLINDED DEER

Jim Shope from Rapid River, Michigan, reports that he encountered a white-tailed doe in Delta County during the fall of 1985 that was blinded by tumor-like growths covering its head. The animal was stumbling around aimlessly, unable to see, and was destroyed.

The growths are called fibromas and are frequently caused by virus transmitted from biting insects. Shope said he's seen the growths on deer before, but never that many.

Richard P. Smith

Thomas Indrebo

■ CHOPPING BLOCK ANTLER

In the October 1987 issue of Deer & Deer Hunting, I read with interest the article in the "Deer Browse" section regarding the antler that was found wedged in the fork of a tree. It appeared that the buck struggled to free himself and, in the progress, broke the antler as well as part of his skull.

I have collected deer antlers for many years and a few years ago a friend of mine made an unusual find. I often speculated about the antler he found until I read the article in this magazine. My friend had been using a large section of an oak tree as a chopping block. It appeared to be from a crotch or forked section of the tree. One day the chopping block split apart, revealing a deer antler which had been completely concealed inside the tree. This antler also appeared to be fractured from the skull. The oak tree had been dead for some time prior to being cut down. We estimated the tree to be fifty to sixty years old at the time it died.

Thomas Indrebo

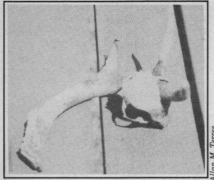

Allan M. Terres

■ UNUSUAL SHED ANTLER

Recently, while scouting my hunting area in Gloucester County, New Jersey, I found a shed antler that was quite unusual. There was a small skull impaled on the antler. No other bones were found in the vicinity of the antler. The skull appears to be that of a small fox or dog.

The area where I found the antler is normally quite wet, frequently covered by several inches of water. Due to our recent drought, although the area remains damp, there is little or no standing water. As evident in the photo, the nose of the skull and most of the antler are covered with algae, indicating it was under water for a period of time. Perhaps this explains why it hadn't been eaten by rodents.

I theorize that the buck fought with the other animal, hooked it under the jaw and drove the antler through the skull and out the eye socket, thus impaling the animal on his antler. I imagine he carried this dead animal until the body eventually fell away from the skull.

Allan M. Terres

Abe D. Miller

■ QUADRUPLETS

This five-year-old doe held in captivity gave birth to four fawns on 28 May 1984. According to Abe D. Miller of Baltic, Ohio, "she raised them all and they are all doing fine." While two to three fawns are quite common, the odds of a mature doe giving birth to four fawns and successfully raising them in the wild remain very small. One recent study indicated that only one percent of mature does will have triplets and that triplets have to come from areas with a superabundance of food.

Gary A. Redmon

■ LUCKY BUCK

Lucky Buck is an unusual buck, apparently abandoned shortly after birth. With its umbilical cord still attached, it was found by Deputy Conservation Officer Larry Elliot in a South Carolina marsh five years ago.

The buck has several unusual characteristics. What is most unusual about this "lucky buck" are his hooves. They are widespread, soft, and curl upward. Larry tried to improve the buck's hooves by trimming them, but they continued to grow soft and rubber-like and curl. This makes it difficult for the buck to run, so he is still cared for by Larry in a private wildlife park.

Lucky Buck's other unusual characteristics are that he sheds his velvet a month earlier than other bucks and he is smaller in size than other bucks in the park as well as bucks native to the area.

Gary A. Redmon

Richard P. Smith

■ TRIPLE-HEADER

On 25 November 1985, *Deer & Deer Hunting* Field Editor Richard P. Smith photographed a most unusual episode of deer behavior. While few deer hunters ever encounter two bucks fighting, Richard observed and photographed an even rarer event — three bucks engaged in combat.

Richard reports that the episode took place on a rather cold day (0°F) in Michigan's Upper Peninsula. Because of the cold temperature, the bucks' faces and heads were coated with ice at daybreak. Prior to the arrival of the third buck (the smallest of the three), the two large bucks would alternately lick the ice on each other's faces and then fight. Mr. Smith suspects the younger buck got drawn into the site of the fighting by the intensity of the activity.

■ DEER KILLED BY LIGHTNING

In early October 1983 a Marquette, Michigan bow hunter, Sanfred Olson, came upon three dead deer in a field. At the time, Olson was walking across the field after leaving his deer camp to go bow hunting early in the morning.

The three deer were all yearlings — one buck and two does. The deer were apparently killed by lightning during a thunderstorm the previous night. The accompanying photo of one of the does clearly shows the lines on her body that

Richard P. Smith

marked the course of electricity followed through her body.

Richard P. Smith

Maine Fish and Game Department

■ 461 POUNDS ON THE HOOF

This white-tailed buck, shot in 1955 by Horace Hinkley, had a dressed weight of 355 pounds, which puts him at an estimated 461 pounds on the hoof. According to the records of the Biggest Buck in Maine Club, Hinkley's buck still remains the largest buck ever shot in that state. Indeed, it is one of the largest whitetails, in terms of weight, ever shot anywhere.

It was shot on a rainy day in November; the year was 1955. Lennie Rue recalls the tale:

"Horace Hinkley and his wife, Olive, were hunting on the Kennebec River near Bingham, Maine. It was a good hunting day because a hunter could move through the woods silently and there was only a light breeze to move scent around. Mr. and Mrs. Hinkley took stands on opposite sides of a ridge. At about 9:20 that morning, Hinkley fired at a buck but missed. A few minutes later, Olive Hinkley's rifle cracked, and after a few minutes she shouted that she had downed a big buck. Hinkley, certain that there were more deer in a thicket of scrub beech where he had missed the first one, remained where he was and did not respond. Suddenly a huge buck came crashing out of the brush toward him. Hinkley dropped the animal with one shot. It was so heavy that the Hinkleys had to get help to haul it out.

"The buck was not officially weighed until three days later. The weighing was performed by Forrest Brown, an official state sealer of weights and measures, and there were two witnesses. Hog-dressed, and after three days of drying out, it still scaled 355 pounds (160.8 kg.). Bob Elliot, of Maine's Department of Game, originally calculated the live weight to be at least 450 pounds (203.8 kg.) and more probably 480 pounds (217 kg.). Records of the Biggest Bucks in Maine Club officially established the weight at 461-1/2 pounds. The buck's rack was excellent, but not in keeping with its body size. There were eight points on each side, with a spread of twenty-one inches (53 cm.) and a beam length of 24.5 inches (63 cm.)."

Several bucks have come close to this record. One thinks of Dean Coffman who shot a 440-pound Iowa buck in 1962. Or Robert Hogue who reportedly shot a buck in Sawyer County, Wisconsin in 1924, that had a dressed scale weight of 386 pounds (174.8 kg.) and an estimated live weight of 491 pounds (222.4 kg.) Unfortunately, Hogue's buck was not officially witnessed. One also thinks of the huge southern whitetail taken in Worth County, Georgia, in 1972 by Boyd Jones. Hog-dressed, it weighed 355 pounds (160.8 kg.) with an estimated live weight of 443 pounds (200.6 kg.).

Minnesota, however, claims the all-time record with Carl J. Lenander's buck shot in 1926. Field-dressed, it scaled 402 pounds (182.1 kg.). The Conservation Department calculated its live weight to be 511 pounds (231.4 kg.), making it the largest whitetail ever officially recorded in North America.

Rob Wegner

■ DEER TOES

Have you ever seen a snake with two heads? A white tom turkey? How about an antlered doe? No?

Even though these "freaks" of nature are rare, they do occur in several animals.

Gary Beeland of Jackson recently found a new deviation from the rule during this past deer season; Would you believe a white-tailed deer with three toes on one of his feet?

In November 1984, Gary killed a Scott County six-point buck which appeared to be normal in every respect except one. He had three toes on his left hind foot. The deer weighed 155 pounds.

How could such a thing happen? We don't really know, but we can offer some good guesses. Here's the story.

The common ancestors for all land vertebrates had five toes. Many animals — raccoons and man among them — have kept all five toes on all their limbs. Over evolutionary time, other animals have lost their thumbs and have only four toes on each foot. Examples would be foxes, cats, and dogs.

Members of the deer family, for example, have evolved with adaptations for running with speed. Although deer also possess four toes on each foot, the consequences of this evolutionary development have resulted in only two functional toes, whose toe-nails have lengthened to form split hooves.

Deer toes are the evolved third and fourth digits of their five-toed ancestors which still roamed the earth as recently as 30 million years ago. (Note: life on earth is over 3,000 million years old.) The dew claws are simply remnants of the second and fifth toes. The first toe or thumb is completely gone.

So where did Gary Beeland's deer get the extra toe? Since both dew claws looked normal, could the extra digit (toe) be an evolutionary throwback showing development of the thumb from the deer's long lost past? Possibly. The new toe is about where you'd expect to see a thumb if a deer had one.

Horses have also been known to possess multiple toes in addition to their typical one hoof. The single hoof is the evolved third toe, from their five-toed equine ancestors. It is recorded that Julius Caesar even owned a horse with hooves that were cleft like toes. The seers of the day said that Caesar would be lord of the world. Jay Gould in his book, Hen's Teeth and Horse's Toes, says that Caesar raised the horse with great care, and was the first to ride it.

Scientists at first thought that all the extra horse toes were developments of the degenerated second and fourth toes which are usually present only as short splints of bone above the hoof. However, after closer examination, in only about one-third of the multiple toe cases were added digits toes were simply duplicates of the

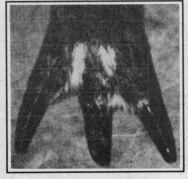

Gary Beeland's 155-pound deer came complete with a left hind foot that sported three toes, one too many.

This toe is believed to be abnormal. It is possibly a mutation which appeared from the animal's past.

normal hoof due to some type of mutation.

Although developmental patterns of an animal's past may often remain in a dormant state, variations from the norm will usually show up as mutations due to other causes. Chances are that Beeland's three-toed buck was just an accident of nature rather than an evolutionary ghost from its past.

The longer and closer we look at wild things, the more mutations and accidents we'll observe. Deer teeth also exhibit differences that most people are unaware of. To obtain age, Department of Wildlife Conservation biologists look at thousands of deer jaws every year. A few of deer jaws will contain more teeth than normal and some will contain fewer.

Freaks, such as three-toed deer, are obvious examples of the variations that regularly occur in nature. Although discoveries of such deviants get most of the attention, they simply point out the underlying and wondrous variety that the truly observant can routinely see in the wild.

David E. Steffen
Mississippi Outdoors
March/April 1985

■ BUCK-RUBBED FENCE POST

In November of 1981, I spent some time photographing whitetails at the Quivera National Wildlife Refuge in the center of Kansas. While easing through the tallgrass uplands one day, I stumbled onto a huge six-point buck chasing a doe. I followed the trail for some distance until discovering an isolated fence post that someone apparently overlooked when dismantling a fence line. The post seemed to have attracted the attention of at least one feisty buck. Why the buck rubbed such an unyielding object I couldn't guess.

Two years later I moved to Idaho but in the fall of 1988 I returned to Quivera and rediscovered the fence post. Seven years of rutting bucks had shaved it mighty thin. I wonder how many more it can survive these repeated assaults?

Ron Spooner

Unusual Antlers of
🦌 Saskatchewan 🦌

Garry Donald, Trophy Deer of Saskatchewan, 1985

A non-typical with an antler protruding just above the eye.

Garry Donald, Trophy Deer of Saskatchewan, 1985

This big whitetail was taken by A. Linder in the Dafoe area

Garry Donald, Trophy Deer of Saskatchewan, 1985

This moose-like whitetail was taken by Harvey Wolowsju. It is six inches from bottom to top.

■ INCREDIBLE VITALITY

Do deer have more lives than a cat? Glen Taylor, a conservation officer in New Hampshire, has long suspected as much. Now, he is convinced that the vitality of a whitetail is at least as great as the vaunted life-force of the proverbial cat.

Taylor's conviction stems from what has become for him a distasteful, though routine, job—the picking up and disposing of deer that have been illegally killed. Hence, he was expecting nothing unusual when this past fall he took possession of a gun-shot doe near his home in West Canaan.

But upon examining the animal and dressing it thoroughly, Taylor ran into something he had never seen before. In the upper chest cavity, and encapsulated in gristle, was a three-inch piece of a stick, as big around as a broom handle. It lay only an inch or so from the spine, at which point it must have penetrated a lung. There was no hole or any other mark or sign on the outside to show how the stick had gotten there, thus indicating it had been in the deer for some time. Despite what must have been excruciating pain and irritation, Taylor learned only that up to the time it was shot the whitetail apparently was living a perfectly normal life.

This story will doubtless seem improbable to some, but one person who will not hesitate for a moment to accept it is Leonard Lee Rue III. In his definitive book, *The Deer Of North America* (1978), Rue cites an instance which is not only similar but identical right down to the last detail.

Ernest E. Robinson
5 February 1987

■ LONG-LIVED DEER

On 5 May 1980 Claude Bowes of Big Moose, New York, found the remains of a female white-tailed deer that had been trapped and ear tagged near his residence on Big Moose Lake on 22 December 1967 when it was at least 1.5 years old. Therefore, during the winter of 1979-80 it would have been at least 14.5 years old. It appeared most likely that the deer had died of malnutrition. Nevertheless, it lived to a noteworthy old age, although it did not set a longevity record.

J.J. Ozoga, in Michigan, reported recapturing and releasing two female white-tailed deer more than fourteen years after they had been trapped and tagged as fawns. L.L. Rue III reported several captive females that lived more than 16.5 years and a "semi-tame" doe in Maine that was killed by a rutting buck at the age of 18.5 years. However, M.A. Gordon noted what might constitute an all-time record. This was a female shot on an estate in Orange County, New York, because she had severe hair loss on her face, neck, and ears. She was determined, from Giemsa-stained tooth sections, to have been between nineteen and twenty-three years of age and was carrying an eighty-day-old fetus.

Benjamin F. Tullar, Jr.
New York Fish And Game Journal
January 1983

■ HOW A DEER SLEEPS

A stag dozing, while he chews the cud, rests with his head well up in the air, and is more or less alert to scents and sounds. When he has finished his cud and feels very sleepy, he stretches his head out on the ground in front of him. When he feels perfectly secure, and able to indulge in a deep sleep, he lies curled up like a dog with his head turned to his tail. The writer and a friend, on a hill tramp, once found a stag in this position so sound asleep that it needed shouts to wake him.

Allan Gordon Cameron
The Wild Red Deer of Scotland, 1924

Charles J. Alsheimer

■ A TALE OF TWO DEER

It is amazing what the whitetail can endure. Encounters with automobiles, lightning, woven-wire fences, predators and hunters represent just a few of the dangers they come up against in their quest for survival.

My personal experience in observing these encounters has usually been after the fact. The sight of auto-deer collisions and a host of other accidents can leave a lasting impression. One personal example of the whitetail's survival potential took place a few years ago on the opening day of New York's gun season. I harvested a six-point buck early in the morning and later, when I skinned and butchered it, discovered a three-bladed broadhead between the shoulder and chest cavity. A sack, of sorts, surrounded the broadhead. As I recall, the deer showed no signs of injury as it came my way through the woods. I've since heard of similar stories, but it wasn't until 1985 that I was able to observe the whitetail's truly miraculous will to survive. My first encounter came during July while photographing deer from a blind at the edge of a hay field. Just before dusk, a buck came out of the woods to join some feeding does and fawns. Though at first the buck was some distance from me, I noticed he was having trouble walking. When he crested a knoll,

I could see his right front leg was missing. To walk, the buck seemed to bow his back and thrust his shoulders forward in one motion.

When he grazed to within forty yards of my blind, I got a good look at him through my 400mm lens as I took pictures. His right leg was gone below the knee and the leg had healed into what appeared to be a hard callous. From the photos you can see that the buck's rack is deformed, especially on the right antler.

Just before dark on that July evening the wind shifted, giving me away even though the deer never saw me. All the deer bolted and in the process I was able to watch the buck run for about 300 yards. Though he ran with a slight limp, he seemed to be able to keep up with the other deer. What struck me most was that it appeared more difficult for the buck to walk than run.

At the time, I couldn't tell whether the buck's injury resulted from a hunting or a farm accident. In agricultural areas, deer injuries are common during the haying season. In talking to the landowner, I learned that the buck was probably the same one a hunter had shot two years earlier. He also told me that, in addition to the buck, there was a doe with a broken leg living on his farm. The landowner observed the doe lying on the ice in March of 1985 and figured it probably had fallen and broken the leg then. Though he thought the break would heal, I found out later in the fall that the doe was doomed.

In early November, I returned to the hay field where I photographed the buck during July and got some more interesting photos. I had scattered apples around in front of my blind in hope of getting some good close-ups. However, the sight of my foreign-looking blind kept all the deer farther away than I'd hoped. But the doe with a broken leg showed herself and came closer than the other deer. While she devoured the apples, not fifteen yards from my blind, I was able to photograph the break on her left leg.

Through my long lens I could clearly see that the break was compound. Though she looked gaunt, she didn't appear to be

Charles J. Alsheimer

in pain. As she walked straight away from me, her leg snapped out at the break point when she put her weight on it. The amazing thing was her apparent resistance to pain. If the injury was painful, the doe didn't show it.

On the same day I photographed the doe with the broken leg, I again photographed the three-legged buck. This time he came closer to me than in July, though he didn't stick around as long. But during the short time he was at the hay field's edge, I was able to learn more about him. His neck was swollen and he appeared in prime rutting condition. There were several does close by but he never went after them like I thought he would. Instead, he was content to just feed.

I could see that the leg had been taken off just below the knee joint and the callous seemed larger than in July. Several times the buck actually put his weight on the leg as he walked and grazed. As would be expected, his right shoulder showed considerable atrophy while the shoulder supporting his left foreleg was very muscular.

As the last rays of sunlight waned on that beautiful November day, I decided to try something. I opened the back of my blind and stood up. Immediately all deer spooked. The three-legged buck brought his head up, snorted once and ran full speed toward the woodlot. Though he didn't bound like the other whitetails, he seemed to be able to run faster than I remembered him doing in July.

I had been witness to two very unusual deer injuries, one caused by man and one by nature. It's doubtful the doe made it through the 1985-86 winter, but the fate of the buck seems to be a different matter. He had survived one hunting season on three legs and, from all appearances, had as much chance as the other deer of making it through another season.

The whitetail is an incredible creature. I've spent thousands of hours observing, photographing and hunting them and I continually come away amazed. Whether on three legs or four, their will to survive in the midst of our changing world is phenomenal.

Charles J. Alsheimer

■ UNUSUAL STAMINA

Our hunting party experienced an unusual display of one whitetail's cunning, stamina and will to live during the 1985 deer hunting season.

While hunting on Thanksgiving Day, we came across a fresh blood trail in the snow at about 11:00 A.M. The tracks revealed that this was a large deer with a broken right rear leg. After a considerable wait, it became evident that the person responsible for the wound was not on the trail, so we began following the rather meager blood trail at a modest pace and were shown white-tailed deer evasion tactics that were almost human.

Whether intentional or just by coincidence, this deer circled and backtracked on the other deer tracks and on his own blood trail several times, ran over two separate gut piles and then on the bloody drag trails for several hundred yards, and ran with other wounded deer, all in the first five hours of the chase which covered approximately three miles. All this time, we never did get a glimpse of the deer, although several times we were close enough to hear it crash off through the half-frozen alder brush swamp. If not for contact with another hunter just before dark who asked if we were on the trail of "that huge buck," the chase probably would have ended right there.

Since we didn't want to risk chasing the trophy into another hunter during legal shooting hours, we decided that night trailing would provide our best chance at tagging the buck. What transpired next was up an eight-mile, cross-country jaunt through all types of cover and terrain in the dark during which, at one point, the desperate buck swam and waded, or drifted, down the Kewaunee River for about five hundred yards.

It was sunrise the next morning when the buck crossed the same river at a point further downstream on a sheet of ice barely thick enough to support his weight. But, this buck wasn't done yet. Next, he took refuge under a bunk feeder in a fence-enclosed barnyard, practically right in a farmer's backyard! After chasing him back into a nearby woodlot, we finally inflicted the killing shot at about 7:30 A.M. The buck weighed in at 182 pounds. His ten-point rack had a spread of 18-1/2 inches. No meat from the right rear leg was salvageable — the large upper leg bone was completely splintered. When all was said and done, our hunting group covered more than twelve miles and spent seventeen hours on the trail of the extraordinary animal. The identity of the "hunter" responsible for the initial wound was never discovered.

The moral of the story seems to be that having a sighted-in gun and knowing its effective range should be the top priority of any conscientious hunter so that episodes of this nature can be kept to a minimum. Horror stories of crippled deer left to die slow agonizing deaths by careless hunters, as this beautiful buck undoubtedly would have, just provide more fuel for the anti-hunting fire.

Tom and Bob Karl
Kewaunee, Wisconsin

■ FISHY DEER

A small controversy has started on whether deer eat fish or not. I base my idea that they do on an article in the Binghamton Press (Feb. 7, 1967). The article was written by Frank Dolan. The article went like this:

"Observers have watched deer eat trout and go at the catching and brunching as though they were in the habit of dining on such delicacies every day.

"Another qualified observer has reported seeing deer eat black suckers. The deer would take the fish in its mouth, head first and munch away until it was completely devoured and do it as casually as any other fish-eating animal. These observations were made in late spring, a time when there was no shortage of browse or other foods."

As Roscoe is in the Catskills, on the famous Beaverkill River, it is an area of much hunting and fishing. This controversy is spreading among my friends.

Charles Buchholz
Roscoe, New York

■ DEER RESCUE IN UPPER MICHIGAN

I had an opportunity to help in the rescue of a whitetail doe this spring that was stranded along the rocky shoreline of Lake Superior north of my home in Marquette, Michigan. Here's what happened.

The doe ran into the cold waters of Lake Superior to escape dogs. To reach the water, she had to descend or jump off a rock cliff that was four to five feet high in some places, but much higher in others.

A local homeowner who saw what happened, removed the dogs from the area. The whitetail waded to shore after the dogs were gone, but was apparently unable to get back up the cliff. The homeowner called me four hours later when she was still there. I, in turn, notified the Department of Natural Resources and a pair of conservation officers responded.

At first, an attempt was made to herd the deer down the shoreline to a point where the rock cliff diminished to almost nothing. The animal would be able to walk off on her own once she reached that point. That plan didn't work, however.

The doe walked back out in the water at one point, instead of following the shoreline. The rest of the time she faced us ready to fight. One of the officers used a tree branch, then a pole, for a while in an effort to push the whitetail along the shore. She frequently struck out at these objects with her front feet.

A rope was eventually employed to subdue the doe. Once she was down, one officer grabbed her front feet and I grabbed the rear ones. The second officer held her head. We then carried her down the shore and over the cliff at a low point.

The doe was too weak to get up when released, but she eventually regained enough strength to stand up and walk off. Hopefully she fully recovered and should have given birth to fawns by now.

Richard P. Smith

Richard P. Smith

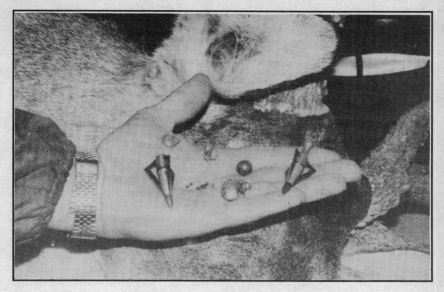

Taylor holds the arsenal of other shooting efforts in his trophy deer — two arrow heads, several bullets and a sprinkling of shotgun pellets.

■ RUGGED BUCK

Missouri deer are tough—on the hoof at least—as one white-tailed trophy from the Midwestern state was packing two arrow heads, four lead slugs and a dose of shotgun pellets when finally brought down by a bow hunter.

The hardy Missouri deer not only toted the amazing amount of weaponry under his hide, but also hefted a trophy rack that earned state and national honors for a Missourian.

Curtis Taylor, a forty-six-year-old veteran hunter, dropped the trophy-racked deer during the first historic weapons deer hunt last January at Squaw Creek National Wildlife Refuge in northwest Missouri.

"I've been hunting deer and turkey since I was about nineteen years old— some twenty-seven years—and this had to be the most unusual among my thirty-six deer and fourteen wild turkeys," said Taylor.

Taylor lives near the Missouri town of Savannah, a community of 3,500 located about forty miles southeast of the federal refuge where he collected the deer during the first-ever white-tailed deer hunt on the government area.

"Everyone thought that deer was a tough old boy, even to the eatin' level, but it was good and tender venison. He was plenty fat and just as tasty-tender as most of Missouri crop-fed deer. He was only a three-year-old — the biology folks checked all the deer taken during the special hunt — so he wasn't even in the prime of his life," Taylor observed.

"He weighed 205 pounds liveweight, including the arrow heads and lead slugs he was carrying," the hunter said. Taylor and other veteran hunters, including Missouri conservation officials, still marvel at the 205-pound deer's capacity for survival.

The hunter found two arrow heads in the deer's body. Both broadhead points had been broken from the arrow shafts and both were fairly fresh wounds.

The lead muzzleloader ball may have been from a special primitive weapons event, while three other lead slugs were apparently from a high-powered rifle and perhaps a smaller caliber. Shotshell pellets were small, about No. 8s, and probable the result of some irate farmer who discouraged the whitetail from nibbling on crops.

"The big lead slug was found by the taxidermist when he was mounting the rack. It was near the base of the antlers. All the bullet wounds, including the pellets, had healed," Taylor said.

The wounds didn't appear to affect the deer as it showed no physical problems as it ambled towards Taylor before he dropped the whitetail with an arrow.

The Missouri hunter was among an elite corps of only nine archers to collect a deer during the special hunt. A total of forty-two archers and fifty-four muzzleloader shooters participated in the historic event. They removed fifty-two whitetails from the refuge during the hunt, designed for recreational and management purposes.

Taylor's refuge deer qualified for Missouri state Big Buck Club honors and also for national Pope and Young ranking with a rack that measured 137 points.

The rack received national recognition during a recent deer rack measuring session, conducted by personnel of the Missouri Conservation Department with the help of college students as part of their studies for a career in the field of conservation.

A previous archery deer kill, a whitetail Taylor took in 1986, had a rack that totaled 127-7/8 points to also make Pope and Young listing.

"I've had a lot of comments on the refuge deer, a lot of compliments and a remark from one hunter who said 'the old boy must have been so tough you'd have to cut the deer steak gravy with a knife.'" Taylor grinned.

Bill Bennett

■ BUCK KILLED BY ANOTHER BUCK

Barry DeCharme of Marenisco, Michigan was on the way to his deer blind to finish preseason preparations a week before gun season opened when he found a dead buck along the trail. He called Conservation Officer Gary Lindquist from Wakefield to report the find and they determined the whitetail had been killed by another buck. Lindquist said there were four puncture wounds from tines under the dead buck's front leg that they discovered when skinning the carcass.

The heart was punctured by one of the tines and another broke a rib. One of the dead bucks antlers had been broken off near the base, too, and a search failed to turn it up. The antler that was intact had four points and the CO estimated the deer would have weighed "well over 200 pounds." Lindquist said there was a 15 to 20 foot circle of trampled ground where the two bucks fought.

Richard P. Smith

■ AN UNUSUAL CAUSE OF DEATH OF A WHITE-TAILED DEER

Herbert Dill of Mud Lake National Wildlife Refuge, Holt, Marshall County, Minnesota, procured the antlers of a white-tailed deer, Odocoileus virginianus, that had become entangled in bog birch (Betula pumila) and died. The deer was found dead by Laurence Gutterud on 8 November 1958. Several pieces of the birch were wound around the bases of the antlers and securely knotted. Apparently the deer had been rubbing its antlers to help rid them of velvet. There were strands of velvet intertwined with the birch. The antlers and part of the skull were sent to the Minnesota Museum of Natural History, where they bear the catalog number 4483.

Harvey L. Gunderson
Journal of Mammalogy (1961)

DEER HANGS ITSELF IN YEW TREE

On March 15, 1952, while studying the winter range conditions of elk and deer on the Lochsa and Selway river drainages, the writer found a mule deer (Odocoileus hemionus) which had hanged itself in a yew tree (Taxus brevifolia).

The yew tree was growing below an abrupt bank at the edge of Deadman Creek (300 to 350 yards from the Lochsa River). A cover of crusted snow approximately three feet deep recorded the series of events leading to the fatal accident. This deer was able to travel on top of the crusted snow and, from the abrupt bank, browse parts of the yew otherwise beyond reach. Undoubtedly over-zealous in its attempt to get the choice twigs of yew, the deer walked to the very edge of the snow-capped bank, and while it was stretching to reach the twigs the snow gave way beneath the animal. It plunged forward and was hanged by the neck in the fork of the yew tree.

Bobcats had visited the accidental kill and feasted on the hind quarters. The stomach contents revealed that this deer had been feeding heavily upon yew browse. This big game range has been heavily used by elk which have taken much of the browse within reach of deer, thereby forcing deer into closer utilization of browse.

Edwin B. Caswell
Journal of Mammalogy (1953)

WIRE IN A DEER'S LIVER

A piece of wire was found lodged in the liver of a white-tailed deer killed by a hunter on the Archer and Anna Huntington Wildlife Forest Station during an experimental harvest in 1967. All female deer were brought intact to a checking station for removal of reproductive tracts, and each was routinely examined for gross abnormalities or intestinal parasites, including gross dissection of the liver to determine the incidence of liver flukes (Fascioloides magna). One liver, from a female estimated to be 4.5 years old, had an essentially circular lesion approximately twenty millimeters in diameter near the surface. The lesion appeared similar to those containing flukes in the livers of heavily infested deer. Upon dissection a piece of 19-gauge wire, 0.89 millimeters in diameter and 4.4 centimeters long, was discovered three to five millimeters beneath the surface. The deer appeared to have been in good health. Its live weight of 152 pounds was typical of females of this age or older.

In the opinion of Dr. C.G. Rickard of the New York State Veterinary College at Cornell University it is likely that the wire was ingested, piercing the wall of the reticulum as that organ contracted, and lodged in the adjacent liver. Wire of this sort could have been picked up at any of over a hundred exclosures used to demonstrate effects of browsing activity. These areas were fenced with galvanized two-inch-mesh chicken wire.

George F. Mattifield and
Walter Buckley
New York Fish And Game Journal
January 1969

STRANGLED DEER

Refuge Keeper Isaac Baumgardner makes the following report: "Found a deer hung by its neck in the crack of an old stump in an old salt lick. It was a yearling fawn (male) and had been there possibly several weeks. Salt had been placed on top of this old stump by someone. Due to the stump being high it was necessary for this small deer to stand on its hind feet to reach the salt. Evidently it slipped or was pushed off balance by another deer and caught its neck in the crack."

Pennsylvania Game News
September 1934

■ FATAL FOOTFALLS

In disputes over space, often in feeding areas, both does and bucks will resort to "flailing," or standing on their hind legs for short periods of time and striking out with their front feet. Apparently, these two Michigan bucks had been fighting in this manner when, dropping to the ground, one pushed the other's foot into the crotch of a tree with enough force to wedge it and his own foot there permanently. Although it's not uncommon for white-tailed bucks to lock antlers during fall fights and subsequently die of exposure, these two bucks — who had already lost their antlers — met their end in even stranger fashion.

Richard P. Smith

■ EAGLES SLAUGHTER DEER IN FORESTS OF CENTRAL IDAHO

Salmon, IDA., March 8. — (AP) — Out of north central Idaho's wilds came a veteran trapper today with a story that savage eagles have slaughtered deer throughout the winter in the primitive Salmon river canyon country.

Many kills of big game, said Elmer Purcell, are the work of the huge birds of prey — not of coyotes, as had been generally believed.

"I myself found seven full grown deer that have been killed by eagles over a 20-mile area recently," Purcell said.

"The eagles dart down, fasten their claws in a deer's back and tear the muscles with their beaks. They keep repeating this, wheeling away and then rushing back, until the deer breaks down in the back."

A full grown mountain sheep was slain in the same manner, Purcell said, while he watched from a distance too great to permit his aiding the animal powerless to defend itself.

Williston Herald
8 March 1937

■ DEER AND SNAKES

C.E. Aldous reports that a student assistant assigned to the Allegheny National Forest during the summer of 1937 saw a doe milling about in a restricted circle. Suddenly the deer leaped into the air and descended with all four feet together. On the ground was found a weakly writhing rattlesnake about two and one-half or three feet long, badly mangled.

This apparent dislike of snakes has been repeatedly observed. Perhaps it is similar to some human aversions to spiders and snakes: "I just do not like them and so I kill every one I see." In Pennsylvania some experiments were conducted to test a deer's dislike for snakes. As a result, R.D. McDowell (1950) wrote: "Do deer trample snakes to death? Perhaps a doe, in defense of her young, may. However, every penned deer we held, regardless of age or sex, exhibited the utmost terror of all snakes. A piece of rope, held in the hand and moved to simulate a snake, would prevent a buck from charging when a club wouldn't."

C.W. Severinghaus and E.L.
Cheatum, 1956
In the Deer of North America

■ A RESCUED WHITETAIL

In early January of 1971, Bill Carey who farms south of Vermillion, Alberta, was coyote hunting along the Battle River near his home. In a particular field he had been seeing forty or more deer feeding regularly, including several good white-tailed bucks.

About 2:00 P.M. while driving, Bill noticed what appeared to be a dead deer in that field and assumed someone had shot it and left it. He had a snowmobile in the back of his truck, which he promptly unloaded and drove out to see what had happened. As he neared the deer, he realized that it was, in fact, two bucks with interlocked antlers. One was very much alive and one was dead and partially eaten by coyotes.

He realized how rare this sight was and decided to get a camera, return, photograph the spectacle, and then free the living deer. He found a friend at home and together they returned to the scene. They photographed the deer as the living buck dragged the carcass in an attempt to get away from the two men. The buck dragged the carcass of the dead buck backward in a retreat toward the timber, but was stopped when he hit a barbed wire fence. The fence halted his progress long enough for Bill to get photos.

Then the buck broke the strand of wire that was trapping him and began moving again. At this point, Bill and John Rudd roped and hogtied the buck and sawed several inches off one main beam of his antler. This freed him of his burden. They then released the deer. It arose and headed for the timber. When he reached the trees, he stopped momentarily and looked back at the two men who saved it. He then lifted his tail proudly and vanished into the bush.

Bill Carey considers this episode the most intriguing event he has ever encountered in the wilds in all of his years hunting, fishing and trapping.

Russell Thornberry
Trophy Deer of Alberta, 1982

■ FRACTURED ANTLER

Enclosed is a photograph of an antler discovered October 12, 1986 on Kelleys Island in Erie County, Ohio. The antler was wedged in the fork of a Red Willow, the circumference of which was slightly more than eighteen inches. The condition of the tree made it obvious the deer had been "rubbing" when the antler became caught. The ground around the base of the tree was substantially disturbed indicating strenuous efforts to free himself. Even though this occurred in an area of thick, brushy second growth with little to moderate deer activity, this particular tree has shown evidence of vigorous rubbing each of the past three years.

John D. Kinn

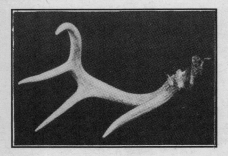

■ STUMP CHEWING

Deer frequently chew at old stumps. Their work here is often hard to distinguish from that of the bear, which tears these old stumps apart mainly to secure the ants found in there. A bear usually tears the stumps into larger pieces whereas a deer chews at exposed corners and leaves a different mark. It seems likely that deer do not chew stumps which have been recently nosed over by a bear. If the work is that of a bear one can usually find some faint trace of its teeth on the soft wood splinters and debris, occasionally its claw marks on the larger pieces and now and then its excrement in the immediate vicinity. If deer have been at work their sharp hoof marks usually can be found in the earth beside the stump, and sometimes dung pellets occur.

Other old logs as well as stumps frequently were found torn apart by deer in all the localities studied, but especially on the west slope of T-Lake Mountain and around the shores of Lizard Lake, west of T-Lake. At these two points numerous such stumps and logs were found within a relatively small area. Just why a deer chews at a stump of rotten wood is hard to determine unless it derives from this source a certain amount of mineral matter. In the case of decayed logs they are possibly able to secure roots which have penetrated the soft wood. These logs are comparatively easy to tear apart. In this connection William Monypeny Newsom ('26) mentions that deer sometimes go into a burnt-over area soon after the fire; perhaps the ashes attract them in somewhat the same way as a salt lick.

Townsend & Smith
White-tailed Deer of the Adirondacks (1933)

■ A LOSER

Last fall, during the rutting season, Deputy Vaughn Ulrich observed a buck in a field with several does. The buck was showing quite an interest in the does, but they did not want anything to do with him. Then a skunk ambled out into the middle of the field. The buck saw the skunk and decided it should not be there. He charged the skunk, driving it backwards and several times actually tossed it up in the air with its antlers. The skunk used its main method of defense, but it did not seem to affect the deer. The buck was finally able to chase the skunk out of the field, but when he returned to the does, they not only still would not have anything to do with him, they wouldn't even let him get close.

W.A. Bower
Pennsylvania Game News
June 1982

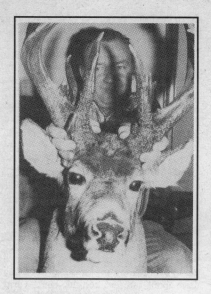

■ A FIGHTER

This incredible buck was taken in the Drayton Valley area of Alberta by Burt Smythe on 26 November 1979. The circumference of the bases of both antlers measured a full eight inches. The measurement around the burr where the antlers meet the skull measured nearly twelve inches in circumference.

Burt said that he watched this buck fighting with two other white-tailed bucks at the same time before he made his shot. He also observed that the testicles of this buck were extremely underdeveloped, which may have had a bearing on the unusual stag-like antler growth.

Russell Thornberry
Trophy Deer of Alberta, 1982

■ DEER AND EAGLES

Deer normally appear undisturbed by low-flying eagles except during the fawning season. At this time some eagles search for fawns and several observations indicate that does are aggressive in their attempts to drive eagles away from the vicinity of young fawns.

On the morning of 19 June 1957, William Alldredge, who was helping with fawn tagging, observed twin fawns disappear in some low brush. Shortly afterward, a golden eagle flew over, a few feet above the ground, and as one of the fawns started to flee, the eagle swooped down and bowled it over. Almost immediately three nearby does hurried to the bleating fawn. The eagle flew away and the fawn appeared uninjured upon regaining its feet.

On the morning of 25 June 1952, Spencer Whitney, also assisting with fawn tagging, observed an eagle in Lyman's Canyon alight on the ground near where twin fawns had been observed shortly before. In a matter of seconds, a doe appeared, frightening the eagle away. On the following morning Whitney observed an eagle on Partridge Mountain that flew into some scrub oak cober where twin fawns had disappeared shortly before. Whitney heard a fawn bleat but a doe immediately appeared and drove the eagle away.

W. Leslie Robinette, et. al., 1977
The Oak Creek Mule Deer
Herd In Utah

■ A BIRD INGESTED BY A WHITE-TAILED DEER

White-tailed deer have been observed eating fish that fishermen have thrown on the shores of streams and ponds. Muntjac deer have been observed chewing antlers and bones. In addition, a red deer has been observed killing and eating a Manx shearwater, and red deer were thought to have preyed upon shearwaters on a number of occasions.

In August 1969, a 128-pound two and one-half year old white-tailed doe from Herkimer County (New York) was autopsied for suspected arsenic poisoning. While sorting the rumenal contents, several pieces of tissue resembling the breast muscle of a small bird were found along with several bits of feathers and two bird legs. Dr. Edgar M. Reilly of the New York State Museum examined a fairly intact leg and thought it might have been from a rufous-sided towhee. The doe had been feeding on blackberries and blackberry vegetation. Tests for arsenic were positive.

Whether the arsenic poisoning had affected the behavior of the doe and caused her to ingest to bird is unknown. The bird may have been found dead and eaten accidentally, but the remains gave considerable evidence of mastication without rejection. Although the doe was in good flesh, she was lactating and may have had a deficiency in salts and/or proteins. Perhaps deer learn to use dead or helpless animals as a source of nutrients. This may be particularly true among deer that are living in the nutritionally poorer areas of their range.

New York Fish and Game Journal
January 1970

■ DEER VS. BOBCAT

For several days a doe and her two fawns were seen in a certain location in the chaparral vegetation near Prescott, Arizona. On the morning of August 27, 1953, the doe was observed standing in one spot, and the fawns were bedded about 100 yards away. As the doe was being watched, she grew excited and wheeled and trotted about at the sight of a mature bobcat walking up the grassy bottom of the valley. By now, the bobcat had passed 150 yards to the side of the fawns, and there was, consequently, no reason to think he was molesting them. Nevertheless, the deer raced toward the bobcat. The bobcat jumped out of her path, ran the short distance to a dense clump of brush, and darted in, with the deer about ten feet behind. For several minutes the doe ran around the clump of brush, stopping now and then to peer inward. For several minutes more she stood nearby, then walked up the slope to where her fawns were lying. The bobcat did not come out of the thicket during this time.

Throughout the encounter the bobcat was obviously afraid of the doe. It would be important to know how common such behavior of mule deer is and how successful it is in repelling bobcats. The behavior of both animals in this case, and in the cases reported by Linsdale and Tomich, suggests that mule deer may by such attacks prevent a considerable proportion of the predation attempts of bobcats upon the fawns.

William R. Hanson
Journal of Mammology, 1956

SCIENTIFIC WHITETAIL FACTS

Your hunting skills and hunting success will improve when you know the facts. **DEER & DEER HUNTING** delivers the latest in whitetail research presented especially with the deer hunter in mind. Each issue is 100% dedicated to Whitetails and whitetail hunting. Be on the leading edge...Subscribe today.

**Published 8 times a year.
Satisfaction guaranteed.**

Name _____

Address _____

City _____

State/Zip _____

ABAE8C

☐ One Year $17.95   ☐ Bill Me Later

☐ Two Years $31.95   ☐ Payment Enclosed

(Your paid subscription will include a FREE copy of the Deer Hunters Equipment Annual.) ~

BUSINESS REPLY MAIL

FIRST-CLASS MAIL PERMIT NO. 12 IOLA, WI

POSTAGE WILL BE PAID BY ADDRESSEE

DEER & DEER HUNTING
700 E STATE ST
IOLA WI 54945-9984

Stan Cope

■ PIEBALD DEER

On 11 January 1983, I rattled up and killed a small white-tailed buck that seemed typical in all features except for the color of his coat. He was about seventy-five percent white. The head and shoulders were the natural grayish-brown color and the rest of this body, including all four legs, were as white as the underside of a whitetail's tail.

Since that day, I have been hounded with questions as to why this unusual color existed, were the deer's parents white, was it an albino, and numerous others. I would greatly appreciate it if you could provide some information that might help answer these questions.

Stan Cope
Union Springs, Alabama
21 January 1983

Dear Stan,

The deer in question is termed a piebald deer. Piebald deer may have small patches of white where the hair would normally be colored in the typical shades of gray and brown. At times, as in your case, nearly the entire deer will be clothed in white.

Either or both of this deer's parents could have been normal colored, albino, or piebald. This unusual coat is a genetic trait, and it is quite likely that other piebald deer will appear in the same area in future years.

Al Hofacker

■ INTERLOCKED MULE DEER

On 5 November 1971, Mr. Edward Wesslen was looking over his land and fences near Blackfalls, Alberta when he found two mule deer bucks which had been dead for several hours. In their death struggle, the two bucks uprooted 100 feet of barbed wire fence and posts and tore up the ground around the scene of the battle, evidence of their ferocious fight for freedom. The Fish and Wildlife Department was advised of the find and the remains were collected. Eventually the two heads, still ensnared in the barbed wire that cost them their lives, were given to the Provincial Museum where they were photographed by Russell Thornberry. A special thanks to the Provincial Museum for making this story and photo possible.

Russell Thornberry
Trophy Deer Of Alberta, 1982

■ FREAK FACE MASK

This most unusual male deer was killed by Frank Kacsinko on 6 November 1965 along the Little Bow, east of Carmangay, Alberta. There was nothing abnormal about the deer except the antlers, according to Kacsinko, and the buck was fat and appeared healthy in spite of the strange formation.

Russell Thornberry
Trophy Deer Of Alberta, 1982

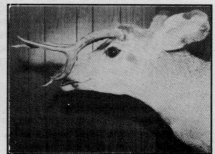

■ "TUNED-IN" DEER

Ten points on the rack of a deer shot near Arena, Wisconsin on 30 October 1983 aren't the only reason the head will make a memorable mount. Antenna stick out on either side of the deer's head, attached to small radio transmitters behind each ear.

Bow hunter Richard Nemetz of Brookfield shot the deer near his cottage north of Arena near the Wisconsin River, and contacted Larry Severtson of the Department of Natural Resources to show him the unusual feature.

Severtson did some investigating and came up with the story on the buck with radio transmitters.

The deer was live-trapped in the Madison Arboretum the previous February or March, wired for radio, and released south of Arena. Bill Ishmael, UW-Madison graduate student in wildlife ecology, and Dr. Rob Wegner, editor of Deer & Deer Hunting magazine, wanted to study movement of one animal. Only one was released.

Ishmael has followed the deer's movements ever since release. It travelled about four miles in the first three days after its release.

Within one week, the deer had moved about one mile north, to a big marsh north of town near the Wisconsin River. It has stayed in that vicinity ever since. Severtson estimated the area to measure something less than a square mile.

"There's a little pocket in that marsh and it's been there almost every time Ishmael has checked," Severtson said. "In fact, he thought if any deer was going to make it (through the hunting season) it would be this one, staying in that marsh."

Photo cells in the radio transmitters charge them up for about one night's worth of signals. The tracker was always in his car or on foot in the vicinity when on the trail of the deer. Each transmitter had a different signal, in case one malfunctioned.

Ishmael was disappointed the deer was shot, since he had not even followed it for an entire year, Severtson also reported. The deer was about two and one-half years old. Severtson is fire control assistant at the Tower Hill DNR station.

Home News
Spring Green, Wisconsin
2 November 1983

■ DEER BUCKS STATUE

It must have been a real knock-down, drag-out battle.

Rueben and Evelyn Storlien awoke last week to find two deer lying in their yard with antler locked.

One was mortally injured but still alive. The other didn't move at all. It never had; it was a cement statue of a deer with antlers.

Mrs. Storlien said no one saw or heard the confrontation, which ended with the cement deer on top of the live one. Apparently, the latter had charged its foe and both fell to the ground. The injured deer had to be destroyed.

Chicago Sun Times
22 September 1985

Richard P. Smith

■ UNUSUAL BUCK BAGGED

Every fall hunters shoot some unusual whitetails in the U.P. such as does with antlers or animals of either sex that exhibit abnormal coats like albinos or piebalds (partially white deer), and this fall was no exception. But one of the most unique deer tagged by a hunter during 1988 that I've seen was a buck bagged by a bow hunter in Mackinac County during December.

Mark Eby from St. Ignace is the successful hunter. He was in a tree stand in a cedar swamp on the evening of December 17 when he saw two deer approaching his stand. As they got close he made out spikes on the head of the lead deer and he decided to try for that animal, turning his attention from its antlers to placement of his arrow.

The buck was angling away at a distance of fifteen yards when Mark drew his sixty-pound-pull bow, aiming for a point behind the whitetail's shoulder. His arrow went higher than expected, severing the spine, dropping the deer instantly. Not until the hunter reached the fallen whitetail did he realize it wasn't a typical spike-horn.

The slender, five-inch spikes Mark saw from his stand grew out of the center of Circular-shaped, knobby growths. Both spikes and the growths that they grew from were covered with velvet. It was obvious from the deer's antlers that he wasn't a normal buck and Mark discovered what was responsible for the abnormal antler growth when field dressing the animal.

It had no testicles, even though he was a normal male otherwise. Without testicles, production of the male hormone testosterone would have been inhibited, resulting in abnormal antler growth. An increase in levels of testosterone during the fall is responsible for the shedding of velvet from antlers of normal bucks.

The deer Mark bagged with his bow proved to be an old animal. It was estimated to be 11.5 years old, based on tooth wear, by a DNR Wildlife Biologist at Sault Ste. Marie. The buck had a dressed weight of 165 pounds.

Perhaps the buck lived so long because it didn't grow antlers long enough for hunters to see during most of its life. In fact, 1988 may have been the first time the unusual buck grew spikes that were over three inches long. Since deer with antlers less than three inches are protected during gun season in Mackinac County, it would have been illegal for hunters to shoot if its antlers were smaller than they were this year, even if someone other than a bow hunter saw them.

I've only seen and photographed one other U.P. buck that lacked testicles and it was not many miles from where Mark shot his. This particular buck was a live animal that visited a feeder every winter for five years. Each year it had smooth, lumpy growths on its head in place of antlers that remained basically the same from one year to the next.

A close examination of this whitetail with binoculars revealed that it lacked testicles. There is a chance that buck and the one Mark shot could be the same one due to its advanced age and close proximity.

Richard P. Smith

98

■ PETRIFIED ANTLERS

This white-tailed deer rack narrowly misses Boone and Crockett standards. What makes it unique, however, it that the antlers are more than 1,000 years old. They were found by a farm hand, James Cooper, on the old homestead of Miles P. Hibkle near Balls-Franklin, Missouri in the year 1900. Cooper found them at a time of low water levels of the Missouri River in a bend of the river that had caved into the water. The antlers were petrified. Wildlife specialists at the University of Nebraska aged them. The right antler had two large drop tines that were broken off.

The Professional Bowhunter Magazine 1984

■ DEER SLIDE TO THEIR DEATHS DOWN A SNOW BANK

On November 10, 1952, a report was received that several deer had slid to their deaths down a snow bank just below Bishop Pass, Inyo County, California. Bishop Pass is situated about nine and one-half miles southwest of the town of Bishop, at an elevation of 11,972 feet, which is about 500 feet above timberline. It constitutes a main migration route for Inyo mule deer (Odocoileus hemionus inyoensis) over the crest of the Sierra Nevada. Deer winter low along the eastern slope of the Sierra and summer high on the western drainage.

On November 12, I hiked into the area with four others to investigate. We found 26 deer — 6 bucks, 17 does and 3 fawns — dead in rocks below an icy snowfield about one-quarter of a mile north of Bishop Pass. Some deer had died prior to a light snowstorm on November 7, but most had died subsequent to it.

Remains of winter snows often persevere in shaded sites at high elevations through summer and fall. This particular snowfield had been transformed into solid ice by successive thaws and freezes during summer months. It was about 150 feet long and tilted at an angle of nearly 45 degrees. The storm of November 7 deposited four to six inches of powder snow on the surface. Though deer had fallen prior to this, the new snow unquestionably aggravated the situation by making the glare ice.

Deer attempting to cross were unable to obtain traction and so plummeted the length of the ice to crash into a jumbled area of sharp talus blocks below. The rocks were bloodstained and strewn with splintered antlers and bits of flesh. Limbs, heads, necks and backs of deer had been fractured in a variety of combinations and some body cavities had been punctured by sharp rocks.

Bloodstains in the trail below showed that additional deer had been severely injured. Deer continued to migrate over the pass until November 14, when a heavy storm closed the route, so it is likely that others died in the same fashion. The route across the icefield was, fortunately, little used. The majority of the migrants followed a horse trial which was free of obstacles.

Many losses suffered by deer, such as this, are completely uncontrollable due to chance occurrence. It is seldom that we have the opportunity to determine an exact cause or even that loss took place. Old residents state that nothing similar has been known to have occurred previously in this section of the state.

Fred L. Jones
Journal of Wildlife Management 1954

■ THIS DEER THINKS HE'S A DOG

The deer's name is Bucky, but it could just as well be Rover or Fido because the yearling buck thinks he's a dog.

Ever since Bucky was a fawn being raised by the David Schiavo family on Lake Mary in Michigan's Iron County, dogs have been the deer's constant companions. The Schiavos have a black Lab name Ben and Mr. and Mrs. Robert Martin, who live nearby, have a Collie named Smokey.

The Schiavos obtained Bucky from the Department of Natural Resources when he was about a week old, according to Mike Schiavo. He said some people from Chicago picked the fawn up thinking it was an orphan. The rural setting where the Schiavos live is perfect for raising a deer. The animal has been permitted to roam freely most of its life.

Nonetheless, Bucky prefers the company of dogs and people to its wild relatives. He frequently sleeps with the dogs outside in the Schiavo or Martin yard, although this past winter the deer spent a lot of time in the Martin's garage with Smokey.

The deer and dogs romp and play together, too. Last winter Bucky and Smokey routinely took walks on the ice of Lake Mary to visit with fishermen. Anglers who fished the lake regularly and became accustomed to their visits got in the habit of carrying graham crackers with them as treats for Bucky.

Mrs. Martin said the unusual deer also likes sweets such as cookies and donuts as treats. However, Bucky's favorite food is dry dog food of any kind. When the dogs eat, he eats, too, and if he finishes before his canine companions, he tries to horn in on their meal.

Smokey doesn't usually stand for that though. His friendship with the deer doesn't go that far. If Bucky tries to snitch some of Smokey's food, the dog snarls at the deer as a warning, which Bucky usually heeds.

The deer's taste for dog food should be enough proof that the animal thinks it's a dog. However, Bucky's diet isn't totally like that of a dog. He hasn't shown any inclination for chewing bones, not yet at least, and he does eat commonly accepted deer foods such as woody browse and grass.

Bucky is sure to have come in contact with other deer during his walks around Lake Mary, according to the Martins. Other whitetails frequent the area. However, Bucky apparently doesn't recognize or accept himself as one of them. That may change in the future though as Bucky matures and becomes interested in does.

At the present time, Bucky wears-

appropriately-a dog collar with a bell attached. Mike Schiavo said that the buck's antlers may be sawed off this fall before hunting season begins, to reduce the chances of a hunter shooting the deer. He said Bucky may also be painted to serve as further protection.

Richard P. Smith

■ DOG NURSES DEER

My neighbor has a terrier dog ("Muffin") and about the time the puppies she had were six weeks old this fawn's mother was killed by an auto — resulting in the fawn being orphaned.

My neighbor has a wildlife rehabilitation license so the state game biologists took her fawn. They also took her two baby raccoons which were about three days old. The gal (Cynthia Palmer) is a bit of a free spirit so she thought she would see if the dog would nurse the two coons and the fawn and adopt them as her own. She (the dog) did just that — nursing the fawn and two coons till they weaned.

I did not know what Cynthia was doing, or trying to do, until one day when I was driving past her farm and saw the scene. Luckily I had my cameras with me because as I later found out the dog would seldom nurse in the open.

I'm sure you'll agree, it's incredible. I'm sure most wildlife biologists would doubt such a thing could ever happen. But as you can see from the photo the dog adopted the coons and fawn as her own and literally raised then from the time they were given to Cynthia until they wandered off into the woods for good.

The fawn returned to the wild for good after two and one-half months while the coons stayed around a bit longer. Cynthia didn't pen the animals so they were free to come and go as they pleased.

Regards,
Charles J. Alsheimer
Bath, New York
19 October 1981

Richard P. Smith

■ DEER IN CHINA SHOP

Just like a "real good shopper," a deer wandered through Buster Powell's china shop the other day without touching or buying anything.

The deer "came down the third aisle, took a left, took another left and went right out the door." Powell said, "I'm glad he got out of here. We've got displays all over."

The deer, which appeared to be slightly wounded, avoided Powell's displays.

Chicago Sun Times

■ OLD DOE BAGGED IS RECORD

When Dennis Vissering of Three Lakes, Michigan took aim at a deer during October of 1987 with a bow and arrow in southern Ontonagon County, he had no idea the whitetail might be a potential state record. After all, it was a doe and not any bigger than normal.

What was different about that deer though is it was older than most. After successfully making the twenty-two-yard shot at the doe and recovering it, Dennis discovered that its liver was full of flukes and teeth were worn to the gums.

DNR Wildlife Biologist Rob Aho at Baraga examined the doe, which had a dressed weight of 104 pounds, and said it had to be at least twelve years old, based on tooth wear. Tooth wear is not an accurate way of aging old deer, so Aho took a tooth from the deer for processing in the lab by Paul Friedrich. The exact age of deer can be determined by counting the rings in a cross section of a tooth.

Friedrich determined the doe was 14.5 years old, probably making it the oldest whitetail taken by a bow hunter in the state. Dennis said the doe was accompanied by a fawn at the time she was shot, so she was still producing offspring.

DNR Deer Researcher John Ozoga at the Cusino Wildlife Experiment Station in Shingleton has records of a doe that continued having fawns until thirteen years old. That doe was part of a herd kept in a square mile enclosure at the research facility until she was almost thirteen and then released in the wild. Ozoga said she gave birth to a set of twins in the wild and was shot illegally later that year.

Ozoga said does that reach thirteen and fourteen years of age still manage to breed normally, but not many wild whitetails live that long. The oldest doe Ozoga has records on lived in the wild all of her life and was almost seventeen when he last saw her in Alger County. He initially captured and ear-tagged the doe in a winter yard as a fawn on 20 March 1955 and recaptured her in the same yard on 12 March 1969 when almost fifteen. Two years later, he saw her again.

Most older does manage to escape hunters, according to Ozoga, making severe winters a more important factor in their chances of survival.

Richard P. Smith

■ MYSTERIOUS DEATH

Indiana's 1988 archery season was only a week old when Jennifer Deter noticed something strange in the middle of a 3/4-acre lake near her home in Warrick County.

"At first I thought it was a cardboard box floating in the lake," said Jennifer. A closer inspection revealed the floating object to be that of a huge twelve-point buck.

Jennifer then phoned the game warden who later took a small boat out to bring the buck in.

It was expected to find a wound, but the buck's body appeared to be in excellent condition. The conservation officer also checked the hooves of the deer to see if there was any cracking, which is a sign of Epizootic Hemorrhagic Disease (EHD). Several cases of the disease were reported in the county just prior to the previous year's archery season.

The possibility existed that maybe the deer was first struck by a vehicle and then went in the lake, however, the buck was skinned and there was no bruising or marks to indicate it had been hit.

It was finally decided that the probable cause of death was a heart attack, since there was some hemorrhaging in the body cavity. The buck apparently had went into the seventeen foot deep lake, and while swimming across suffered a heart attack. Drowning had also been ruled out.

Although Jennifer and her family are not deer hunters, they decided to get the buck mounted.

Due to the two unusual brow tines, it was scored as a typical ten-pointer. The buck's unofficial green score was 155-5/8, and had an inside spread of twenty-one inches.

John Trout, Jr.

■ DEER VS. COUGAR

The cougar or mountain lion seems immune to attack by all but the largest predators, such as grizzly bears. As is well known, the principle food of this large cat is deer, and cougars seldom occur where some species of deer is not present. Perhaps it is not surprising that, occasionally, the deer fight back, as one might surmise from the incident reported here. The veracity of this account is open to question, and I have a disinclination to add further to the great mass of myth and legend already associated with the cougar. Still, there are circumstances in this case that suggest its credibility.

On the eastern slopes of Glacier National Park, Glacier County, Montana, the mule deer is relatively common. Current estimates place its population at about 800 head. The cougar is present throughout the Park in limited numbers, although it is seldom seen. At the Many Glacier Ranger Station an unidentified camper reported the following episode on the afternoon of July 1, 1954. The observer was fishing at nearby Redrock Lake when a commotion on the shore attracted his attention. A mule deer doe was launching a vigorous attack on a cougar. Several times she leaped into the air and landed with all four feet on the prostrate cat. At first opportunity the cat jumped to safety in a tree above, grasping an overhanging limb seven feet above the ground, as determined by later measurement. No mention was made of the final outcome of the encounter. It was not indicated whether the cougar was an adult or juvenile; nor whether the doe had a fawn nearby, as would seem likely.

The observer had lived in the State of Washington for some fifty years and claimed to be well acquainted with these large, long-tailed cats in the wild. The authenticity of his fragmentary report may well be doubted. However, on July 13 another camper reported seeing what appears to have been a cougar in the same general area, on the south shore of Fishercap Lake, at about 5:00 P.M. This man claimed no prior acquaintance with the species, but merely inquired casually if it was common in the area and if it was destructive to other wildlife. His description fitted the cat perfectly.

Richard H. Manville
Journal of Mammology, 1955

■ "BUTTERFLIES" FROM A DEER'S MOUTH

Many years ago my parents had quite a collection of old books on various subjects, dating from 1700 to 1850. They were destroyed by fire some time about 1890. Among those old volumes was one which impressed me greatly, being a story of the strange beliefs and queer superstitions of a still earlier age, among which was related a tale of how at certain seasons, butterflies emerged from the mouths of deer. The article was illustrated by crude drawings copied from the old volume quoted, and ridiculed such a strange statement as the superstition of a very primitive age.

Strange to say, and quite by accident, I discovered that the old tale is true.

I was running a "pack train" at one time during my younger days, sometime about '87, and in those days, when we needed meat we simply went out and got it; no game laws then — in fact they were not necessary until later when the hide hunters began operations.

So I went out from camp one evening in early June — how I used to love those evening rambles — and soon saw a nice buck standing probably one hundred yards away. I was a fair shot in those days and taking careful aim with my Winchester 40-60, I broke his neck.

As was leaving camp one of the boys asked me to bring in the tongue of the animal in case I got a deer. After I had bled the animal and removed the entrails I split the larnyx preparatory to cutting out the tongue, and found inside of that organ, at the upper end of the windpipe, two insects in the pupal stage, probably an inch in length and about the diameter of the end of a medium-sized person's little finger. I thought it rather strange as they seemed to be lodged there and about to enter the chrysalis stage.

About three weeks later I killed another buck, and having my previous discovery in mind I examined his larnyx and found one insect in the chyrsalis form with wings folded and seemingly about ready to emerge.

Since then I have examined the throats of many deer and, although not always present, in the majority of cases have found from one to five when in the pupal stage, and one to three in the chrysalis period.

I came on to a yearling doe on one occasion in the early part of December that had just been killed by coyotes, and upon examining her throat I found fifteen or twenty larvae apparently of the same species, so judge that all but a small number deposited are expelled during that period. I believe that the eggs are deposited on the leaves of the shrubs upon which the deer browse and are taken into the throat that way — only a small portion surviving. The fully developed insect leaves the deer's throat about the latter part of June.

I have often heard the natives ask why deer hardly ever accumulate any fat until after June, and I really believe that the presence of these parasites is the explanation, as every hunter knows that a small number of deer occasionally found to be very fat during the winter and spring months, while the majority are in poor condition, whether the feed is good or bad.

I was attending to an irrigation ditch in an out-of-the-way part of my place on the North Fork of Salmon River on one occasion about June 20th. Early in the evening, hearing a slight noise, I looked up and saw a large doe coming almost directly toward me and seemingly in distress; trying to expel something from her throat, she held her head down nearly to the ground and came within ten or twelve

feet of where I was standing. She passed by me and was choking so that she walked right against a wire fence. That startled her and she leaped over it and made one or two bounds across the adjoining field. She then seemed relieved and taking a normal pose and natural gait she walked away. I fully believe that she expelled one of those insects at that time.

Forest and Stream
Herbert Finley
April 1925

A "maned" white-tailed buck shot by Mike Jaskaniec near Blue Mounds, Wisconsin.

■ "MANED" DEER

Mike Jaskaniec of Madison, Wisconsin may not have reason to brag that the nine-pointer he shot last fall was "as big as a horse" but he certainly can say that it looked a little like a horse. The white-tailed buck had a definite "mane" of dark hair growing down the back of its neck.

Mike shot the buck with his bow on 11 November 1983 from a tree stand on his farm in rural Blue Mounds, Wisconsin. His farm is in the same area where another unusual buck was bow-killed in 1979 by Dennis Shanks (Deer &

Deer Hunting, October 1980). Shanks' buck received a Pope & Young score of 231-5/8, high enough to become the new state record non-typical whitetail.

The maned buck was traveling alone on the cold, windy morning when Mike brought him down with a lung shot. He estimated the deer field-dressed at 140 pounds and might have been 2.5 years old.

This is the first case of a "maned" deer that we are aware of. We would be very interesting any other reports and/or photos from hunters that have harvested deer showing this strange characteristic.

William E. Ishmael
Department of Wildlife Ecology
University of Wisconsin-Madison

A "maned" doe photographed by Richard P. Smith near Grand Marais, Michigan in early 1984.

■ DEER'S BIOLOGICAL CLOCK OFF

Mama deer's biological clock may have malfunctioned because she gave birth to twin fawns during one of the coldest weeks of the year.

The Ohio Division of Wildlife says white-tailed deer fawns are normally born from mid-May to July after a 200-day gestation period.

Gildo M. Tori of the Division of Wildlife said this particular doe is approximately six months off, definitely an abnormal occurrence.

Richland County game protector Bill King says several people reported seeing the deer and two fawns near Bellville January 27, just hours after birth.

Division of Wildlife biologists were concerned that the fawns would not survive the harsh weather, but subsequent visits by King indicates the fawns are healthy and moving about.

King plans to keep an eye on the hardy twins and hopes to get close enough for a photograph.

"Most deer are born in mid-May to July with the majority born in June and that's just something nature doesn't stray with," said Tori. "Does only come into heat in the fall and that's when they are bred and it takes 200 days to have the fawn.

"This deer might have had some sort of hormone imbalance and came into heat, maybe last summer," said Tori. "Male bucks are always receptive and always fertile, of course. One apparently came across the doe in heat in the summer and bred her."

Tori said the fawns were born in sub-zero weather.

"The only thing they are eating is mother's milk and they obviously stayed real close to her and she kept them warm enough. They were last seen last Friday.

"The fellow that found them said they were still wet. They has just been dropped. He left them alone and the mother came and took care of them," Tori said.

"Usually during severe weather the deer will lay down for days at a time. The doe apparently laid down and kept the young ones warm and they're making it," Tori said.

The Parkersburg Sentinel
Parkersburg, West Virginia
13 February 1985

■ UNUSUAL DEER DEATHS

During my twenty years of hunting the white-tailed deer, I've been able to pursue my share of big, heavy-racked bucks. Fortunately, I've been able to slip my tag on a few of these heart-thumping trophies. However, more often than not, no matter how hard or how smart I hunt them, many of these wise old grandaddy bucks escape me.

Sometimes other hunters kill these deer that foil my best-laid plans, but frequently these monster bucks just seem to vanish off the face of the earth, never to be heard from again. What happens to them? That's the sixty-four thousand dollar question and one that I've pondered in my mind hundreds of times.

The dreaded poacher, of course, always is a possibility, but usually I rule this out since I feel these individuals would have the rack out bragging about it in pretty short order, revealing that the buck was dead.

Highways could be another factor. We all know that thousands of deer per year are killed on our nation's roads, and unquestionably this could happen to a trophy whitetail, especially during the rut. Without doubt, he could be hit and severely injured by a vehicle, then stumble into the woods and die hours, or even days later, unknown to any hunter.

Another way a big whitetail could die, and a way I like to feel a few of them do, is from old age. It seems only right that a few heavy-beamed, long-tined trophies should grow so wise and wary as to escape all hunters, eventually dying of natural causes, probably pneumonia.

For some strange reason, of all the ways a trophy buck might die unknown to the hunter pursuing him, the electrical storm is the one I fear the most. I cringe every time a thunderstorm sweeps through my area. I can just picture a big, nocturnal buck in late October bedded on a strategic point. Just as darkness envelops the forest, a thunderstorm moves in from the west. The great buck

Brad Herdon

rises from his bed, then cautiously works his way along the ridge to his favorite white oak tree that is just starting to drop its sweet acorns to the forest floor.

The buck and the greatest fury of the storm arrive at the oak almost simultaneously. Just as the gray-faced monster lowers his head to vacuum up the succulent food, a bolt of lightning arcs from the sky toward the tallest tree on the ridge — the white oak. Death is instantaneous. The buck crumples to the ground, to decompose and act as food for the new acorn sprout that must grow for at least seventy-five years to replace the now-dead oak from which it fell.

I suppose my imagination runs a little rampant occasionally, especially when it comes to trying to figure out what could happen to the wallhanger bucks that elude me year after year. However, an accident so bizarre as to be beyond my consideration — or anyone else's for that matter — killed four deer this past spring in my home region of Jackson County, Indiana.

This happened when an early season wind storm buffeted the hardwood forests the night of April 6. The fifty and sixty mile-per-hour winds played havoc with the trees in what was to be one of the most destructive wind storms to pass through southern Indiana in the twentieth century.

Near the small town of Clearspring, a group of deer calmly grazed in a secluded pasture, oblivious to the fury of the storm. A small, two-wire power line, supported by wooden poles, passed through the middle of the pasture. One of the poles, weakened by years of usage began to crack, eventually breaking under the force of a strong gust. The noise of its falling was muffled by the ferocity of the storm so the deer were unaware of their impending doom.

For a power line to fall and kill one deer would be unusual, but when this line fell, four deer were in its path and died from electrocution. The line had just been put back up when I arrived to photograph this rare accident, but the picture shows how the deer were standing in a straight line when the wires fell. The long dark line in the pasture was caused by the grass being burned by the high voltage. If you look close, you can see dark or burned areas where the electricity arced from the deer's bodies to the ground.

Brad Herndon

■ CROSSBREEDING IN DEER

Evidence of crossbreeding between white-tailed deer and mule deer has been discovered in West Texas, researchers say.

"Hunters and scientists have long known that the two species were intermingling in the Trans-Pecos River region of Texas and have often wondered if the interbreeding could play a part in the dwindling number of mule deer in that part of the United States," Dr. Steve Carr of Texas A&M University said.

Carr led a Texas A&M research team that examined genetic composition of more than 100 deer, including white-tailed deer and mule deer in West Texas.

"Surprisingly, on one Pecos County ranch, the two species were genetically identical," Carr said. "Our hypothesis is that hybridization occurs most often between white-tailed does and mule deer bucks."

During the research, mitochondrial DNA from white-tailed deer in South Carolina and mule deer from California were also examined.

"The simplest way to look for hybridization (in deer) is to find genetic differences between the species involved and then to look at the suspected hybrid population for evidence of genes from both species," Carr said.

"Mitochondrial DNA is inherited solely from the mother, which makes it possible to determine the direction of interbreeding between species."

The research may help better manage the $100 million-per year deer hunting business in Texas, Carr said.

Houston Post
24 May 1987

■ MAN WALKING ON ROAD TRAMPLED BY EIGHT-POINT BUCK

A 160-pound deer with eight-point antlers gored and trampled to death a man walking along a rural road, authorities said in October 1990.

Charlie Jackson Coleman, 61, of Caldwell, Texas, was hunting for antique bottles along the side of the road when he was attacked by the buck, which was still standing over the body hours later when sheriff's deputies arrived.

The deputies said they shot the buck when it charged them.

An autopsy determined that Coleman died from a crushed skull and had more than 100 hoof and puncture wounds over his back, abdomen and face, police said.

"It was the most unbelievable thing I've seen," Burleson County Chief Deputy Tom Randall said. "It was more of a massacre than an attack."

Another buck had charged three surveyors earlier that week near Beaumont, 50 miles east of Houston, pitching one of them 20 feet into a creek.

One of the men said he wrestled the deer to the ground and his partner slit the buck's throat with a machete.

Don Steinbach, Texas Agricultural Extension Service wildlife and fisheries specialist, said the case was "very unusual," but that deer are more likely to become aggressive if they have been tamed.

"If deer have been domesticated and aren't afraid of people, they do get aggressive when they come into rut," he said.

Milwaukee Sentinel
Oct. 31, 1990

■ FAWN SURVIVES TWENTY-FOOT FALL

In Mountain City, Tennessee, a fawn hopped a railing and fell twenty feet to become Johnson County Hospital's first patient in over a year.

Although the hospital is closed because of financial trouble, a few people are working in the facility as efforts to reopen continue. Recently, maintenance supervisor Bernest Trivette and a helper were in the basement when they heard a thud and then a squeak.

They found the fawn rolled up under Bernest's car in the garage area. According to hospital administrator Kevin Hodge, "There's a railing nearby, over which it apparently jumped, not knowing it was a twenty-foot drop."

Trivette carried the stunned fawn into the hospital and placed it on a stripped bed. Amazingly no bones appeared broken, and the deer had only minor scrapes and bruises. "It wasn't too long before it regained its faculties," Hodge said. "It had apparently just knocked itself silly for a little bit."

Rollin Moseley

■ TAGGED DEER ELUDE HUNTER

Despite a record deer kill in Wisconsin during 1990, big numbers of deer are probably still walking that state's woodlots and forests. Consider, for example, a radio-tag study being conducted in the state's Northwest by the University of Wisconsin. Last summer and fall, researchers located 91 deer they had previously fitted with radio tags. The group consisted of 52 does, 21 bucks and 18 fawns in deer management units 6 and 20. After the archery and firearms seasons ended, the researchers determined that four does, five bucks and one fawn were killed by firearms hunters; one buck was killed by an archer; two does were killed illegally; and one doe was killed by a car. Another doe likely drowned after breaking through the ice on a lake.

In other words, hunters killed only 12 percent of the group. Further, this means hunters killed only 8 percent of the group's does, 29 percent of its bucks, and 5.5 percent of its fawns.

Orrin J. Rongstad, professor emeritus at UW-Madison, made these comments in a progress report in February 1991: "In spite of the fact that (the state) had a 16-day (firearms) season and (distributed) a large number of antlerless permits, hunter-related mortality was the lowest since our study began in 1986. I located 50 antlerless deer the week before the hunting season in Unit 6. Of these 50, only one buck fawn was killed. I located the other 49 the week after the season, alive and well, in the same areas they were in before the season."

This doesn't mean the rest of the state experienced similar results, but it does show that deer in the northern forests are skilled at eluding hunters.

Pat Durkin

■ UNUSUAL DEER ATTACK

Dr. William Robinson from Marquette, Michigan observed an unusual interaction between a healthy whitetail and one he hit with a broadhead while bow hunting last December.

Robinson arrowed the whitetail, which proved to be a buck that had already dropped its antlers, on December 28. He thought the hit was a good one and after a short wait followed the wounded whitetail into a cedar swamp. There was no difficulty following the deer because snow covered the ground.

The injured buck was eventually spotted lying down. The deer saw Robinson at the same time, however, got up, and walked off. But the deer laid back down within view of the hunter. While Robinson waited, another deer happened along in the vicinity of the injured one.

Upon detecting the wounded buck, the healthy whitetail went up to it and began striking it on the head with its front hooves. The deer that was under attack moved in an effort to get away, but the aggressive deer persisted, following until the deer laid down again and then continued its attack.

Robinson suspected that the second deer was also a buck with antlers shed, but had no explanation for the attack. Perhaps it had something to do with interaction between the two animals earlier and/or the vulnerability of the wounded buck. At any rate, the healthy deer eventually broke off its attack and left the scene. Robinson then moved in and claimed his deer, using another arrow to finish the weakened whitetail.

Robinson felt the outcome would have been the same without "help" from the second deer because the attack didn't appear to have injured the dying buck any more than it already was.

R. P. Smith

■ BOLD DEER

The 1981 Wisconsin gun deer season taught me a lesson to be learned. I had the experience of being knocked over by a deer.

On Thanksgiving Day, my hunting companions and I decided to make a drive through a small patch of thick brush. I was elected to be one of the standers. The brush was too thick to stand in so I decided to stand on a fire lane, hoping I would get a shot at a deer crossing it.

As I was standing there, I could hear my companions approaching from the right. Figuring it was getting near the end of the drive, I didn't expect to see any deer. All of a sudden, however, a deer burst out of the brush and knocked me on my back. Laying in shock for a few moments, I managed to get on my knees in time to see a nice buck disappear into the woods.

The lesson to be learned is that one should always be prepared to see a deer at any time or any place.

Jeffrey F. Jasinski
Milwaukee, Wisconsin
12 March 1982

■ BREAKING TRAIL

I was doing some winter camping in the mountains of Utah when I saw three deer making their way through the deep snow. Number one deer would lunge forward for about fifty feet, then lie on his side in the snow while numbers two and three passed. Number two would then take the lead for fifty feet, with number one at the tail end. Finally, number three broke trail followed by one and two.

With binoculars, I watched these three animals alternate in breaking trial for about a quarter of a mile. Had one deer done all the heavy work, he would soon have become exhausted and helpless.

Henry E. Leabo
Lancaster, California

■ RUBBING POLE

Research biologists have shown that "buck rubs" serve as special signposts, of particular social importance during the white-tailed deer's breeding season. These marks likely help delineate a buck's breeding range, serve to inform other deer of his superior presence and enhance prospects for social order during the whitetail's otherwise hectic breeding season.

Each rub not only appears as a showy blaze, where bucks scrape away the tree bark with their antlers (and head), but because all deer possess specialized forehead skin glands, it also carries the distinctive scent of the maker. Interestingly, tests indicate that mature, socially high-ranking bucks exude greater amounts of this forehead glandular secretion than younger males or females and that relatively few breeder-bucks are generally responsible for most of the rubs within a given area as a means of advertising their high dominance rank.

Bucks normally prefer to rub trees and shrubs in the one- to four-inch diameter range — especially those that are really debarked — but on occasion tackle sizeable timber. Repeat rubbing of the same stem within the same or even successive rut seasons is relatively uncommon, as the buck more likely rubs a new stem nearby on return visits.

In October 1974, while conducting observational studies of buck rutting behavior in our Upper Michigan square-mile Cusino deer enclosure, I observed a 4.5-year-old buck as he squared off with a large pole supporting overhead high voltage lines and thrashed it with his antlers. Many bucks have since then come and gone from the enclosure, but each autumn this one pole (of twenty-four available along the three-quarter-mile long right-of-way) shows unusually heavy and repeated rubbing by antlered bucks, as evidenced by the pole's shredded condition in the accompanying photo.

Given what scientists know about buck-rubbing behavior, I'm somewhat at a loss to explain the unnatural and persistent use that bucks have made of this particular pole — as a rubbing post — during the past twelve years. I assume that it serves as a scented signpost of sorts, but why bucks would select a marker treated with foul-smelling wood preservative and tar, and rub it with such dedication, in preference to naturally growing saplings, remains a mystery.

John J. Ozoga
Michigan Out-Of-Doors
November 1986

■ STEALING CORN

Brian Landrum, Field Supervisor for the Division of Wildlife, was working at Lake St. Mary's on Saturday, 27 May 1984 when he spotted some frantic "picnickers." It seems this group of people had wandered away from their table full of food when one of them looked back and saw two "raiders" helping themselves to the corn. The raiders were white-tailed deer which were scared off by the picnickers. One of the deer ran past some cottages and the other one jumped in the lake and started swimming. (Guess no one ever told him to wait at least one hour after eating before going into the water.) A crowd of people gathered around to see what the deer would do and it eventually made good its "escape" by taking refuge on an island. Officer Landrum saw the same deer later on and it again ran down to the water and leaped in. . . is it too late to enter the Olympic swimming trials?

Jim Wentz
Wildlife News
Ohio Department of Natural Resources

■ DEER DOES IN DEPUTY

Deer were really roaming the rural roads in Erie County, New York, one night recently.

"Deer are on the move," Sheriff Kenneth J. Braun alerted his deputies via radio.

And Deputy Sheriff David Karney knew what his boss was talking about.

Karney was already investigating an incident near Holland, New York, where he had to dispatch a badly injured deer which collided with a motorist's car. The motorist was unhurt and his car was undamaged.

Shortly thereafter Karney received a radio message to investigate another accident involving a deer.

Then, while driving near Sardinia, New York, to that accident scene, a deer jumped in front of and damaged Karney's patrol car. Karney was not injured and the deer disappeared into the woods.

Grit
5 March 1985

■ DEER BAGS HUNTER

Several years ago I went hunting snowshoe hares with two companions in January. Late in the afternoon we were hunting our way back out to our truck and were spread out approximately 100 yards from each other. As I neared the truck, I came upon a field of standing corn which was loaded with feeding deer. About the same time that I noticed the deer, they spooked. Apparently they saw the other two hunters and our hounds.

I quickly knelt down in the three-foot snow drifts and started counting the number of deer running out the far end of the field. Because I was kneeling in the deep snow, I could not clearly see much of the corn field. All that I could see was the far end of the field where the deer were exiting.

All of a sudden I heard the noise of running deer very close to me. As I turned towards the noise (while still kneeling), I was shocked to see several deer charging straight toward me.

By the time I realized what was happening, the first deer (a large doe) in the group smashed head on with me. Her shoulder hit me squarely in the face and chest area and I was knocked over backwards. I quickly rolled myself up into a ball, tucking my head down tight against my knees to protect myself from the rest of the deer following the lead doe.

Then the other deer (six or seven of them) jumped over me as I was lying on the ground. All of them except for the very last one; that one didn't jump high enough to completely clear me. Her feet somehow got tangled up with my legs and she went crashing to the ground beside me.

Luckily, she missed me when she fell, but the scope of my .22 rifle was not so lucky. She broke it as she regained her feet before running off.

This all happened within a period of a minute of two. As I laid on the ground, I tried to figure out what had happened. Then I heard the laughter of my two hunting buddies. They witnessed the whole episode and were enjoying it to the fullest.

Then soon realized that it may not be so funny after all when they saw that I was hurting. They quickly came to my aid.

The first deer that hit me did a pretty good job of it. She gave me a nose bleed, a black eye and some very sore rib and shoulder bones.

Looking back on all of this now, I understand why my buddies laughed so hard. It must have been quite a sight to see — all those flying bodies, both deer and hunter.

After calming down, I realized exactly what had happened. Because of the deep snow cover, the deer never saw me kneeling until it was too late. I also made the mistake of kneeling until it was too late. I also made the mistake of kneeling in one of the main deer trails of the area.

Thus, when the frightened deer took off, some of them used the trail as an escape route. Unfortunately, I was in the wrong place at the wrong time.

Even though several years have passed since that cold day in January, my hunting companions still won't let me forget that day. They really seem to enjoy telling others about the time they saw a deer bagging a hunter.

Michael D. Winkel

■ BUCK ATTACK

Back home in Texas, Benjamin Kirkland roped calves and rode bulls, but now he knows that's wimp stuff compared with rassling a big ol' Minnesota buck.

"I thought sure enough I was a goner," he said of his encounter last week with a 225-pound, eight-point deer, which attacked him in the woods near Elk River.

Kirkland, twenty-six, of Lufkin was returning to his motel around dusk after working on a nearby pipeline when his eyes fastened on a buck, grazing in a field a few hundred yards behind his motel, about thirty miles north west of the Twin Cities.

"Where I'm from, deer just don't get

as big as that," he said. "This looked like a monster to me."

Crawling behind an embankment, he planned to sneak up behind the buck and get a good look without being detected. But when he reached the spot where he thought the buck should be, there was nothing.

He stood up to walk away, and there it was about thirty steps away, staring at him. Kirkland froze.

"Generally, a buck deer like that is going to break and run to get away from you. He's supposed to be way scareder of you than you are of him."

The buck charged, slamming its antlers into Kirkland's ribs.

Kirkland fastened his legs onto the antlers, covering the buck's eyes, and the two fell to the ground.

"He'd get up and run around in circles, dragging me on the ground. Then he runs me into a tree, hard, as hard as he could run, and slams me into it."

Kirkland grabbed hold of the pine tree and scampered up it. "I knew that tree was going to save me — it was the only way out."

Kirkland figures he sat in the tree for forty minutes before people at a nearby shopping center heard his cries for help and called police.

Elk River Patrolman Dave Sievert showed about ten minutes later and called in a State Patrol officer and a reserve officer.

When the buck lowered its head and started charging, Sievert fired the first of four shots that killed it.

The Department of Natural Resources on Wednesday gave Kirkland the antlers as a souvenir of Minnesota. Kirkland thanked him and promised, "I won't bother no more of your wildlife."

Kirkland plans to have the antlers mounted and hang them beside the tattered blue jeans and leather vest he was wearing, "and tell stories about it the rest of my life."

Houston Chronicle
3 November 1988

■ DEER SHOOTS HUNTER

A seventeen-year-old Avera, Georgia youth was hospitalized in fair condition recently after being shot when a deer apparently kicked a gun.

Jefferson County Sheriff Zollie Compton said the youth was shot around 9:00 P.M. when he and three other youths on their way home from a hunting trip.

Sheriff's investigator Mark Williamson said the youths had shot two deer and had loaded them, along with their guns, in the back of their pickup. Williamson said one of the deer apparently kicked a loaded 12-gauge shotgun and the gun went off. He said the pellets went through the cab of the pickup and hit the victim in the back.

Williamson said the youths were charged by the state Game and Fish Commission law enforcement division with hunting from a public road, hunting from a vehicle and hunting deer at night, as if the one hospitalized didn't have enough trouble already.

Rollin Moseley

■ CLOSE ENCOUNTER

It was a close encounter that the participants, human and animal, are not likely to forget anytime soon.

Two brothers are traveling a country road near Mobile, Alabama. Philip Vinson, 18, is driving his two-door Escort sedan. His brother, Daniel, 15 is in the front passenger's seat.

They see a deer at the side of the road. As they are passing the animal, it leaps through the window on Daniel's side of the car sending glass flying. The deer lands in Daniel's lap.

Philip has difficulty finding a place to pull off the roadway while dodging the frantic deer but eventually succeeds in stopping the car.

Somehow, either through Daniel's struggles with the animal or through its own efforts, the deer is in the rear seat.

"I was eating a Butterfinger," Daniel said. "I beat on the deer with it."

After the deer was in the rear of the car, Daniel grabbed the car keys, opened the rear hatch and got the deer out of the car through the hatch.

The deer ran. Philip said the animal was small, three to four feet high.

Daniel received scratches and cuts from glass or deer or both and his clothing was torn.

The windshield of Philip's car was broken in the melee and the head liner of the vehicle was torn in two places. Whatever caused one of the tears also punched up the car roof directly over the rip. There was damage to the dashboard in the glove compartment area.

Neither of the brothers recall seeing antlers and it is believed most of the damage was inflicted by the animal's hooves.

By that afternoon, the Vinsons were able to make jokes about deer seasons and deer hunting without guns.

"They were scared to death," their mother said. "They pounded on the door (after the accident). Their faces were white and Daniel was bleeding (his nose was bloodied in the fray)."

The brothers involved in the close encounter of the deer kind are the sons of Mr. and Mrs. Horace Vinson.

Rollin Moseley

■ DEER COLLIDES WITH RACE HORSE

Even the least superstitious person would admit that "Friday the 13th" cast a sinister glance the way of jockey Brian Peck at Turfway Park on 13 January, 1989. In as peculiar a scene as ever witnessed in sports, two deer crossed the main track while the fourth race was proceeding down the backstretch at the Northern Kentucky oval.

The first deer crossed safely in front of the oncoming twelve-horse field. However, the second deer collided broadside into the pacesetter, Top Booking, ridden by Brian Peck. The mare was literally "tackled" from the side causing Peck to be catapulted twenty-five feet forward and be rolled over by his mount.

With a heap of horse, deer and rider prone on the main track, the other eleven riders were a split second from a "miracle," the horse sprang up and continued running, the deer was bumped hard twice but then wobbled to safety into the forest that makes up half of Turfway Park's 365 acres, and Peck was brushed by only one horse, which did not cause further injury to him.

Peck did suffer a compound fracture of his right forearm in the hard spill to the track. He was operated on Saturday morning at Booth Memorial Hospital and a steel plate and two pins were placed in his arm to promote healing. Peck, seventeen, was expected to be out for at least two months to recuperate.

Television footage of the incident was seen nationally by sports viewers on CNN, ESPN and local network sports telecasts and interest grew due to the spectacular nature of the video.

"I saw something streak across the track, but I wasn't sure what it was," stated rider James Bruin who's mount Irish Honor was third along the rail down the backside. "Then I saw another one (deer) ... it was the size of a yearling. The horse hit it hard, like a Mack truck.

"A lot of credit goes to the rider in front of me (Perry Ouzts). If he had not been able to get around him (Peck) ... there was no way I would have been able to get around him (Ouzts). The four or five horses behind me wouldn't have been able to make it either."

The power of "Friday the 13th" made a believer of 9,000 race fans in Kentucky and millions watching TV video that evening from coast-to-coast. Sportscasters and racing fans from across the country have called Turfway Park seeking to acquire the freak footage.
Turfway Park Racing Association

■ DC-DEER

Long before Dulles International Airport was built in 1962, deer romped around what was then a largely unpopulated area in the northern Virginia countryside just west of Washington. As airport officials know only too well, the deer have not been intimidated by jumbo jets into giving up entirely their old haunts.

A mid-morning incident last Sunday in which a New York Air DC-9 jetliner struck and killed two deer while landing at Dulles was the most serious encounter so far. None of the thirty-two passengers or crew aboard the flight from La Guardia Airport were injured, but a tire and a wing flap were damaged. Dexter Davis, the airport manager, says employees in the tower report seeing deer near the runways several times a week, usually in the dark of night. Operations officers are dispatched to chase the animals away. "It's unusual for the deer to show up in the daytime," Mr. Davis said.

No one knows how many deer roam the 10,000-acre Dulles site. The Federal Fish and Wildlife Service has canvassed the area but was unable to come up with an exact count.

But one thing is sure. The deer population thins considerably during Virginia's official deer hunting season, from about the third week in November until early January, when the more than forty Dulles police officers, equipped with hunting licenses, are given carte blanche to shoot on sight to fill their home larders.
New York Times
24 July 1985

■ PHENOMENAL DEER/VEHICLE COLLISION

Indiana records hundreds of vehicle/deer collisions each year. As in other states, many collisions occur during the rut, when bucks are most active. On 12 November 1989 Bruce Aigner of Warrick County experienced a dramatic collision.

He left his parents' house near dusk and headed west on State Road 62 in his 1985 truck. His four-year-old daughter was lying down in the seat and had nearly fallen asleep when suddenly a loud crash and explosion of glass occurred. Bruce had no idea what happened as he struggled to gain control of the truck. The vehicle veered to the right and went down an embankment, finally coming to rest in a ditch.

His daughter was crying and very upset, but Bruce was relieved to see she was okay, particularly after noticing the windshield was shattered and peeled back at the top of the cab. Bruce was covered in blood, however, and unaware how serious his injuries were.

With the help of other motorists they finally managed to get out of the truck through the passenger door window.

Two young men who knew Bruce had been following a short distance behind him just prior to the accident. After checking him over, one of the young men asked if Bruce had been deer hunting that day. He explained he hadn't as they pointed to a large-bodied whitetail laying in the bed of the pickup truck.

Another driver approached Bruce and explained he had just hit a deer while traveling east bound. Bruce continued to inspect his truck and found the rear window of the cab also ripped out.

They soon pieced together exactly what had happened. The driver of the other vehicle had apparently struck the deer first, sending it into the air and through the windshield of Bruce's truck. It continued to pass through the cab, crashing through the rear window and finally coming to a halt in the back of the truck.

A wrecker eventually arrived, confirming the deer to be a buck as it drove over one of the antlers and punctured a tire. The two young men soon located the other antler of the eight-point buck.

Bruce was later treated at a nearby hospital for lacerations of his face, hands, and legs. Several pieces of glass were removed from his eyes, though he suffered no permanent damage. His daughter escaped injury, as did the driver of the car who struck the deer first. Bruce's truck suffered $4,500 in damages. Investigating officers offered to give the deer to Bruce, but he declined. The two young men were awarded the 150-pound, field-dressed deer.

John Trout, Jr.

■ DEER HYBRIDIZATION

Texas A & M University wildlife biologists have embarked on a project to document cross-breeding between two different species of large mammals living in the wild.

The researchers are studying genetic differences between white-tailed and mule deer to look for evidence of hybrids. The work is significant because hybridization among large mammals is rare and because it may lead to better management practices that would enhance Texas' $600 million a year deer hunting industry.

Dr. Steve Carr, A & M research scientist, explained that wildlife biologists have long known that the two species were intermingling in the Trans-Pecos region and have wondered if interbreeding could be a reason for the dwindling number of West Texas mule deer.

Dallas Times
13 January 1985

■ A WELL-CAPTURED BUCK

On 20 November 1982, while deer hunting in Fairfield County, South Carolina, an unbelievable mishap could have ended in tragedy for me. While stalking deer, I came upon an enormous oak tree on the edge of the clearing.

Seeing several briar thickets laced with honeysuckle vines nearby, I knew this was an ideal place to find a bedded buck. Knowing this area had the markings of an old home site, I cautiously entered this half-acre of tangled vegetation. Having hunted around abandoned home sites in the past, I was fully aware of the possible existence of an old, open pit well.

Taking each step carefully, I constantly scanned the thickets in front of me for a fleeing buck. Not paying attention to every step as I should have, I accidently stepped directly into the middle of an old well shaft. Seeing the rock-lined shaft go by my face as I fell, I knew I was doomed.

Expecting to fall twenty to twenty-five feet, I stopped suddenly at around eleven feet. Luckily, this was a very shallow well.

Thinking that I had not fallen to the bottom, I was afraid to move. As I looked down to see how far the bottom was, a dark grey object was directly below me. Before I had time to react, the object sprung up between my legs. As it was dark in the well shaft, several seconds passed before I recognized that the animal was a deer. To avoid being injured by the hooves of the alarmed deer, my first instinct was to shoot the deer, but the narrow shaft prevented me from maneuvering my shotgun into position. Then I thought I could kill it with my knife, but it occurred to me that we both were trapped. Sizing up the situation, I pulled the panic-stricken deer down under me and climbed the rock-faced wall of the old well to safety.

For more than a minute I stood staring down the well shaft watching the young buck try to leap to safety. On each attempt he fell back. At this time, I knew if I didn't get the deer out soon, it would kill itself. Knowing that my hunting companions were nearby, I yelled for help.

One of my companions fortunately had some strong cord which he quickly looped on one end. I re-entered the well with the utmost caution. I was able to tie the back legs of the deer together and, as the deer was pulled up, the front legs were tied together. After lifting the deer from the well, I tied all four legs together so the deer could not kick. We examined the buck for injuries. It had a small cut on the top portion of its tail and was bleeding some from the nose. The deer was in good shape and had apparently not been in the well very long, a few hours at most.

Examining the bottom of the well, I found the skeletal remains of a four-point buck which had been fatally trapped in the well. Also, there were turtle shells and other unidentifiable bones at the bottom of this death pit.

We attempted to transport the deer home to look after his wounds and then release him. But when we got home, which was less than an hour's drive, the young buck had died, apparently from shock.

This was quite an experience for me and I advise any hunter, especially those who hunt, alone to be very cautious when hunting around old home sites. You may not be as lucky as I was.

M. Wayne Archie
Fort Mill, South Carolina

■ "BAMBI" STARS ARE MAIN COURSE

A Yalta film studio's production of "Bambi" has been thrown off the schedule after three of the four deer used in the filming ended up on someone's dinner table, a Soviet newspaper reported yesterday.

After the deer vanished from the movie set in the Crimea, where Felix Salten's children's book is being filmed, a police investigation revealed they had been stolen by three men who slaughtered them for a birthday feast, Selykaya Shisny reported.

The three deer slayers were sentenced to four to six years in prison, and the film studio was awarded about $6,000 in damages for the loss of its stars, the newspaper said.

The Plain Dealer
6 February 1985

■ THE CRAZY MOON

The summer of 1982 looked very promising for my pursuit of white-tailed deer photographs. A secluded area inside the Sioux City city limits was being visited by four bucks regularly. As fall drew near, the two largest bucks became rather tolerant of my presence and I was able to get some late evening photo opportunities on a nightly basis. One buck became so trusting that I was eventually able to approach quite easily. Unfortunately, late evening light conditions never offered me many quality shots.

With the Iowa bow season just around the corner, I began to devote my time to practice and scouting my own hunting area many miles to the north. I couldn't help wondering about what the future had in store for the city-bound whitetails and I hoped my interference would not prove detrimental to their well-being.

After a successful season, I once again tried to locate my elusive friends. On November 1, my first morning out, I did locate the fine nine-point buck that had grown to trust me like no other wild animal has ever done. Unfortunately, he lay dead on the shoulder of the road, hit by a passing auto during the night. The rut was in full swing and natural desire was stronger than instinctive caution. The time of the "Crazy Moon" led to his death. He was the third road-kill in just six days. That night I returned to where he had been hit and found one antler that had been knocked free by the force of the collision. One final gift from an old friend.

Two nights later, I heard of yet another deer-auto collision just a quarter-mile from where the last buck was hit. I arrived at the scene too late to see which of the small herd was killed this time. This was November 3 and I knew that by this time three of the four bucks had been killed and reports of this latest incident proved to be another nine-point buck. He was the last remaining buck in the area. It's rather ironic that this in-town sanctuary would prove to be the demise of all four bucks.

The rut soon passed and so did my quest for photographic subjects in their home territory. I hoped the rut had been successful for the many does in the area.

In February 1983 at the yearly banquet of our local bow hunters club, the story continued. A new member whom I had never met walked in with a pair of antlers. I recognized those antlers instantly. Jerry Hoelker had heard of my

photography of the local whitetails and was curious if I knew their history. Well, you guessed it, they belonged to the nine-point buck killed the night of November 3. Jerry was given the road-killed deer to put to good use. Since my last sighting, the antlers had changed remarkably. What was so unusual about the antlers was that the left side was totally entwined with stainless steel wire. The buck had apparently escaped a poacher's snare or possibly encountered the wire while foraging in the abandoned dump site in the area. Because of my close relationship with the deer, Jerry graciously offered me the amazing antlers.

Occasionally I catch a fleeting glimpse of antlers in my old haunt. Perhaps someday they and their offspring will grow to tolerate me and my photographic escapades also. Maybe this ending is just the beginning.

Mike P. Grenier
Sioux City, Iowa

■ DEER GOES BERSERK

Wildlife officials destroyed a deer, raised as a pet, that went berserk and gored three people in Cross Plains, Tennessee.

"I have never seen anything like that in my life," said Ida York of Brownsville, Kentucky, one of the three people wounded in the attack. "He just gored me like everything."

Mrs. York said she and her granddaughter, Charlotte Swann of Cross Plains, had car trouble and were walking past a home when "this great big deer just jumped out of nowhere and ran us up on the porch.

"I started hollering at my granddaughter to pull me up in a tree, because I knew he wouldn't come up there," she said. "When she turned around, he got her in the behind and in the leg and then came at me again. She had to have thirty-six stitches herself."

Mrs. York was admitted to the hospital with severe puncture wounds on both legs.

The animal also reportedly attacked Will Gregory of Cross Plains, who had apparently brought his granddaughter to pet the deer. Authorities said Gregory suffered a puncture wound in his left thigh but the child was not injured.

An unidentified Robertson County woman raised the buck, officials said. Mike Murdock, the Tennessee Wildlife Resources Agency's Robertson County game officer, said the attack wasn't that unusual.

"It's really just typical behavior of some deer who have been raised in captivity," Murdock said. "They just go berserk." They get so full of themselves and they're ready to hurt people. They have no fear of people. Out in the wild, naturally, deer don't act like that."

Murdock explained what usually happens:

"People pick these little fawns up all the time and say, 'Well, his mama left him, I'll help him.'"

Unfortunately, these beautiful little fawns grow up to be mean and ornery.
Rollin Moseley

■ PUZZLED GROUNDHOG

In the early part of the 1986 archery season, I was in a tree stand in the corner of a woodlot bordered on one side by a corn field. On another side, a power line cut through and on a third side was a country road. Twenty paces from me was a crabapple tree laden with apples. I had observed a good buck in this area frequently during the summer; the immediate area was loaded with deer sign.

Near midday I heard a rustling of leaves in the direction of the crabapple tree. Straining to see the source of the noise, I finally spotted a large groundhog on the far side of the tree. As I watched, he climbed the tree and began walking out on the limbs to get at the apples. I was fascinated by how well he climbed

around without breaking branches or falling.

After about fifteen minutes, I heard sounds of another animal coming from behind me. I looked and saw the buck was headed directly toward me. I watched as he passed directly beneath me and headed to the base of the crabapple tree. It seemed as if the groundhog had rung his dinner bell.

The buck began to eat the apples almost as fast as they hit the ground. After a few minutes, the groundhog stopped and the buck, finding no more apples, moved off and watched as the groundhog descended the tree. The groundhog searched in vain beneath the tree for his apples. He returned to the base of the tree and looked around as if to ask, "What's going on?" He then climbed the tree again.

As soon as he was aloft and began knocking down more crabapples, the buck returned. Apparently the sound of the apples hitting the ground attracted the buck. The scene was repeated a few times, until the groundhog finally gave up. It was funny to watch him leaving, making sounds as though he was complaining.

The button buck watched as the groundhog moved off and then returned to the base of the crabapple tree and inspected the area. Finding no more apples, he looked in the direction of the departed groundhog for about twenty strides and then gradually wandered off in a different direction.
John S. Moreton

■ DEER IN THE BEANS

A trophy deer is every hunter's dream ... but it might be a farmer's nightmare. Nearly ninety percent of farmer deer damage complaints to the Missouri Department of Conservation are because of deer in soybeans. So, is it a real problem?

Maybe not. Recent research on the effects of soybean browsing white-tailed deer indicates it really doesn't affect soybean production. Of course, if the deer eat the beans to ground level, it will, but they seldom do that. Russell Garrison and James Lewis, of the Georgia Cooperative Wildlife Research Unit at the University of Georgia, took a look at deer in the beans.

They simulated deer damage by artificially defoliating soybeans at various stages of growth. "Treatments included removal of thirty-three, sixty-seven and 100 percent of the leaves, removal of terminal buds, and repeat defoliations in various combinations," says their report. Essentially, there was no loss of production. They also studied five soybean fields with a history of deer depredations.

"The majority of heavy deer browsing occurred before the fourth week of plant growth," they say. "Deer defoliations of 100 percent would have amounted to only forty-two cents an acre loss and only in portions of the field utilized by deer."

They recommended no deer control permits when deer browsing is within five meters of a field edge and also recommended that biologists let farmers know that soybean plants can withstand browsing without a loss of yield. "The biologist should also make the farmer aware of hunting lease income that could offset losses due to deer depredations," they concluded.

All Outdoors
14 October 1988

■ "HOMING" DEER WALKS TWENTY-ONE MILES

A homesick doe has proved that white-tailed deer may be endowed with homing instincts often seen in pigeons or abandoned dogs.

The doe was one of a group of deer trapped at Lyndon B. Johnson State Park in Gillespie County and released in a deer restoration area in Hunt County in East Texas, according to Texas Parks and Wildlife Department officials.

The deer adapted well to her home, but apparently lacked fear of humans and

had become a nuisance to local residents whose spring gardens she raided.

To solve the problem, Game Warden Larry Boyd of Quinlan and Biologist Carl Frentress of Athens decided to move the animal to another location. They selected a release site in Henderson County about sixty miles away.

After tranquilizing the deer, they placed brightly colored tags in her ears and transported her to the new location.

The second day after the release, the deer was seen heading north eleven miles from the release site, and the following day the animal surprised an automobile garage owner by walking into his establishment near Canton, about twenty-one miles from the release site.

Frentress said a line drawn on the map from the release site through the location near Canton showed the doe was exactly on course to get back home. At that point, Frentress became worried about hazards to the traveling doe's life, so arrangements were made to place her in a deer-proof enclosure at a game ranch between Canton and Wills Point.

"Had her travels not been interrupted I believe she would have returned to her original location in Hunt County within a week," Frentress said.

Frentress theorized that the deer's homing instincts may have been reinforced by the handouts of food she received in Hunt County. Or, there may be a distance threshold, since she had never attempted to leave Hunt County.

Texas Parks & Wildlife Officials

■ BUCK RAMS VEHICLE

District warden Dick Knapp, Jamestown, North Dakota, shares this unusual hunting story that happened to a North Dakota State Highway Patrolman who was bow hunting at one of his favorite spots north of Jamestown.

Dale Elbert was on stand the morning of September 3 when he shot a six-point white-tailed buck at fifteen yards. After being shot, the buck entered a cornfield adjacent to a shelterbelt and made his way back through heavy cover to a gully, where Elbert had parked his vehicle, a 1983 Toyota station wagon. His route of escape blocked, the buck rammed into the vehicle and inflicted $264 worth of damage to the front left quarter panel. After striking the vehicle, the buck rolled down the hill and lay dead at the bottom.

North Dakota Outdoors
November 1984

■ DEER HUNTER, 1; COYOTES, 1

No one ever said nature was a friendly provider, but when Jackie Gau of Lake Andes, South Dakota went deer hunting last fall she learned a lesson in just how stern nature can be.

Jackie and her husband, Bruce, were hunting a shelterbelt in the Pease Creek area north of Geddes when she noticed something ahead of her. As she approached, she realized it was a deer carcass.

Thinking it must have been wounded earlier, and was now perhaps the remains of a predator's meal, she took a closer look. That's when Mrs. Gau saw a live five-point buck standing in the cedars. And the two deer were attached at the antlers.

She called for help from her husband but when he didn't respond she shot the exhausted five-pointer.

All around the two deer were blood and hair, and the ground was covered with coyote tracks. She said all that remained of the dead deer was the head, one front leg, the spine and some hide.

Apparently the two deer locked antlers in a rutting battle, and when one of them died it became the victim of coyotes. The deer that Jackie shot must have used most of its strength keeping them at bay while they took turns eating parts of its final opponent.

South Dakota Conservation Digest
53(4): 1986

■ PAJAMA BUCK

Jack Lundgren from Baraga, Michigan stayed home instead of going deer hunting on opening day of gun season (November 15) because he was sick, but he got a trophy buck anyway. He saw a buck chasing a doe from the window of his house shortly after daylight. After retrieving his rifle from the basement. Lundgren went outside in his pajamas, hoping to get a shot at the buck. He did get a shot and brought down a nine-pointer that had a dressed weight of 226 pounds.

Richard P. Smith

■ BEAR KNOCKS AROUND DEER HUNTER

Deer hunter Tom Walsh says a hungry 325-pound black bear picked him up and "swatted me like a badminton birdie," but he escaped with only minor injuries.

Walsh, of Iron River, Wis., said the sudden attack occurred last fall in the Long Lake area of the Chequamegon National Forest while he was hunting deer with bow and arrow.

Walsh, 29, noticed a bear was feeding on corn that was set out for deer. Cautiously, Walsh checked for other bears, counted six, and then suddenly the attack occurred from a male bear he had not spotted.

The hunter figured the bear hurled him 10 to 15 feet.

Walsh estimated the bear weighed at least 325 pounds.

Walsh said he put his hands over the back of his head, played dead and the bear came over to him, rolling him on his back.

"He drooled in my face and snorted. It smelled like death warmed over," Walsh said. The bear then ambled away, allowing Walsh to escape.

The hunter was treated at an Ashland hospital for a sprained ankle, cracked ribs, a slightly bruised kidney and a claw mark on one leg.

Game Warden Mark DiSalvo said it was hard to say why the bear attacked Walsh.

"Perhaps the animal was protecting its food or it just picked up Walsh's scent too late and was startled," DiSalvo said. "I've been that close to bears before and have never been attacked."

■ WARDEN FINES SELF

Alabama Conservation Officer Chester Pugh, a man who practices what he preaches, recently fined himself for violating state game laws.

Pugh, formerly the game warden in Marengo County, was hunting doe on a managed area in the county and had two doe tags with him. He said he shot two deer — one was a doe and the other an unantlered buck — and realized he had violated Alabama hunting laws.

Since the season was only for female deer, shooting the buck was a fish-and-game violation.

Pugh, captain of the game and fish division in the Russellville area of northwest Alabama, signed a personal arrest warrant, took himself into custody and then paid a $69 fine.

Rollin Moseley

■ ALMOST GOT AWAY

Dave Bigelow from Gwinn, Michigan, got a surprise when he recovered an eight-point buck he arrowed on 29 November 1985. The buck had a crease on the side of its head from a rifle bullet. Dave was the hunter who fired the bullet that left its mark two weeks earlier.

Bigelow is primarily a bow hunter, but he occasionally hunts deer with a rifle. Traditionally, Michigan's gun deer season opens on November 15 and runs through November 30. Most people hunt with firearms, of course, but hunting with bow and arrow is legal as long as the hunter possesses a gun deer license.

It is not unusual for Dave to hunt with a bow during the gun season, but he hunted with a rifle on opening day of the 1985 deer season. He eventually saw a buck that stopped behind a tree with only its head visible. Attempting to kill the buck instantly, Dave tried for a head shot, but the buck ran off after the shot.

Dave switched to his archery equipment after that buck got away. On November 29, he was hunting from a different stand than the one where he shot at the buck with his rifle, but the locations were not very far apart. Bigelow had no idea the bow-killed buck was the same one he shot at with the rifle until after examining the carcass. The flesh wound had already begun to heal.

Richard P. Smith

Photos by Richard P. Smith

■ CARS CLAIM BOONE & CROCKETT BUCKS

Rural Stearns County, Minnesota resident Robert Bastien was into his fourth season of trying for a record book buck with both bow and gun when his wife Karen connected on the megabuck by accident. Karen was on her way shopping in the family car at 1:30 P.M. on 26 October 1986 when their paths crossed. She drove up out of a dip in a township road as the trophy whitetail crossed the pavement. The buck appeared so suddenly there was no time to stop or swerve and the vehicle clobbered him.

The closest Robert had been able to get to the eleven-point buck while hunting him was sixty yards.

After the purchase of a $15 permit from the Minnesota DNR, the Bastiens were allowed to keep the deer, which dressed at 206 pounds. Its antlers had an inside spread of 29-1/5 inches at the time it was killed, but shrunk to 26-3/4 inches by the time the rack was officially scored.

Final score for the typical antlers is 192-6/8, well above the 170 Boone & Crockett minimum. However, the rack won't be listed in state or national records because the skull plate between the antlers was cracked during the collision with the Bastien car, disqualifying the antlers for listing in the record book.

Another buck with a fourteen-point rack qualifying for Boone and Crockett records was hit by a vehicle in the city limits of Sault Ste. Marie, Michigan on 18 or 19 October 1986 and was confiscated by the DNR. The mounted head, which scores 181-2/8, is on display at the DNR office in the Soo.

Richard P. Smith

Richard P. Smith

■ LOCKED ANTLERS

The last days of Michigan's 1986 gun deer season held more excitement for brothers Eric (17) and Dave (16) Nordern from Rock than they expected. Each of them filled their tags with trophy bucks whose antlers interlocked while fighting.

The excitement started early in the afternoon on November 29. At about 1:30 P.M. Eric left home and began the 1.5-mile walk to his deer blind. He was carrying some apples to feed the deer and his .30-.30 rifle. The young man neglected to carry his rifle in a similar midday walk on opening day and saw a buck that he could have shot.

After dumping the apples, Eric headed for home. He had only gone a short distance when came upon a confusing mess of fresh deer tracks in the snow. Then he heard a commotion in the swamp bordering the logging trail he was walking on.

The young hunter investigated and caught glimpses of two huge bucks fighting. Unaware that the bucks' antlers were locked together, Eric took aim at the larger of the two whitetails as they thrashed about in thick cover. Eric fired all four bullets he had with him, but the bucks continued to fight, oblivious to his presence.

Eric ran home after emptying his rifle and probably covered the mile or more in record time. He excitedly told his father and brother about the two bucks, exchanged the .30-.30 for a 12-gauge shotgun and buckshot, and the three of them returned to where Eric had left the bucks.

The bucks were still in the same location. After looking at them, Eric's father realized they were locked together. With that knowledge, Eric and Dave moved in close enough to make sure of their shots. Eric tagged the larger buck, a twelve-pointer. The other buck was a close second, having eleven-point antlers.

If Eric hadn't stumbled upon the fighting whitetails, the animals probably would have eventually died of exposure.

Richard P. Smith

Richard P. Smith

■ CALL HIM "LUCKY"

Francis McCarthy of Marquette, Michigan, is one of the lucky deer hunters who bagged a buck during firearms deer season, but he had more luck than most.

The buck McCarthy tagged was a trophy whitetail with ten points. The buck was 6.5 years old and dressed out at 181 pounds. It was how he got the deer that luck really played a role.

McCarthy was on his way to deer camp November 18, traveling south on a paved county road, when he spotted the big buck in a large clearcut on the Sands Plains. The time was about 9:00 A.M. After pulling off to the side of the road, he grabbed his rifle and three cartridges and maneuvered into position for a shot.

He rested his rifle on some bent trees and aimed carefully, holding the scope's crosshairs on the animal's shoulder. Only after he fired all three shells, did he realize the distance was 300 to 400 yards and he should have been aiming higher.

Out of ammunition, McCarthy snuck back to his vehicle as fast as he could, grabbed more shells and returned for another crack at the trophy deer. A doe the buck had been standing with was still in sight, but the buck was gone. Sneaking ahead, the excited hunter soon located his quarry when it raised its head and the antlers flashed in the sun.

At that point, the buck was closer, 100 to 200 yards away, and calmly feeding. Despite his excitement, Fran's fourth shot was on target. He had his buck before actually doing any hunting.

McCarthy is a measurer for Commemorative Bucks of Michigan. Now he has a trophy buck of his own to enter in CBM's records.

Richard P. Smith

■ A DAY TO REMEMBER

It was Sunday and my family and I spent the morning fishing for walleyes in Rainy Lake on the Minnesota-Ontario border. We caught enough walleyes for a tasty shore lunch so 1:00 P.M. found us on top of a rocky ledge overlooking the lake, with fresh fillets sizzling in the skillet. Our daughter, Shawn, was down next to the shoreline and heard the noise first. Frightened, she ran up the ledge. "Mom, Dad, something big is crashing through the brush and headed our way!" We all stood up and listened. It was loud, and it was coming our way fast. Thinking it might be a starving bear that smelled our cooking, I told my wife, Dorothy, to grab Chris, the baby, and head for the boat.

Shawn quickly joined them there. My sons, Tom and Don Jr., and I stood our ground. I grabbed a large stick while both boys picked up some boulders. We were ready!

The large animal was closely following the shoreline. It broke into the opening on a dead run and headed straight up the incline toward us and the camp stove. It was a huge buck deer! The thick velvet on its rack made the antlers look larger than usual. The boys and I quickly scattered as the buck leaped over the camp stove, took three bounds down the rocky incline and was in the water and swimming. Before we could regain our senses, another large animal emerged on the path of the buck. At a full lope, and almost ghost-like, a black and grey-coated timber wolf bounded up the incline. The moment the wolf saw us it veered left and disappeared into the woods. What a sight! What an experience for the whole family. After excitedly talking about the "once-in-a-lifetime" experience, we finally remembered the fish fillets sizzling away in the frying pan. They were just right! Fish sandwiches with onion slices, baked beans, small whole potatoes and cold pop from the cooler — what a meal, and it seemed to taste better than ever. It was a day the family will long remember.

Don C. Carey
International Falls, Minnesota

■ DIANA

With my husband, an archery enthusiast, I was visiting the National Gallery in Washington. Both of us admired Renoir's beautiful painting of the nude Diana and the deer which she had just slain. I moved on, but my husband continued to stand meditatively in front of Diana. A little embarrassed, I wondered if people would notice how long he had been staring at the nude.

At last he turned from it to say thoughtfully, "You know, that arrow would never have killed that deer."

Patricia Klein

Jerome Martin (left) and Sam Mathews with their two ten-point deer. (Photo courtesy of "The Pike Press")

■ LOCKED BUCKS MAKE FOR UNUSUAL HUNT

A Sangamon County deer hunter got the surprise of a lifetime while hunting Pike County (Illinois) during the second half of the firearm season. Spotting a nice buck grazing on grass as it came across the top of a hill, he put a well-placed slug into the animal. As the big buck went down, another stood up beside it. Only then did Sam Mathews, Riverton, realize the buck was not grazing; it had its antlers locked with another buck. His hunting partner, Jerome Martin, Pleasant Hill, shot the second buck, and the two dragged the animals out of the woods, still locked together. They stated they had a heck of a time loading the deer in the truck. The deer weighed approxi-

mately 225 pounds each field-dressed.

The two bucks, both having ten-point antlers, have been donated to the Illinois State Museum, which plans to do full mounts of the two deer and display them in Champaign.

Bucks locked together at the antlers are not uncommon during the late fall. During this time of the year, male deer are fighting for mates. They occasionally lock their antlers and both deer usually perish from exhaustion and starvation.

Outdoor Highlights
7 January 1985

■ WHAT'S IN A NUMBER

Some numbers are more significant than others, especially with the passage of time. Take the back tag number from George Reid's Michigan gun deer season license last fall, for example. The number 1578982 didn't mean much more than any other license number to the Cedarville resident at the time he purchased it. It took on a new meaning, however, after opening day of the season.

He filled his tag that day, November 15, with a 7-point buck that he dropped at 8:00 A.M. It was the 9th buck he bagged from that particular stand and 1982 was the last year he scored there!

Richard P. Smith

■ THE IVAN RHODES STORY

There wasn't another hunter within sight or earshot of Ivan Rhodes all day on opening day of the 1978 deer season. Ivan had planned to hunt with his father and brother near Bonny Reservoir in Yuma County, but they had applied for the lim-ited permits in separate envelopes and were not drawn with Ivan. They spent opening day on Western Slope hunting mule deer.

The area Ivan hunted on the eastern plains is interlaced with ravines and branching lateral fingers. By late afternoon, all he had to show for his efforts was a pair of sore feet. He hadn't even spotted so much as a doe, let alone any sizable bucks that he had heard inhabited the area. After one last break, Ivan began working his way back to his vehicle. He had only gone fifty yards when he spotted what appeared to be the ribs of a cow's skeleton in a small brush-covered depression. They were gray-white in color and only about thirty paces away. When the "ribs" suddenly shifted slightly, Ivan realized he was gazing at one of Colorado's most remarkable trophies. It was a massive white-tailed buck bedded down for the day and facing downhill. Ivan instantly lined up the crosshairs of his .30-06 on the buck's neck just below the ear and fired. Charging forward, Ivan found his Boone and Crockett buck lying in the brush.

As there was only about an hour of daylight left, Ivan caped out the head and positioned the animal so that it would drain and cool during the night. Realizing that the car was still two miles away, he began his hike out.

The next morning Ivan returned to the buck early and spent five hours packing it out, one half at a time. The two halves later weighed 190 pounds. Not only did Ivan's whitetail score high enough to make the Boone and Crockett record book, but it became the first Colorado whitetail taken by a hunter to do so. The buck scored 182-5/8 points and ranks as the 72nd (two-way tie) largest whitetail ever taken.

Jack and Susan Reneau
Colorado's Biggest Bucks and Bulls, 1983

■ DEER HUNTER BUCKS THE ODDS AND BAGS SECOND DOE WITH ANTLERS

It's getting so that Bruce Schuelke never knows for sure what kind of deer he's shot until he takes a close look, a real close look.

Schuelke, 3914 Nimitz St., a food service employee at Luther Hospital in Eau Claire, Wisconsin, hunts near Grandview in Bayfield County.

A big deer sporting a huge rack of antlers came trotting up to Schuelke who was 5 1/2 miles back in the woods.

Schuelke shot the deer and went over to dress it out.

"I spread its legs, and I couldn't believe it," Schuelke said. "It was a funny feeling."

The 9-point "buck" was a doe!

Schuelke dressed the deer, carefully leaving in reproductive organs to verify the story he would have to repeat over and over to the people who would stare at the animal in disbelief.

Department of Natural Resources employees at the Hayward Ranger Station, where Schuelke registered the deer, confirmed the animal's sex.

"It definitely had no male organs," said Thomas Judd, a DNR forester. "Wardens looked at it, too. It is quite extraordinary."

The deer's rack has a 22-inch spread, and the animal weighed 211 pounds field dressed. Live, it probably weighed close to 260 pounds. Its age was estimated at 4 to 5 years.

Schuelke shot the big deer about noon Monday, and quit dragging it out at 7:30 p.m. Monday. He returned to finish the haul Tuesday morning.

An imbalance of female hormones will result in a doe growing antlers, but the mathematical chances for this happening are very small.

"Every year, you hear about one being shot, but usually it's a small spiked doe, and the spikes are fuzzy with velvet," said Terry Valen, a DNR biologists at Eau Claire.

"The mathematical odds for a doe having antlers this size have got to be pretty damn small," Valen said.

Under state law, hunters are allowed to shoot deer with an antler spike at least 3 inched long. Does can be shot only in either-sex hunting zones, or in "hunter's choice" areas open to taking of antlerless deer with a special "hunters choice" permit.

Schuelke bucked (no pun intended, of course) the odds once before. In 1963, he shot a doe with a single spike antler while hunting in Iowa County.

The chances of one person getting two antlered does? Even IBM's best wouldn't tackle that.

Dave Carlson
Leader-Telegram
26 November 1980

Richard A. McCurdy, Jr.

■ 200-POUND CLUB

Frank Prato from Trenton, New Jersey did something in 1986 that no other deer hunter has ever done since the state has been keeping records on deer. During the 1986 fall archery season, Frank killed two monster bucks that both weighed more than 200 pounds.

October 4 was the first Saturday of the

1986 fall archery season. Frank arrived at his tree stand before daybreak. Right after it got light, Frank heard deer coming his way. He saw several does coming from a field down into the woods. Following behind them, he saw another deer and, for one quick second, he saw a set of long tines going through the woods. Frank was pretty sure it was a nice buck approaching. The buck continued on until he reached a clearing about twenty-one yards away. When the buck reached this point, Frank was already at a full draw. He whistled to the buck and it stopped in its tracks. At that point, Frank's arrow penetrated right through both lungs and stuck in the ground. The buck ran through some thick cover and dropped about thirty yards away.

"When I first saw him on the ground, I just could not believe the size of his body," Frank remembers. The buck had a beautiful ten-point rack with split brow tines and scored 110 typical Pope and Young points. He weighed in at 220 pounds, field dressed.

About two weeks later, Frank was hunting in the same area in hopes of getting a shot at a huge nine-pointer he was pursuing. On October 25 Frank climbed into his tree stand at 4:30 P.M. No sooner did he pull up his bow and settle down, when a doe walked right by and closely behind her he spotted a large-bodied deer approaching. "I just knew had to be a buck, the body was so big, " Frank said. Once the deer cleared the cover, all Frank could see was antlers. It was the big buck he had been after.

As the buck approached the deer lure he had out, Frank kept repeating to himself, "pick a spot." The buck was only about six yards away when Frank placed an arrow right through the buck. The arrow hit the liver on one side and exited through the lung on the other. The buck ran off about forty yards and stopped to look back. Watching closely, Frank was worried that he had made a bad shot on the buck. As Frank was watching the buck, he heard a branch snap and he looked off to his right to see another nice buck approaching. When Frank looked

back toward the wounded buck it was gone. Frank got down out of his stand about ten minutes later and found the big nine-pointer on the ground in the exact spot where he had last seen him standing. The buck weighed in at 224 pounds and scored 130 typical Pope and Young points. Frank was the first hunter in New Jersey to enter two bucks in one season for the state's 200-pound club.

Richard A. McCurdy, Jr.

■ ONE SHOT ... TWO BUCKS

My 1984 deer season began as it typically has each year since 1958. Art Benson, Bob Niver and I pointed Art's motor home north to begin the the 250-mile ride from Neenah to Clam Lake. For the last three years, my son, Matt, also joined us.

As we rode along, I thought of the changes that have taken place in the last twenty-six years. Originally we hunted out of a Baker-style tent, in 1968 I bought a pickup truck camper, in 1974 Art bought a larger pickup camper, and this year he traded it in on a twenty-six-foot motor home. The number of deer hunters in our area actually decreased through the years. I suspect that this holds true in most of the northwestern part of the state. I encourage more deer hunters to make the effort to camp and hunt in the National Forests of northern Wisconsin and hope my son continues this tradition into his generation. The attributes of this type of "quality" deer hunting have been written about by many people. This story is about such a hunt but with a "once-in-a-lifetime" twist.

Clam Lake is located on the northern watershed where rain falling a few miles apart can take greatly differing routes to the Atlantic Ocean. It can flow north into the Great Lakes system or south to the drainage basin of the Mississippi River. The preservation of the Wetlands in these drainage systems must be maintained by coming generations. It's near the edges of these wetlands where we spend most of our hunting hours. The big bucks enjoy travelling along the edges of the wet areas and if they stay there, our chances of seeing them are very slim because of the heavy cover.

We arrived at our campsite near the remnants of a horse barn that probably goes back to the twenties when horses were used to skid out logs. Bob and I had "any-deer permits" which we would consider using after opening day.

Saturday, opening day, was brisk in the morning (18°) but there was no wind. Art went to his stand by Moose River, Bob sat in the hardwoods where he got a nine-pointer last year, I went to the edge of some hardwoods where I shot an eight-pointer last year, and Matt sat about 250 yards from me. I remained on my stand until about 9:00 A.M., then took a walk until about noon. I ended up on the hard-wood ridge Bob had been on. Climbing a windfall provided a good view of the hard-woods blending into the birches, aspen and spruce. After about ten minutes, a doe came poking along the edge of the hardwoods about 100 yards away. This was the only deer I saw that day. Bob saw two does in the morning, but Art and Matt saw none.

Sunday's weather was about the same as the previous day and Matt saw a ten-point buck briefly on a ridge about two miles east of the camper. No one else saw any deer.

On Monday Matt and I decided to go back where he saw the buck on Sunday. It's a tough walk back there, but the deer sign is always good. Matt headed for the hardwood ridge and a windfall he liked. I decided to wander to the south and explore some areas that were new to me. For the first time in my life, I took a 35mm camera along. I've considered hunting with a camera for the last several years and thought I could practice on some Canada jays, chickadees, or other birds.

I moved north on an old logging trail that was being taken over by young spruce. Deer had been moving through many places in the area. As I walked through a spruce-crowded area, a tree about fifteen feet off the trail shook violently. I thought a grouse was in it, ready to take off, so I flipped the case off the camera and got ready for a close shot. When the tree shook again, I spotted the back half of a large deer. I couldn't see the front half clearly because of the brush and it seemed to have its head down. Since I carried an either-sex permit, I didn't really have to check for antlers. I aimed for a spot I guessed was near the front shoulder. At the report of the rifle, the deer fell. I pushed my way through the brush and looked at the dead animal. I could hardly believe my eyes!

There lay two dead bucks with their antlers locked together and tangled in a couple of two-inch saplings. One had his eye open so I touched it with my gun barrel but there was no sign of life. As it turned out, the buck I shot (ten points, 170 pounds dressed out) had killed the other one (eight points, 190 pounds) by piercing the heart area with a tine. It then dragged the dead buck about fifty yards through the woods before the dead one became caught in the saplings. Then the living buck couldn't move forward or backward, nor raise his head. The one buck had been dead about two days and was not salvageable as meat.

I called for Matt and he soon joined me. We backtracked the drag trail to the area where the battle took place. The two bucks had dug up a twenty-foot square area. Apparently they had sparred around and around a five-inch diameter maple tree. This is where we found the first signs of blood.

We gutted out the good deer and cut the head off the poor one. I hiked out to the road and then down the road about two miles to Harold Schonscheck's camp. He and I rode a motorcycle for about 3.5 miles over roads and trails to get to the deer. He dragged it with the cycle for about a mile to a spot where we could pick it up with a truck. Occasionally the racks dug into the ground so hard that it lifted the cycle's front wheel off the ground, but the racks did not disengage from each other.

Back in camp, we hung it in the big old spruce by the horse barn. That old spruce has had a lot of nice bucks hung in it but never a combination like this. When I registered the deer at the check station in Loretta, they said it was a first-of-a-kind for them and took pictures of it.

This fall we will again make the trek to the Chequamegon National Forest hoping for the unexpected during the annual deer hunt.

Les Talo
Neenah, Wisconsin

▪ SELF DEFENSE

It was just a little buck, only a year-and-a-half old. It was an eight-pointer, but the rack had only an eleven-inch spread.

It won't hang on David Wade's wall, but he'll never forget it, because this was one buck that fought back.

Wade, thirty-eight, of Atlanta is a hard-core bow hunter. He uses a long-bow, shoots instinctively and still hunts (stalks) rather than sitting in a tree stand.

He was creeping through the woods a couple of weeks ago on the Berry Creek archery-only section of Rum Creek Wildlife Management Area in Monroe County when he had the biggest adrenaline rush of his life.

Wade said he was in a particularly brushy spot, "an area so thick you had to crawl," near a game trail. He cleared a spot big enough to kneel down and he waited.

Pretty soon, a doe came bounding up the trail, and it was followed a short time later by a young buck.

Wade, at the time, was looking for a certain deer he had been trailing, and he stood, arrow nocked and ready to shoot, to get a better look. The buck saw movement behind him, turned and spotted Wade.

Instead of raising his tail and running away like deer usually do when they spot humans, the buck lowered his head and charged at Wade.

Moving through sheer instinct, Wade lifted his bow, drew the 79-pound Big Red Long Hunter, anchored the cedar arrow to a point on his jawline—he doesn't remember doing this—and shot. The arrow hit the deer five feet from Wade.

It went in the buck's neck and penetrated down to his lungs.

Momentum might have helped the buck finish his charge, but the big cedar arrow got his attention and turned him. He barged into a tree, broke the arrow shaft and ran.

Wade and his hunting partner, George Steel, found the buck about fifty yards away.

He said he didn't even want to shoot the little buck, that he had been stalking a big one.

"I had seen a monster in the woods," Wade said. "He was about three times as big as the one I shot and looked like he had about a twenty-two inch spread."

Why would a young buck charge like that? It is a rarity.

"I've never heard of it happening," said David Waller, Assistant to Game & Fish Chief Leon Kirkland. "I've heard of wounded deer attacking when a hunter approached, but not this."

One theory Wade has is that maybe the big buck had been chasing the smaller one. Maybe.

"I've thought about it a bunch," Wade said. "I just don't know."

One thing he is sure of: He was involved "in a chain of events that almost got me hurt."

Kent Mitchell
Atlanta Journal
29 November 1987

■ TOUGH TRACKING

Dan Ossmann will remember this deer hunting season for a long time.

His story starts last Wednesday when he went behind his house to start hunting.

"I started out by getting caught on a fence," he said laughing. "Then walked quietly to my stand and climbed up. I was trying to get situated when I heard a noise in the brush."

Ossmann just had time to pull his bow up and set his arrow before an eight-point buck showed up. He got off one shot that hit the deer near the ribs and the buck ran off.

He tracked it a little ways, but decided to wait until the next morning to continue the search. Ossmann tracked the buck to its bed, but it wasn't there. Thinking he had lost it, he circled around and finally picked up the trail again.

When he finally located the buck, it was in heavy brush. He circled the deer trying to get a finishing shot. He worked his way to within ten to fifteen feet of the buck and the next thing he knew he was on his back with the deer over him.

"I couldn't believe he could move that fast," he said. "He had me pinned down with his horns planted on either side of my thigh." Luckily though, the deer was worn out so it didn't do any damage.

"I had to wrestle him down by holding onto his horns like a steer," he said. When he finally managed to free himself, Ossmann used his hunting knife to finish the buck and then headed back to the house for help.

"When the deer hit, he broke my quiver and arrows went flying everywhere. One cut across my hand and cut my finger," said Ossmann. Fortunately, he had a glove-type covering over his palm that saved his hand from being injured badly. He did require ten stitches in his finger.

With the help of his neighbor, Karl Kemp, Ossmann got his deer cleaned and hauled back to his house.

He said he never had time to be scared because everything happened so fast. But instead of the same old story of so-and-so got a buck, this time it's "the buck almost got me," he said laughing.

Marge Guyette
Appleton Post Cresent
17 November 1986

Dan Brockman

■ DOUBLE-VISION BUCKS

Twenty-two years ago bow hunting wasn't the popular sport it is today, but it was growing steadily. Dick and Mary Sosnovske were a couple caught up in the excitement of the fast-growing sport.

Perhaps living on a dairy farm in the midst of some very fine deer country near Gleason, in northern Wisconsin, led to their interest in bow hunting. Or, perhaps their interest in the outdoors and appreciation of nature kindled their interest in the new sport. Whatever the reason, Dick and Mary soon became part of the sport which gave them momentary fame.

Early one morning in late October, 1964, the phone rang at the Sosnovske farm house. One of Dick's cousins—who, on his way to work, had spotted two huge bucks fighting in a field near the Sosnovske farm—called Dick because he knew Dick and Mary had licenses for the archery season, which was open at the time.

When they arrived at the location of the fight, it immediately became apparent that the two bucks' antlers were locked together. As Dick, Mary and a hunting partner approached the bucks, the ten-pointer stood up and tossed his head back, throwing the other buck up over his back. The two bucks were later judged to weigh more than 200 pounds each. The fourteen-pointer, now dead as a result of a broken neck and crushed skull, prohibited the escape of the other buck. One arrow, from twenty feet away, took the trophy of a life-time.

After field dressing the two bucks (the fourteen pointer was still warm and had apparently died when the other buck tossed it into the air), the trio struggled to drag the two bucks to Dick's pickup and load them in the back for the trip to town. In town, the word spread quickly and soon a crowd gathered around the two fallen trophies. During the next few days, the story was featured on television and in newspapers across the state.

The bucks were mounted as shoulder mounts, locked together as they were found. In fact, the antlers were locked so securely that the taxidermist couldn't even separate them to work on the bucks.

I believe the ten-pointer is the more impressive of the two, with its long, thick beams and long symmetrical tines. The buck scored about 145. The fourteen-pointer has shorter tines and thinner beams but is still very impressive with an approximate score of 145 also. The size of the racks, coupled with the huge bodies of these bucks, makes either one an excellent trophy; together they're a trophy of a lifetime.

When I visited Dick and Mary in late 1985, more than twenty-one years after the bucks were taken, the excitement was still evident by the sparkle in their eyes and the excitement in their voices. Mary no longer bow hunts, but Dick manages to squeeze in a couple of hours of bow hunting around his farm chores. He admits that the events of that October morning are a tough act to follow.

Dan Brockman

■ WAITER, THERE'S A DEER IN MY SOUP!

From our "Guess Who's Coming To Dinner" department: Patrons at a coffee shop near Johnson Sauk Trail State Park were surprised one evening recently when a 150-pound white-tailed buck plunged through a picture window, cleared a booth and knocked down a diner seated at a table.

The yearling darted behind the coffee counter where Bob Tapprich, manager of the Sauk Trail Inn coffee shop, wrestled it to the floor. Tapprich and a patron held the deer down while another customer bound the animal's leg with nylon rope.

"I knew if he got back among the customers we were in trouble," said Tapprich, who jogs to stay in shape but nevertheless had trouble subduing the animal. "I thought I was in pretty good shape from jogging," he said. "But I wasn't in shape for that. One person could never hold one. There's no way."

Local police and conservation officers removed the whitetail and took it to Johnson Sauk Trail State Park, where it was released.

The deer was not injured in the incident except for a loosened tooth and some cuts around its mouth. The customer that was bowled over by the animal was uninjured, and damage to the coffee shop was confined to the broken window.

Illinois Outdoor Highlights 1984

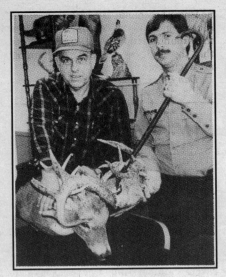

■ RISKY RESCUE

A father-son outing became a deer mission for Missouri Conservation Agent Russ Shifflett and his father, Ray. It began as a sight-seeing tour of Squaw Creek National Wildlife Refuge in Northwest Missouri, where the pair hoped to spot some of the hundreds of white-tailed deer roaming the federal site. "To say the least, Dad got more than he bargained for," said the agent, who patrols the federal refuge as part of his state duties.

The older Shifflett got the viewing opportunity of a lifetime when he helped his son separate two large bucks, their antlers locked from a sparring bout. He also got to test the strength of the winning buck, which shoved him through the snow with Ray grasping the ten-point rack.

Both bucks were trophy-sized whitetails. The larger, a fourteen-pointer, died of a broken neck. His antlers were still locked solidly with those of the ten-pointer, which had been dragging the dead deer, "probably since early that morning," the agent said. There were several spectators, so the younger Shifflett asked two men to drive into a nearby town and get a

hacksaw in case they couldn't get the bucks apart with a pry bar he kept in his car.

While his father anchored the dead animal, Russ applied the crowbar to the tangled tines. That ten-pointer didn't want to cooperate. When Russ got near, he got ornery. "He kept trying to hook me with his antlers, even though it meant dragging the other deer, and Dad," said Shifflett.

"So, Dad and I switched deer. He got a firm grip on the live buck and I finally managed to pry them apart." Russ stepped back and Ray slid back, pushed through the snow by a rather upset buck.

"He was still a bit tired, and bewildered, but he sure didn't lack any strength," the older Shifflett said.

"I now know what it means to have a tiger by the tail, or a deer by the antlers. I couldn't let go, and Russ couldn't help me. The buck shoved me backwards for several yards until he got me against a tree. I could get a solid foot hold there, so I twisted his rack to one side and jumped clear." The buck shook his head, got his bearings and took off for the nearby woods.

Bill Bennett
St. Joseph, Missouri

■ IDENTICAL TAGS

What would you think of the odds are of someone being issued the same license and backtag number for deer hunting two years in a row?

"I couldn't believe it when I saw it," said "Moon" Mullen of Appleton, Wisconsin.

When you consider the fact that over 230,000 Sportsman's Licenses are sold in Wisconsin each year and these are distributed by thousands of offices and retail outlets in every major city and crossroads store—the odds go up.

"Those odds would be astronomical," said Bud Gourlie of the Department of Natural Resources public information office at Madison.

"I wouldn't believe something like that could happen," Nita Randerson of the Outagamie County Clerk's office staff.

"Moon," an Appleton postman who said, "Don't use my given name (LaVerne) because nobody will know me," discovered the rarity when he went to put his new backtag on his deer hunting jacket.

"The first three numbers caught my eye, because they were the same, but then I noticed all six were the same. That's when I thought it had to be something unusual," he said.

Unusual is right.

According to the DNR, latest figures show that 230,240 Sportsman's Licenses were sold in Wisconsin. In Outagamie County, close to 8,000 are issued and there are thirty-five different agents in the county who distribute licenses.

At the clerk's office, Randerson said that the chance of the same outlet or agent getting the same numbered licenses in succeeding years would be practically impossible." Some places get their licenses on different dates, and some run out early and come and get more. We have thirty-five agents in the county who handle licenses," Nita pointed out.

Mullen purchased his 1987-88 Sportsman's License on September 1. His license and backtag number is 189-506. In 1986, on August 26, he bought his license at the same place and the number was identical.

"Moon" has been hunting deer since 1948 and he, along with a group of local hunting buddies, tramp the woods near Sayner in Vilas County. "I'm one of those savers," Mullen said. "I have all my old deer hunting backtags and I also have the old metal tags from when I didn't get a deer. When I went to put the new backtag on my jacket I just happened to glance at the number. I guess I'll have to make a special place for these two."

Making the odds of this happening even greater was the fact that the Coast to Coast Store was issued its Sportsman's Licenses on August 15 in 1986 and wasn't issued the permits until August 26 this year. "Just think that if we did have the same numbers, what would the chances be of that particular store getting the same ones," Randerson said. "And add to that the fact that out of all the licenses they sell, this hunter would happen to get the same one. It's unbelievable."

"I've never heard of this before," Gourlie said. "We have had people on a special list who ordered the same low number year after year as sort of a prestige item, but these were situations that were handled directly through the DNR license section. Sort of like getting your personalized license plates for a vehicle. But, for someone to purchase their license at a regular retail outlet and then get the same number two years in a row — well, it would be impossible to speculate on the odds of that happening."

Jim Harp

■ REPEAT PERFORMANCE

It was the first week of November 1986 when Randy Bruntjens was all set to bag the biggest buck of his hunting career with bow and arrow. The whitetail was only fifteen yards away feeding. It wasn't in the best position for a shot, though, so he had plenty of time to watch and count the points on its antlers. There were nine.

After ten to fifteen minutes, the buck finally turned broadside and Randy took the shot. He saw his arrow hit high in the shoulder. The impact from the sixty-pound bow knocked the buck off its feet, but it got right back up and took off.

It was after dark by the time Randy, his brother and brother-in-law returned to look for the buck. They found no blood. The next morning, Bruntjens returned with reinforcements and they found the beginning of a blood trail 150 yards from where the deer had been hit and followed it as far as they could — about a mile.

Randy spent the next couple of days looking for ravens that may have spotted the deer or any other sign of where the injured whitetail may have gone. He was sure his arrow killed the buck and felt bad about not being able to find it.

Bruntjens was hunting from the same stand again during November of 1987, only this time he had a rifle in his hands. A doe approached and she was followed by a big buck. The only shot Randy had was at the buck's neck and he took it, killing the eleven-pointer on the spot.

When the meat from the deer was being processed, the butcher found a broadhead embedded in the buck's backbone. Randy recognized the broadhead. It was the same one he hit the buck with the year before. Until seeing the broadhead, Bruntjens had no idea he killed the same buck. He was obviously wrong about having killed it the year before.

It still ended up being the best buck of his hunting career. The whitetail had a dressed weight of 197 pounds, was 4.5 or 5.5 years old and very healthy. The broadhead was covered with scar tissue and the wound perfectly healed.

Richard P. Smith

Richard P. Smith

■ FOLLOW THAT DEER!

When you take a shot at a deer and are confident you've scored a hit, it's important to follow the animal as far as possible to increase the chances of finding it. Fatally-hit whitetails will sometimes go much further than expected, and there won't always be a blood trail. Tim Gervae from Negaunee found this out on 10 December 1988.

He was carrying a .54-caliber Hawken muzzleloader that day. Still-hunting quietly through fresh snow on a hemlock ridge in Baraga County, he spotted the body of a deer seventy yards away. Since he only saw part of the whitetail at first, he couldn't tell whether it was a buck or doe. He looked at the animal through the variable scope mounted on his rifle until his arms got tired. He still didn't see its head.

The whitetail finally took a couple of steps ahead and Tim saw a beautiful set of antlers on its head. He aimed for the shoulder and fired. There were five strands of hair on the snow where the buck stood, but no blood. The hair was enough to confirm a hit, so Gervae started following the buck after reloading his rifle with a round ball and ninety grains of powder.

After trailing the big whitetail 400 to 500 yards, Tim found it dead. What's so amazing was the fact that he didn't see one speck of blood over that distance. His lead ball hit where he aimed, going through both lungs, but it didn't exit. This probably explains why there was no blood trail.

Tim's persistence netted him one of the highest scoring bucks taken with a muzzleloader in Michigan during 1988, a ten-pointer scoring 153-5/8. He admits to having doubts about the effectiveness of his shot before finding the buck but is glad he continued after it.

Richard P. Smith

■ FAMILY TIES

A Chase County (Kansas) farmer phoned Game Protector Dave Gentry one evening to say a deer "just dropped dead" in his field. The farmer didn't know what caused the deer's death, "maybe a heart attack," he suggested.

It was dark by the time Gentry arrived with the country undersheriff. Two vehicles were there; in one was the farmer. In the other was an unidentified man — just sitting there. A flashlight search revealed a path in the deep snow, where the deer had been dragged away. About half way to the edge of the field, Gentry found the deer, and a set of human footprints leading away from the carcass into the darkness. Gentry followed the trail until his light beam fell upon a sixteen-year-old boy hiding face down in the snow. He was wet and cold.

"I thought you'd never find me," the young man said as they climbed into Gentry's pickup. "I was about the freeze to death."

The boy refused to tell Gentry who his accomplices were, saying that evidence against him was only "circumstantial." Gentry advised him that it was very strong circumstantial evidence and that deer poaching was a serious offense. That prompted the boy to ask to speak to his uncle — the man in the other pickup. The uncle told him to divulge the entire story; and the boy agreed, especially since the alternative was taking the deer poaching rap by himself.

As it turned out, the boy's father had shot the deer and returned home for assistance in retrieving it. The uncle and the boy were helping him drag the deer to the road, when Game Protector Gentry showed up.

The boy's father ran into the darkness and eventually made it home to safety, and the uncle just sat in his pickup and watched, but the boy wasn't so lucky.

After getting the story, Gentry took the whole party back to the sheriff's office, where he obtained a written account of the entire incident.

Next Gentry phoned the boy's father and told him he needed to come get his son and "clear up a few things." The man flatly refused to come to the sheriff's office.

"You won't even come to get your own son?" Gentry said.

"Don't you get macho with me," retorted the father, remaining immune to Gentry's attempt at shaming him.

Finally, when it became apparent that the man had no intention of coming to get his son and facing possible charges, the sheriff took the boy to another uncle's house.

Eventually the long arm of the law reached the father, and Judge William Dick ordered him to pay $850 for taking a deer during closed season.

Rob Manes
Kansas Wildlife
July/August 1984

Steve Heiting

■ WOULD YOU BELIEVE THIS DEER HUNTING TALE?

One of the most popular men in Glidden, Wisconsin, today is a deer hunter who, until late last year, had never shot a white-tailed buck in his life.

There were a lot of people stopping at Ed Hall's place on the edge of the southern Ashland County community in early December, taking the time to view a wildlife oddity the likes of which they may never see again.

On the afternoon of Monday, December 3, Hall killed a huge buck with his compound bow, a ten-pointer with a spread of 16.5 inches. But that's not all. Permanently locked into place atop the head of Hall's buck are the antlers and head of another buck, one that died in a rutting battle estimated to have occurred in early November.

The antlers of the second buck carry nineteen points on their 19.5 non-typical spread. The head of that buck is completely severed from the body, and Hall said Department of Natural Resources game managers who inspected the deer figure the ten-pointer used its hooves to

decapitate the second deer.

It's an impressive sight, the two large racks meshed together with the heads practically touching.

For Hall, twenty-eight, it's the trophy of a lifetime. "I'm happy. It's the first buck I've ever shot with a bow or rifle," he said.

What probably happened was that in early November when the "rut," or breeding period of deer, was in full swing, the two bucks met in a territorial dispute and battled head-on in the fatal struggle.

When their antlers met, the force of the impact locked the racks together. While not a common occurrence, many such cases have been documented.

Usually, the two deer starve to death unless a human intervenes and saws off one of the deer's antlers to free them. This time, it appears that the front point of the ten-pointer's left antler entered the skull of the nineteen-pointer beneath its right ear, killing it.

Hall and DNR personnel figure the ten-point buck then used its hooves to cut away the dead deer's body. "It's the only logical explanation we could come up with," Hall said. "If coyotes had eaten it, they probably would have gotten the other one, too."

When deer hunters gather to exchange tales of the 1984 season, they better hope Hall is not in their midst. The story of how he came to kill the trophy would undoubtedly beat theirs, hands down.

Hall said that a local trucker, Bob Bay Sr., of Glidden, saw the buck earlier that day and told him about it. Hall returned to the location, found the animal's tracks, and followed.

Unsuccessful in the early bowhunting season, Hall was hoping to fill his tags in Wisconsin's late bow season, which had opened two days before.

About eight inches of snow made for an easy track for Hall to follow. It led him about one-half mile into the Chequamegon National Forest, about six miles north of Glidden, when suddenly the buck jumped from its bed no more than thirty-five feet from the hunter.

"It had its head back ... tipped way back," said Hall, who said he could see the second head right away. "I pulled up, drew the bow back and it put its head down."

The deer was facing Hall. "I was going to try to walk around the side of it to get a better shot, but it started shaking its head like it was going to take off, so I shot," he said.

The arrow struck the deer in the neck, and that's when the hunter became hunted. "Then it reared up and came after me. I ran. It chased me for about sixty-five feet before it fell and turned back into the swamp," he said.

"I was hiding behind all the maple saplings I could find. It was bouncing off trees and everything else.

"I was scared when it came after me. When it charged I was running for my life. I didn't stop running until it stopped crashing behind me," he continued.

With the deer in the swamp, Hall again took up the track. He shot it once in the hindquarters, missed it on a third shot, and then buried two arrows into the deer's chest. It died about 1:30 that afternoon.

"I got him," Hall said was his first reaction.

Hall went to Glidden for help dragging the buck. Don Wanglin and Hall then returned to the kill site and brought the deer out.

Hall's buck, with the head and antlers of the other deer attached, weight 195 pounds field dressed. The deer was in an emaciated condition, and it was estimated its live weight would have been about 300 pounds prior to the rut.

The two deer heads are being mounted as they are by Gary Thimm of Glidden. A cape from another deer will be used as the hide of the nineteen-pointer's head was damaged beyond use.

The bucks will be displayed at D&D Bar in Glidden before being hung on the wall of Hall's rec room at his home.

Steve Heiting
The Daily Press
Ashland, Wisconsin

■ MATCH FOR BROKEN ANTLER

Wildlife biologists tell us that white-tailed deer rarely fight to the death. This being the case, the story that I'm about to recount certainly defies all odds. It has been twenty-four years now since the unusual story unfolded, but it is no less astounding to me today than when first saw it and heard it as a child.

It was a cold November day in 1963 when the late Bob Harkey made his way to his deer stand in the Blue Ridge Cove section of western North Carolina. Here, in the shadow of Mount Mitchell, Harkey had bagged several deer. On this last day of buck season he hoped to get a chance at one of several big bucks that had been seen in the area.

At about 11:30 that fateful morning, Harkey left his stand to return to the car to eat lunch and warm-up. As he was making his way down the mountain he heard a dog bark a short distance away in the thick rhododendron. Dogs were not allowed to run deer on game-management land, but were occasionally used for bear hunting.

Anticipating that the dog might have jumped a deer, Harkey ran to a narrow clearing where he would be afforded one quick shot. Just as he reached a "slick" where logs had been dragged down the mountain, the buck ran into view about seventy yards away. A quick but perfect shot dropped the eight-point, 155-pound buck.

Harkey returned home to dress the deer and remove the antlers. While removing the rack, a small puncture was noticed between the base of the antlers. Upon investigating the wound, the top of another deer's antler was found wedged under the skin and against the skull. The deer apparently had survived a serious wound. Harkey and his companions — Bob Turner, Dick Turner and Euray Lawing — discussed the rarity of this discovery, and how interesting it would be to see the deer that this buck fought. Of course, none of the hunters ever expected to do so.

Two weeks later, while participating in an either-sex deer hunt in the same area, Dick Turner came upon the carcass of a large buck. He made his way through a thicket to get a better look at his find. He immediately became very excited. The dead deer had a large, beautiful eight-point rack. Its only flaw was that it was missing the tip of an antler. Turner wondered if this could be the deer they had all wanted to see so badly. The deer's body was marked by several scrapes and cuts with the death blow apparently coming from a puncture wound to the left rib cage.

Near the dead deer was an area which Turner described as the scene of "a tremendous fight." The ground was pawed and torn by hoofs where two deer had battled gallantly. The battle scene was some 200 to 300 yards down the ridge from where Harkey had killed his eight-pointer just two-weeks before.

Anxious to verify his suspicions, Turner returned to Lincolnton to reveal his find to his hunting buddies. Dick and Bob Turner and Bob Harkey returned to

the area the following day with the broken tip from Harkey's deer's skull. There was a deep sense of anticipation as they worked their way to the deer. When they reached the carcass no one spoke as Harkey slowly fit the two-inch antler tip to the broken tine of the dead deer. Dick Turner described it best. "There ain't no doubt about it! That's it — a perfect fit!" The jig-saw puzzle fit verified the highly unlikely incident.

The eighty-six-year-old Mr. Turner has seen a lot of unusual things in his many years in the outdoors. He has killed over sixty deer, eight elk and three antelope across the United States. He says, "This is the most unusual experience that I can recall."

Wildlife in North Carolina
Mark Taylor
January 1988

■ OBSERVATION OF A WOLF KILLED BY A DEER

Wolves (Canis lupus) probably risk injury while attempting to kill large prey (Murie, 1944; Rausch, 1967; Mech, 1970; Peterson, 1977). Rausch (1967) found that numerous wolf skulls collected in a control program had sustained injuries, probably inflicted by severe blows from moose (Alces alces). Wolves killed by prey seldom, if ever, are found. We located only three such published records, two involving moose (MacFarlane, 1905; Stanwell-Fletcher, 1942), and one involving deer (Odocoileus virginianus) (Frijlink, 1977). In the latter case, the wolf was rabid and apparently was killed by a blow to the head, presumably by a hoof.

This is a second report of a wolf killed by a deer. The wolf carcass was discovered at 10:00 A.M. on 3 December 1983 by Tom Pearson of Isabella, Minnesota, 1.2 kilometers southeast of Silver Island Lake in the Superior National Forest of northeastern Minnesota (Nelson and Mech, 1981). Snow depth was forty-five centimeters, air temperatures varied from -11° to -23°C, and it had snowed just before the wolf was found.

The wolf carcass was lying on a plowed road forty meters from a freshly-killed nine-point buck lying seven meters off the road. Fresh tracks indicated that two wolves had chased the deer down the road as two other wolves came out of the woods and intercepted him. At that location, there were signs of a scuffle and a wolf bed nearby with a small amount of blood in it. Tracks led from the bed forty meters to where the wolf had died. The buck's antlers had three centimeters of blood on one of the tines, suggesting that the wolf had been gored by the deer. Nelson examined the scene on 6 December and found it as Pearson had described except that vehicles had obliterated the tracks on the road where the wolf and deer had fought. The deer was ninety percent consumed, had no skeletal injuries, and had a high fat content in the marrow of the femur.

The local terrain was relatively flat, typical of the region. Thus there was no physical evidence that the buck was unusually vulnerable or predisposed to predation.

The wolf carcass, a female of perhaps one to three years and weighing thirty-four kilograms, was autopsied by Dr. Richard Drolet of the University of Minnesota Veterinary Diagnostic Lab, who stated the following: "The animal had good fat reserves. Extensive hemorrhages were present between the muscles of the right thoracic wall. The thoracic wall was perforated (puncture wound) between the sixth and seventh rib. The thoracic cavity was full of blood. A laceration of about 1.0 centimeter was found in the caudal vena cava. No other significant lesions were observed. Radiograph of the right thoracic wall failed to reveal the presence of fragments of bullets or fractured bone. The lesions observed are compatible with your hypothesis stating that this animal would have been gored by a deer."

The usual defense by deer against wolf predation is to flee rapidly when pursued (Mech, 1984). This account and Frijlink's (1977) indicate that deer will, however, use hooves and antlers as defensive weapons against wolves. In this incident, deep fluffy snow (forty-five centimeters) was probably a major factor in the deer's inability to escape. The fact that the chase proceeded down the plowed road just before the kill suggests that the deer was fatigued and reluctant to enter the deep snow in the woods.

Maternal does have been observed attacking coyotes (Canis latrans) and striking them with forefeet (Truett, 1979; Garner and Morrison, 1980). In addition, small groups of mule deer (Odocoileus hemionus) have been attacking groups of three and four coyotes (Calahane, 1947; MacConnell-Yount and Smith, 1978; Truett, 1979). However, such behavior is probably less successful against larger predators such as wolves that rely on ungulates as their primary prey. Thus, active defense by deer appears to be only a secondary and last resort when the usual escape strategy fails.

Mech & Nelson
Journal Of Mammalogy 2/85

■ WARDEN'S TALE OF BUCK FIGHT

This one you are probably not going to believe, but here goes anyway. It was a beautiful day, and I was on patrol in northeast Iowa. The leaves were turning all their fantastic colors and the sky was deep blue. Gosh it was great to be alive. My radio squawked, and it was the sheriff's office. Abbey, the radio dispatcher could always find me no matter where I went. Checking in, she told me of a call from a farmer's wife way up in the other end of the county. Seems her husband was picking corn and had come across two big buck deer locked together. Said to hurry! Now, there are no straight lines in Allamakee County, but I took the fastest route.

As I pulled up to the bunch of cars parked on the gravel, I could see people with cameras walking around in the picked part of the field. The huge combine was parked right out in the middle. The fella opened the cab door and waved to me, "Come on." It was a fair hike and as I climbed up the ladder on the side he pointed to an area in the unpicked corn.

There they were, two of the biggest bucks I had seen in a long time, locked together in mortal combat. Their antlers had caught straight on, and when they moved sideways, they knocked down about ten rows of corn at a time.

"Have you got a rifle?" he inquired. Oh sure, good time to think about that, Jerry, you're twenty miles from home. Only thing I had along was my issued four-inch .357 revolver.

"Maybe I can get you close with the combine," he suggested, but when he started it up, they just moved away some more — again taking down corn, ten rows at a time. "Don't worry about the corn," he yelled. "I can get that. Just see what you can do about getting them apart. The one's about done in."

He was right. One was down now and being dragged around by the other.

I climbed out and hollered for everyone to get back to the road. I didn't want anyone around for what I had in mind. They apparently had used up all their film anyway and moved back to watch. What a deal. As I climbed down to the ground, the one buck tried to run off, knocking down a big circle of corn. He was solidly anchored to his downed opponent. I approached slowly, but he was watching me with one eye as he struggled in vain. He was about done in, too. Studying the antler, I wondered if I could possibly shoot the dying one's antler off, releasing the strong one. Too darn far for a pistol. Sure wished I'd had a rifle. I tried getting close, but he just ripped and snorted. Well, I thought, old boy, I'm gonna try! I spread my legs, locked up both arms, and cocked the gun. There aren't any posts to steady you in the middle of a corn field.

"That's a mightly long shot, warden!" the voice came from the combine.

"I know!" I replied, but what could I do. Steady squeeze, slowly, WHAM! The strong buck went down like he was poleoxed. Darn! Too low. There was a long groan of disapproval from the people on the road.

"Well, you killed that one deader than a tack-hammer," the farmer mumbled.

"Yep, sure did," I said.

What a thing to do and right in front of everybody, I thought, as I slowly approached the two downed animals. Suddenly the exhausted one tried to get up but was too weak to lift the other one. Now, I was close enough for my pistol.

Maybe I could still shoot an antler off and one would survive. I took careful aim. Don't want two dead ones. Wham! What a reaction. The exhausted one bounded straight up. He was free! Without a backward glance, he bounded out across the corn field amid cheers from the crowd.

Well, at least one made it I thought as I approached the one on the ground. His broken antler lay beside him, splintered and shot off close to his head. As I reached down to pick it up, he opened one eye, but didn't move. I jumped back quickly, still he didn't get up. I thought he was stone dead from my first shot. We stood there in the middle of that field looking at one another.

"Are you going to get up or lay there all day?" I shouted at him, wondering just what I was going to do if he did jump up and come at me. With this, he bounded to his feet, shook his one-antlered head at me and off across the corn he went. You should have heard the crowd. I had a white hat on for sure, as far as they were concerned. I thought I had killed him with my first shot but had apparently only knocked him out.

"That's the greatest exhibition of shooting I've ever seen in my life!" I heard the excited farmer shout, as he banged me across the back, "Can I have that?" he asked reaching for the antler that was still in my hand. Two hits on the same antler; matter of fact, part of the slug was still embedded in part of it.

Talk about luck. I guess the story made the rounds, and like all stories, it got even better with the telling. Now this all took place years ago when I was younger and steadier, too. The ol' gentleman I had given the antler to has gone on, but an ASCS man recently told me his wife still had the antler, She lent it to me so I could take this picture. Believe it or not!

Jerry Hoilien
Iowa Conservationist
September 1988

Richard P. Smith

■ MELANISTIC BUCKS

Dick Giles from Milford, Michigan is probably the only deer hunter in North America who bagged two melanistic white-tailed bucks during his lifetime, and he saw a third one before it was shot by another hunter.

Melanistic deer are color mutations, just like albinos, only they are even rarer than albinos. While albino whitetails are basically all white, melanistic deer are black. Like albinism, melanism is a genetic trait that can be passed on from one generation to another within a deer population, under the right circumstances.

The genetic makeup of some of the deer where Giles hunts in Oscoda County obviously favors melanism, or at least it did, because he saw all three black whitetails in the same general area. He bagged his first melanistic buck during November 1977. It was an eight-pointer that proved to be only 1.5 years old.

His second melanistic buck was also a yearling, but it only had spike antlers. That animal was tagged during the 1981 season while hunting within fifteen yards of the spot where he shot the first mutant.

A third black buck was seen by Giles during 1982, not far from where he shot the other two. He later learned that another hunter, his name unknown, bagged that buck and it had a seven-point rack.

Dick said both bucks he shot had blue eyes and the undersides of their tails were white like a normal whitetail. Taxidermist Joe Newmyer of Michigan Wildlife Studios in Union Lake mounted the melanistic bucks Giles bagged. Newmyer also reports tanning the hide of another melanistic whitetail bagged in Michigan, this one a doe. Mark Bottrell shot the doe during 1984 in Iosco County. The northwest corner of Iosco County and southeast corner of Oscoda County touch.

Bottrell said the eyes of melanistic doe were also blue, but there was no white on the tail like the bucks Giles collected. Coincidentally, Bottrell lives in the same city as Giles — Milford.

Richard P. Smith

■ DEER BREAK-IN WAKES INMATE

A 150-pound deer crashed through a window at the Gordon State Prison recently and landed on top of an inmate.

"In my twenty-eight years in the Division of Corrections, this is the first time I've ever had a break- in," said Len Fromholz, superintendent of the camp in Douglas County south of Superior, Wisconsin.

Officials said the inmate screamed for help and struggled with the deer, waking his roommate and other prisoners. Other inmates and correctional officers got the animal outside, where it ran away.

No inmates were injured, and the Department of Natural Resources public information official Jim Bishop said a warden tracked the doe for about a mile after the incident and believes the animal will be OK.

Associated Press

■ ALLERGIC REACTIONS

Hunters who are allergic to cats and dogs may be susceptible to allergic reactions to deer and elk, according to a study conducted in Montana, where more than 230,000 deer and elk hunting licenses are issued each year. The reactions can be severe. One study participant was a twenty-nine-year old professional hunting guide and horse packer who experienced several acute attacks of asthma while skinning and dressing deer and elk in the field for his hunting guests.

"His asthmatic reactions seriously interfered with his occupation," said Dr. Donald N. Gillespie of Missoula, Montana, whose study is reported in Annals of Allergy, official publication of the American College of Allergists. Dr. Gillespie's study on the little-researched subject of allergies to wild animals was conducted in cooperation with the Mayo Clinic Allergic Disease Research Laboratory in Rochester, Minnesota.

The hunting guide, who had a history of allergic rhinitis (hay fever) and asthma, was allergic to a number of other substances, including pollens, molds, dust, feathers and domestic animal danders. Now, after treatment with medication and a course of immunotherapy, or "allergy shots," his symptoms are controlled and he is back at work in the wild, said Dr. Gillespie.

In another case, the thirty-nine-year old wife of a hunter became violently ill while accompanying her husband on a hunting trip. When a deer carcass was brought into the camp, she developed generalized itching, wheezing, swollen eyes and sneezing. She was taken to a hospital emergency room and responded to treatment with epinephrine.

Before her allergies to deer and elk were diagnosed, she had suffered some puzzling, milder reactions after handling clothes worn by her husband while he had hunted and killed deer, elk or antelope.

"Patients with histories suggesting allergy to wild animals such as deer and elk are not unusual in areas of the U.S. where such animals are frequently hunted," said Dr. Gillespie, who found the fifteen subjects with deer and elk allergies for his study in his own allergy practice and through newspaper advertisements.

The allergic reactions can be caused, for example, when a sensitive person inhales deer dander, gets a deer hair in an eye or has skin contact with the animal's urine or serum.

He said the fifteen subjects, who were studied over a period of four years, had some common characteristics. Skin and blood tests showed that all had multiple allergies to various substances, and all were sensitive to the dander of at least one domestic animal like a cat or a dog. The latter characteristic, said Dr. Gillespie, suggests that patients who are highly allergic to domestic animals but who have had no contact with deer or elk, may be at increased risk of developing allergic reactions after exposure to deer or elk. This was also suggested by laboratory RAST (radioallergosorbent test) inhibition studies on serum.

Interestingly, none of the fifteen subjects reported adverse reactions after eating venison. Dr. Gillespie cautions hunters allergic to deer and elk to wear gloves and masks when skinning and dressing the game. He also warns them against jumping in the back of an enclosed pick-up truck with a carcass for the drive home.

American College of Allergists
27 September 1985

■ SCRAPING BEHAVIOR IN FEMALE WHITE-TAILED DEER

The scraping behavior of male white-tailed deer is well documented. Many researchers have described scraping from direct observation. Detailed study of scrape characteristics and the behavior of males reveals that scrapes are signposts and function in social communication during the rutting period. Scraping by female white-tailed deer, however, has not been previously reported. We here describe three observations of such behavior.

Two observations involved females (one adult and two yearlings) that were offspring of wild deer but had been captured just after birth and reared in pens. These deer were equipped with radio transmitters and released onto a study area in Clarke County, Georgia, within the Piedmont physiographic province. Having been conditioned to human presence, they could be followed and observed at close range without apparent effect upon their behavior. Evidently they were sexually normal, as each was bred by a wild buck in fall 1979 and gave birth to a fawn in late spring 1980.

At 0809 on 27 August 1979, the three females were found together on a wooded hill — mostly mature oak, hickory, and American beech — that they often used. They walked slowly through the area and frequently paused to feed and groom. At 0859, one of the yearlings, which had been released three months before, pawed a depression, about twenty by twenty-five centimeters, in the litter and urinated directly into it using the normal squatting posture. She then licked each of her tarsal gland tufts several times and walked on. No apparent reactions were noted from the other females. At 0923, the three deer bedded in the same area 100 to 175 meters from the scrape.

The second observation was indirect. On the evening of 3 April 1980, the three free-ranging females were lured into an unoccupied 0.24-hectare enclosure, located within their home range, and confined overnight. The next morning, a freshly-made twenty-five by forty centimeter depression, with grass and litter removed, was present inside the enclosure. Soil in the scrape was moist and had the odor of deer urine.

The third instance involved wild deer observed from a tree stand in Taliaferro County, Georgia. The stand was along an old logging road in a mixed hardwood and pine woodland. At 0700 on 6 October

1979, a female, apparently an adult, emerged from a thicket. A few minutes later, a six-point male, smaller than the female, approached her. He stopped sixteen to eighteen meters from the female at a small scrape, which was at least two days old and was near a rubbed sapling. He thrashed some bushes with his antlers and pawed the old scrape into a larger one approximately seventy centimeters in diameter. The female watched him intently and, apparently in response to his actions, pawed an almost identical depression where she stood. The male then joined her, and they moved off together browsing. Neither deer urinated in association with scraping. Scraping is performed at least to a limited extent by female white-tailed deer, and it is not confined to the rutting period. Further study is needed to determine to what extent, if any, female scrapes function in social communication.

T.G. Sawyer, R.L. Marchinton and (C.W. Berisford Journal of Mammalogy, 1982

■ CLEAN VENISON

Well, she probably just wanted it to be clean for the agent to inspect. Why else would she put the deer roast in the washing machine?

Don Ruzicka, conservation agent for Dallas County, Missouri recently did some detective work that Sherlock Holmes would envy. He spotted a single turkey feather in the bed of a pickup truck.

The truck owner said he had hauled the bird for a neighbor. Okay, would he mind if Ruzicka inspected his home freezer?

No problem. He and the man went to the man's house trailer where the man called in to his wife to, "get dressed, the conservation agent is here to check our freezer."

Little warning bells went off in Ruzicka. "I guessed the freezer was on the back porch and went around just in time

to see the woman turning away with something in her arms."

The woman put the package in the washing machine and Ruzicka rescued it and found it was a deer roast. "And I found a frozen wild turkey in the freezer," he says.

All Outdoors 24 July 1987

■ UNUSUAL TALE

Michigan's 1974 firearm deer season brought with it the outdoor experience of a lifetime for an Ypsilanti man and his 15-year-old son.

"The greatest hunting thrill I've ever had," says 43-year-old Darrel Hinkle, who has missed but two deer seasons in the past 27 years.

It was about 1 p.m. November 17 when the two hunters happened upon a sight few ever have seen, or ever will see. The Hinkles were making their way along the edge of a Lake County swamp, heading for a deer stand they had come across during a preseason scouting jaunt.

"I saw the two fighting bucks first," the elder Hinkle relates. "They were in a clearing between the swamp and a pine thicket. Their heads were down, so I couldn't immediately see antlers. David hadn't seen them so I motioned for him to stop. We remain amazed by what happened next.

"The big bucks were straining and pushing, driving one another back and forth 20 or 30 feet at a time. Then they paused for a moment and raised their heads, giving us a good look at a clump of antlers that we realized were locked together. I told David to take the buck on the right and I aimed at the one on the left.

"I fired once and my buck went down. With my shot, the other buck lunged and David missed his first shot. The buck began twisting and turning, actually dragging the downed animal several yards. He really 'cut a shine.'"

"I had to sit down for a few minutes,"

he recalls. "David at first was much calmer than I, but later he got a bit shook up, too."

Fortunately, the Hinkles were able to drive their station wagon to within a few yards of the fallen deer, and two other hunters helped hoist the animals on top of the car, antlers still enmeshed. They stopped at the Alma deer checking station, where astonished DNR wildlife biologists determined that David's 8-point buck was 3-1/2 years old. The position of the two animals prevented biologists from measuring Darrel's buck's teeth to determine its age. It sported, however, an 11-point rack. Each animal's dressed weight was an estimated 180 pounds.

While the Hinkles were at the checking station, DNR Wildlife Division Chief Merrill "Pete" Petoskey happened by.

"I told him the story," says Hinkle. "I also told him that had I been alone and seen those bucks, although I consider myself a law abiding citizen, I might have been compelled to shoot both of them. Petosky pondered that circumstance soberly for a moment, then his face broke out in a grin. 'Don't worry about it,' he said, 'it won't happen to you again.'"

Michigan Natural Resources
January/February 1975

■ DEER BEHAVIOR DURING FOREST FIRES

J. H. Sizer, describing the Mazatzal fire in the Tonto Forest in Arizona in 1921, says: "I encountered a bunch of deer hemmed in by a fire against a rock bluff. These, however, escaped by jumping high over the blaze as I approached, and ran away through the burned area, apparently none the worse off."

Here again deer seem to have allowed themselves to be surrounded by fire. Would they have leaped over the flames and escaped if they had not been disturbed by an intruder, or would they have stayed on the spot and perished?

Frederic Winn, describing the Rose Peak fire in the Apache Forest in Arizona in 1911, says:

"We saw a whitetail doe and fawn run blindly into a fiercely burning tangle of down timber. Both were probably consumed, as we never saw them come out. This incident happened at night. The deer apparently were terror-stricken."

This sounds like a plain case of stampede. But again it is not clear whether the doe was stampeded by the fire only, or by both the fire and the fire-fighters, or only by the approach of the men.

In 1922, while fighting the Rawmeat Cabin fire in the Gila Forest, in New Mexico, the writer saw a blacktail doe come bounding down a mountain side parallel with the front of the fire and just inside the unburned territory. Probably a crew of men had frightened her. She was heavy with fawn and coming straight at me. When she got within ten yards I thoughtlessly threw up my arms. She wheeled sharp toward the fire, leaped into the flames without hesitation, and disappeared. She may have survived the flames of the fire-front with nothing worse than a singeing, but there was at least a mile of hot smoking burned-over ground to cross. She could never have crossed it without scorching her hoofs. If a horse or mule scorches a hoof it means a crack in the skin at the hoof-line, flyblowing of the crack, and slow but cruel death. It must be the same with a deer.

In the case of the doe, it would seem that she knew where she was going until suddenly confronted by a new and unsuspected danger; whereupon she lost her head and perished. Maybe this indicates an answer to puzzling contradictions in the behavior of animals in the presence of fire. Maybe confusion is not immediate, but cumulative.

Henry Van Dyke, in "Fisherman's Luck," has this to say about fires and game: "Let but the trail of smoke drift down the wind across the forest, and all the game for miles and miles will catch the signal for fear and flight." Since he is speaking of the north woods, his statement is probably meant to apply to deer. It implies that flight begins as soon as the scent of fire is caught. This may be true in the north woods, but is not the case with deer in the Southwest. I have seen deer feeding peacefully within half a mile of a big fire that had been filling the woods with smoke for a week. In fact, I have seen where deer went to water across a newly burned area on which snags were still smoking, when they could just as well have gone around it. The same tendency to cross new burns is noted by Show and Price in connection with the Cuyama fire of 1922, in the Santa Barbara Forest of California.

One writer suggests that the new ashes contain salts which the deer relish. I doubt this, because in the Western cattle country the deer are provided with plenty of salt, which is put out for cattle. This is one of the improvements which settlement has made in the potential productiveness of our Western game fields.

If I were to attempt to piece together the evidence at hand, of which the foregoing examples are typical, I would say that deer do not usually flee precipitately from smoke; that they keep out of the way of advancing flames in a leisurely fashion, probably attempting to go around and upwind in the same way as they would do in cases of other disturbance. In doing so they are, of course, liable to be confronted with new fire-fronts in unexpected places and even to be surrounded. They then become increasingly alarmed and often stampede, especially when disturbed by human beings. When stampeded they lose their heads entirely and often perish. When badly harassed by a very severe fire they may lose their fear of humans in the same way they are said to do when hard pressed by dogs, and seek refuge in places occupied by humans. But in ordinary fires this is not the case.

Aldo Leopold, American Forestry, September, 1923

Bill Schubert

■ STUCK

While checking out an area to set up a tree stand during the 1983 bow hunting season, I jumped about ten deer in a wooded area. I immediately ran to the top of a nearby hill, curious to see if I could spot antlers on any of the fleeing deer.

When I reached to top of the hill, I spotted a doe digging and driving with her front legs but obviously not going anywhere. I don"t know if she was one of the deer I jumped or if she had been there for some time. In any event, she was in a real predicament. She was stuck between two trees growing quiet close to one another.

I approached very slowly and deliberately to within five feet of her. I sat and talked quietly to her for about two to three minutes and my calmness seemed to put her at ease, as compared to when I first came up to her as she struggled to free herself. Slowly, I approached close enough to pet her and she didn't even jump. I then decided to place my sweatshirt between her and the two trees to protect her while I went for a camera.

I returned shortly and took several pictures of the doe. I then climbed above here, pried the trees apart, and set her free from her predicament. Without this assistance, it seems very doubtful that she would have been able to free herself. I never expected to encounter anything like this while hunting and probably never will again.

*Bill Schubert
Racine, Wisconsin*

■ OBSERVATION OF A SWIMMING WOLF KILLING A SWIMMING DEER

Whitetailed deer and other ungulates flee into water to escape wolves. Presumably wolves have greater difficulty killing prey when swimming than when on land, so escape to water seems generally to be adaptive. The adaptiveness of such escape behavior, therefore, must depend on conditions yet to be fully elucidated.

This is the first report of a wolf killing a deer while both were swimming. The observation was made by Michael Nelson in the Superior National Forest of northeastern Minnesota. All distances given are estimates. Air temperatures varied from -7°C to 0°C.

On 15 November 1982 at 10:45 A.M., we observed from an aircraft a radio-collared wolf with six other wolves from the Malberg Lake pack. They were walking on the southwest side of Thomas Lake (1.6 km by 4.0 km) on shelf ice that extended five to ten meters. The rest of the lake, except for smaller bays, was unfrozen. An adult doe was swimming in a nearby stretch of water, 1.3 km by 0.8 km, toward the opposite shore away from the wolves; the wolves were traveling on land toward the same shore apparently to intercept her. About 100 meters from shore the deer appeared to realize that the wolves had cut off her escape route and turned back to the open lake.

We returned 3.5 hours later, and the deer still was swimming in the same general area; the wolves lay along the nearest shore. As the doe swam within seventy-five meters of shore, one wolf jumped in and swam twenty-five meters toward her before turning back. The doe then swam parallel to the shore toward an island about 400 meters away. The wolves headed along the shore toward the island, which ice connected to the mainland. The doe reached the island first but remained in the shallows. As the wolves approached to within 100 meters, the doe swam away. One swam after her but only came within fifty meters before turning back.

When we observed the doe one hour later, she was swimming toward the same island, and the wolves were moving to intercept her. This time, however, she swam slower than earlier, and she rested in shallows adjacent to a five-meter cliff that enabled the wolves to approach undetected. The wolves were twenty-five meters from the doe before she bounded toward the open lake. One wolf jumped in and swam after her, soon coming to within two to three meters. At about seventy five meters from shore, the doe turned slightly and the wolf caught her. The wolf swam alongside the doe and attacked her neck and head. In the ensuing minutes, single wolves swam out at two different times toward the pair, but one returned when only ten meters from shore. For about one minute, two wolves were attacking the doe, but then one returned to shore. Only one wolf was attacking as the deer died, about ten minutes after we had observed her swimming toward the island. The wolf towed the doe to shore, and the wolves fed on it. The doe had been in the water at least 4.7 hours since we first observed her.

This account shows that wolves can kill deer when both are swimming. However, other accounts, and the earlier events of the present observation, suggest that it may be uncommon. In April 1973, one of our technicians observed a deer swimming and struggling to climb onto thin ice as five wolves attempted to catch it. Although the wolves were within two meters of the deer, they never entered the water, and the deer eventually drowned. Other researchers reported observations of wolves swimming after deer in March and in August, but both deer were killed on land. In the March incident, wolves entered the water twenty-seven times during 3.5 hours. In all the observations, deer easily swam away from swimming wolves. However, in the present observation, the deer spent at least 4.7 hours swimming in freezing water before succumbing to the wolves.

A common element in these observations is the apparent ability of wolves to gauge where a swimming deer will emerge and to intercept it. Thus not all water may be refuge, especially ponds and small lakes where deer would be visible from shore. The presence of islands and configuration of shoreline would also play a role in escape to water. The deer in Thomas Lake swam to an island, which might have deterred the wolves if newly formed ice had not allowed them easy access.

Thomas Lake has a point of mainland only 0.5 km from the island the deer swam toward. Had she continued to that point, she could have escaped easily because the wolves would have had to travel 4.5 km of shore to reach her and could not have done so before she left the water. The deer had swum for one hour after we first observed her at the island, so apparently she had enough endurance for such a swim but was unable to recognize shoreline configuration that allowed her opportunity for escape.

This research was funded by the USDI Fish & Wildlife Service and the USDA Forest Service, North Central Forest Experiment Station. John Burch and Jeff Renner radio tagged the wolves observed, and Dick Mahl piloted the aircraft. Jeff Renneberg made the 1973 observation referred to herein.

Michael E. Nelson and
   L. David Mech
Journal of Mammalogy
February 1984

■ QUICK REFLEXES

Whitetails react with amazing quickness. Many bow hunters have seen deer "jump the string." In fact, during the 1985 season, a friend told me, with exasperation, of a yearling deer that allowed him three shots—ranging in distance from ten to thirty yards—and successfully dodged each arrow. He was shooting a seventy-pound compound bow, too. Unless it happens to you, it's hard to determine if the deer's reflexes were really that fast or if it's a convenient excuse for a shot missed at close range. Let me relate an incident that removes some of the doubt.

Carrying his compound bow and walking back from his stand after an uneventful morning hunt, a friend of mine came upon a spike buck feeding no more than twenty-five yards away. The deer was broadside with its right side toward Doug. After nocking an arrow, Doug drew, aimed for the right front shoulder and let the arrow fly. Upon hearing the shot, the buck jumped up, turned around and started to dash back the way it had come—all before the arrow hit him in the left flank! Assuming even a modest velocity of 180 feet per second for the arrow, the deer had little more than a third of a second in which to react.

By the way, the broadhead cut enough blood vessels to enable Doug to trail and recover the buck.

Experiences like this have created an awe in me for deer and the speed of their reactions.

Tim Lewis, D.M.D

Dave Tripiciano

Was the injured right shoulder of this deer the cause of the severe mutation of the left antler? Or, do you think this strange antler formation occurred due to genetics, an in-velvet injury, or some other reason?

Dave Tripiciano

While there are many reasons for and causes of deformed antlers among white-tailed deer, in this case I believe the unusual left antler is almost certainly due to the injury of the buck's right shoulder. An injured buck will frequently grow a malformed antler on the side opposite the injury.

Al Hofacker

■ A NON-TYPICAL NON-TYPICAL

After the 1983 New York archery season, Wayne Dickerson of Wayne, New York, shot a rather unusual white-tailed deer. The buck's antlers had more than twenty actual points, as verified by a state conservation officer. The buck weighed 195 pounds.

Except for a large, outward protrusion on the deer's right antler, which is fairly common among whitetails, this deer's right antler could almost be considered "typical." The left antler, however, has to be most bizarre and unusual antler formation I have ever encountered on a whitetail.

When Wayne Dickerson bagged this deer he found that the deer's right shoulder was badly smashed by a shotgun slug during the previous year's firearms season. The deer had been maneuvering quite well, however, on three legs for almost one year.

I have heard several theories stating that the left side of the brain controls functions on the right side of the body, and vice versa. Is it possible, then, that an injury to the right side of the body led to unusual antler development on the left anther?

■ FELINE FRIEND

Early this spring Ethel Brown of rural Parke County, Indiana was outside enjoying the exceptionally warm weather. She enjoys being outside and observing the deer that visit and live on her small farm.

One of the stray cats that hang around her farm had given birth to a litter of kittens across the road under a windfall. On this particular evening, a yearling doe and two other deer came strolling down the road at the same time the cat was crossing the road heading for the house. As fate would have it, their paths crossed right there in the road. To Ethel's surprise neither the deer nor the cat were alarmed by each other's presence. However, she was astounded when the yearling doe put its nose to the cat's nose and they nuzzled each other as if in a form of communication. Then the cat turned back towards the woods with the deer following her all the way to the windfall to see the kittens; after which the deer hung around visiting for a while until it finally returned to the other deer, and they went they on their way back into the woods.

Gary A. Walters

Sportsmanship & Ethics

by Charles J. Alsheimer

Few subjects in America evoke such widespread controversy today as hunting.

In many mixed circles even politics takes a backseat when talk turns to the taking of wild game with gun, longbow, or steel traps. There are many reasons for this controversy. Lack of public understanding, improper media reporting, and lack of team effort on the sportsmen's part in selling the positive side of hunting to the public are just a few of the reasons.

To better understand the ethics and sportsmanship behind the sport millions of Americans love, the history of hunting must be looked at first. Since the beginning of time man has depended on wild game for survival. For the most part, the early hunters, nomadic tribes, and Indians killed only what they required, using the furs for clothing and the carcass for food. From the earliest recorded history man was able to lay down the foundation of ethics, a code fostered from an understanding that if wildlife populations were to survive, excessive harvesting could not take place. This code was very much in effect when the white man came to America in the 1600's.

> "A peculiar virtue in wildlife ethics is that the hunter ordinarily has no gallery to applaud or disapprove of his conduct. Whatever his acts, they are dictated by his own conscience, rather than by a mob of onlookers. It is difficult to exaggerate the importance of this/fact."
>
> —*Aldo Lopold*
> A Sand County Almanac, 1949

The story of hunting in America begins with the Indian. The white man learned much from the Indians in terms of hunting techniques and survival on the frontier. But the Indian's idea of what conservation should be was different from the white man's. For the most part, the white man saw the vast wilderness which spread into the sunset as an untapped resource, one of hidden wealth.

With the arrival of 1800, the white man's quest for the wealth found in furs and meat drove many wildlife species to the brink of extinction. For nearly 10,000 years America's wild game populations remained stable, but this was to change in ninety short years. Progress was America's motto. The "iron horse on rails" moved westward, towns sprang up, forests were cleared, and industry took hold. As a result, mouths had to be fed, so the carnage began.

In the early 1800's wildlife populations were high, with demand for meat also running high. Game laws were unheard of and market hunting was big business. During this period the American bison numbered nearly 200 million.

But things "were a changin'" on the prairie, for the .45/120/550 "Buffalo" Sharps and the Remington .40/90 brought the great buffalo herds to their knees. One man who became a legend at the expense of the buffalo was "Buffalo Bill" Cody, who personally accounted for 4,280 buffalos in 1868 and 1869. By 1890 there were only a few hundred buffalo left in America.

The buffalo wasn't the only victim of the big business called market hunting, for throughout America there was open season on all wildlife. Populations dropped to unheard of levels and in many portions of this great land whole specials disappeared. The white man's quest for big dollars had put the American wildlife scene in total disarray by 1895.

Many who understood what the balance of nature was all about were both shocked and angered by what had taken place. The American Indians, who had lived in harmony with nature from the beginning of time, couldn't comprehend what they were seeing. One old chief, who spoke his piece, sent a letter to President Franklin Pierce in 1855 to show his disapproval of what was happening.

Although the following letter from Chief Sealth of the Duwanish tribe speaks directly to the taking of land, it also conveyed a need for something better than the nature scene was seeing in the 1800's. It is entitled, "Where is the eagle?"

"The Great Chief in Washington sends word that he wishes to buy our land. How can you buy or sell the sky—the warmth of the land? The idea is strange to us. Yet we do not own the freshness of the air or the sparkle of the water. How can you buy them from us? Every part of this earth is sacred to my people Every shiny pine needle, every sandy shore, every mist in the dark woods, every clearing and humming insect is holy in the memory and experience of my people.

"We know that the white man does not understand our ways. One portion of the land is the same to him as the next, for he is a stranger who comes in the night and takes from the land whatever. he needs. The earth is not his brother but his enemy, and when he has conquered it he moves on. He leaves his father's grave and his children's birthplace is forgotten.

"There is no quiet place in the white man's cities. No place to hear the leaves of spring or the rustle of insect wings. But perhaps because I am savage and do not understand—the clatter only seems to insult the ears. And what is there to life if a man cannot hear the lovely cry of the whippoorwill or the arguments of the frog around the pond at night?

"The whites, too, shall pass—perhaps sooner than the tribes.

Continue to contaminate your bed and you will one night suffocate in your own waste. When the buffalo are all slaughtered, the wild horses all tamed, the secret corners of the forest heavy with the scent of many men, and the view of the ripe hills blotted out by talking wires. Where is the thicket? Gone. Where is the eagle? Gone. And what is it to say goodbye to the swift pony and the hunt, the end of living and beginning of survival?"

It almost seems as if Teddy Roosevelt had this letter in mind when he and other truly dedicated sportsmen decided to "take the bull by the horns" and form the Boone and Crockett Club in 1895. These early pioneers of conservation realized that if America was going to ever again have thriving game populations, changes had to be made—and fast.

From Maine to California the year of 1900 found wildlife populations in a shambles. The Boone and Crockett Club's task was monumental, but not impossible. Within a short period of time the trend of the 1800's was halted through the first hunting regulations ever imposed in America. As might be expected, the closing of hunting seasons in some areas was met with resistance by a few. But for Roosevelt and the others the vision was too strong for this to set them back.

The turn of the century ushered in a new beginning. With hunting seasons closed and habitat returning, the whitetail started making its comeback throughout the eastern part of the country. Things were again changing—but this time for the better.

The Boone and Crockett Club's ideals were infectious and during the early part of the 1900's sportsmen's clubs sprang up throughout America. As wildlife populations increased, hunting seasons were opened, giving many the opportunity of hunting for the first time in their lives.

Many sportsmen's groups, not wanting to ever see a repeat of the 1800's, devised ways to help improve the wildlife of North America. By self-enactment of the Federal Excise Tax, hunters began pumping millions of their own dollars into wildlife programs. Ducks Unlimited had such a vision and over the years has raised millions for the improvement of waterfowl habitat. All told, sportsman-related programs have proven to be the salvation of both game and non-game species in America.

However, even with the positive turn-about of the past one hundred years, hunting in America is still very controversial. Prior to World War II America's population base was essentially rural. From this setting came the desire of men to teach their children the ways of the woods. Hunting was a tradition and a challenge, the test of man against beast.

After World War II things changed—America changed. Perhaps the greatest change was the population shift from rural to urban. With more and more young people seeking higher educations, new philosophies regarding our way of life evolved. From this came a new generation of people strongly opposed to the killing of anything. Seemingly, overnight America had a new crop of leaders, many who never knew what the great outdoor experience was all about.

The media boom of the 1960's and 1970's introduced all of America to the reality of life. Realizing good news is not news, the media thrust upon America the negative side of life in living color. Everyone was included and suddenly the good guys were the bad guys. When a number of major figures succumbed to assassin's bullets, a cry went out against all forms of killing. People throughout this great land wanted all guns confiscated. These were truly controversial times and the hunter emerged as one of the biggest villains. With the media showing literally all the wrong reasons for hunting, anti-hunting groups sprang up across the country.

"Continue to contaminate your bed and you will one night suffocate in your own waste."
—Chief Sealth, 1855

For the most part, the anti-hunting fraternity took the hunters by surprise. Certainly the National Rifle Association had warned gun owners and hunters for years that new philosophies in America were emerging, but for the most part the warnings fell on deaf ears. For many years most hunters had the attitude that no one would ever challenge them on the whys and wherefores of their sport. After all didn't gun owners in America number in the millions while the antis seemed to have only a portion of that?

But the antis were organized. They had the media's ear and knew how to appeal to America's senses. The battle came to a head in October, 1975, when CBS televised a special "documentary" called "Guns of Autumn." Sportsmen who watched the program couldn't believe what they were seeing and hearing. When the program ended, I sat in our den in a state of shock—not knowing whether to cry or fight. In just ninety short minutes CBS showed me that the anti-hunting movement is well financed, has a great deal of influence in the news media, and is a real threat to the sport of hunting.

In my opinion, America is made up of three groups when it comes to the sport of hunting—those for it, those against it, and those who are undecided. The issue before all sportsmen today is how to deal with the third group, those who are undecided. I view this as the hunters' biggest challenge of this decade. Why? Because the score is pretty much tied, one to one, with the hunters and anti-hunting fraternity in what I'd call a "Mexican standoff."

As a result, sportsmen must sell the sport of hunting to this third group, the ones who are undecided, if our favorite pastime is to survive. If we can't, then our children may never know the thrills we've experienced and the beauty we've seen down through our autums in the woods.

It is unfortunate that a select few who hunt have not left a very good impression in their communities. The guy who doesn't sight his gun in prior to the season, doesn't properly care for the game that is taken, or brags about the number of deer he wounded, tarnishes the sportsman's image. The impression this leaves with those who do not hunt is devastating to those who do.

I'm continually confronted by people who are against hunting or who are not sure whether they're for or against the sport. Some of these experiences have been akin to being attacked by a swarm of bees. The uncertainty of those who are undecided stems from the mixed feelings they've acquired through what they've read or seen. I hunt with camera, gun, bow, or traps, and I enjoy telling people the positive side of the sport. For the most part, people will listen and understand if spoken to politely and properly. While the sport and experience can be simply explained to some, it needs in-depth explanation for others to understand.

The need for hunting in America today is greater than the mere experience. In my area of the Northeast, man long ago did away with the whitetail's natural predators, the mountain lion, the coyote and the wolf. Because of this situation and increased habitat, game populations have literally exploded before our eyes. Each year thousands of acres of field crops, from corn to soybeans, are ravaged by deer and other animals.

For years wildlife managers have been faced with the problem of too many deer for the range available in many parts of the Northeast. And despite record harvests each year, deer populations continue to grow. The increased number of auto/deer collisions annually in New York and Pennsylvania is an indication of what is happening to the deer population.

Therefore, to control and manage wildlife numbers it is imperative that there be hunting seasons to control game populations. Although hunting is controversial with the antis, it is still the only proven method of controlling wildlife populations in this country. Today, more than ever before, hunting seasons are essential to healthy, well balanced wildlife populations.

Why people hunt oftentimes is not understood by those who do not hunt. To me hunting means far more than the killing of an animal. I spend most of my time in a blind or walking slowly in the woods or fields, often getting wet and cold and more often, never firing a shot or an arrow. It's not uncommon for me to sit in a blind for ten straight hours. The sight of chickadees, chipmunks, sunrises and the smell of freshly fallen leaves on the forest floor are soul-touching experiences. They are the intangibles that memories are made of. And through it all, if I'm lucky enough to see the buck I'm looking for—then it's frosting on the cake.

For others the hunt means the smell of bacon and eggs on the camp stove, and the fellowship around the fire at the end of a long day in the woods. It's the joy and excitement a father sees in a little boy's eyes when they're alone together on a hemlock ridge.

Certainly, if it wasn't for things like these, very few people would hunt. In New York, for example, fewer than ten percent of 720,000 deer hunters are lucky enough to bag their buck each year. You can bet your favorite deer gun that it's more than the killing that keeps these guys coming back to the sleet, rain, snow, and cold year after year.

There's no question that the hunter's image has suffered in recent years because of the publicity our sport has received. The media's open exposure of the "slob hunter" has hurt all of us who pride ourselves in being true sportsmen. However, as bad as the experience has been, it's part of this journey called life and it can be turned into a positive experience if we view it with an open mind.

I'm convinced that anti-hunters, as biased and uninformed as they might be, are not the number one threat to the sport of hunting. The foes all hunters need to be really concerned about are sometimes the ones who claim to be on our team. They're the ones who go about breaking game laws. Illegally taking and tagging deer, hunting without permission and shooting road signs are only a few of their violations. While some brag about their actions, others justify them by claiming they own the land and feed the deer so they "should be entitled to an extra one or two." I sometimes wonder who they are fooling.

In my part of the country, poaching and illegal tagging of deer are two of the most serious problems sport hunting faces today. Because our lenient judicial system has made things very easy for offenders, more and more marginal hunters are being tempted to break the law each year.

One New York Senior Wildlife Biologist told me, "It is amazing how many women's names are on tags in the locker plants across western New York the first week of deer season." No doubt many women are successful, but it doesn't take a genius to realize what's going on. And, until laws and ideals change, the illegal tagging of deer will continue to be prevalent. The sad part is that many, including game wardens, know of such acts but, because of the evidence required for conviction, most violators are never apprehended.

In New York, to prosecute someone who illegally tags a deer with someones else's license so they can continue to hunt, requires either a witness who will testify or concrete evidence. With game wardens literally "as scarce as hen's teeth," most violators are never caught.

Poaching today is a multi-million-dollar-a-year operation and no state in the union is immune from this open sore. With venison reportedly going for over $100 a head, this cold blooded carnage thrives in the darkness of rural America.

There is a well-known statement used by psychologists today that says, "More is 'caught' than taught." Unfortunately, most of these offenders have children, who witness and hear of these acts, and—by "catching" what dad has done—view it as acceptable

---

All told, sportsman-related programs have proven to be the salvation of both game and non-game species in America.

---

behavior. As a result, the number of illegal hunters grows through this father/son relationship or through peer pressure.

So what can be done to check illegal tagging and poaching? Get involved! Perhaps this may sound simplistic to some, but if enough hunters become concerned about the few who are ruining the sport, things will change.

Already, across America, sportsmen are starting funds which are used to apprehend violators as well as being used for rewards. This is a move in the right direction but there is still a long way to go. The need for stronger laws against game violators is long overdue and we need to elect public officials who will see that the laws are changed.

No doubt each of us knows some hunter who's not on the up and up. If it's a friend, approach him as a friend and tell him you don't think what he's doing is good for him or the sport. You'd be surprised how much impact peer pressure has. But one warning:

It's not what you say, it's how you say it that will make the conversation a success or failure, so plan ahead. Surely, if all sportsmen start pulling in the same direction, the antis will find themselves with less and less ammunition to use against us.

It wasn't too many years ago that you could drive to your favorite hunting area and hunt to your heart's content, but it's not so anymore. Each year more and more private land is posted in America and, in the majority of cases, it's a result of carelessness or abuse on the part of a few hunters.

Most landowners in my area would rather not be bothered by posting; but too much litter, too many fences left open, and too many tire tracks in the winter wheat have brought the signs out. With more and more hunters taking to the woods each year, the problem of where to hunt intensifies.

It is my belief that few landowners will turn hunters away if the owner is properly approached. In my area the hunters who meet the most resistance are the ones in gangs. As a result, more and more landowners are turning these groups down, while one or two guys hunting together are seldom turned away.

As inflation erodes the farmer's dollar, some of the larger operations are seeking relief by charging hunters to hunt. For many years Texas has been one area where this kind of hunting has been found. Now parts of the Northeast have started to follow suit.

Unfortunately, the guy who pays the land taxes is often not respected. A point to remember is that the hunter needs him more than he needs the hunter. Get to know the fellow who owns your. hunting grounds. Have you ever considered helping him with the chores or sharing the meat that you take from his land? Try it. You may find that you'll not only be welcome but make a friend for life. One thing is certain: As demands for hunting rights increase, it will be tougher and tougher to hunt like you did last year. Therefore, ethics and landowner relations will play a bigger and bigger part as each season approaches.

It is a known fact that sportsmen don't share the positive side of hunting with people as much as they should. With this in mind, we must convey our message to the ill-advised public. We need to tell people about the 16.5 million hunters in America who contribute $299.8 million yearly for wildlife and habitat conservation, hunter safety programs, and the funding of state fish and game departments. We need to tell everyone that a big chunk of this money goes to help wildlife species which are not even hunted. We need to tell the uninformed that American hunters have contributed $4 billion to conservation projects, including the purchase of 3.25 million acres as wildlife reserves since 1923. And lastly, we need to tell people about the sportsmen in America who saw their deer populations drop to 500,000 at the turn of the century and then, through hard work, brought these populations back to over 10 million in eighty short years.

Does this sound like a pep talk? I hope so, because the hour is upon us. At this very moment forces within this land of liberty want to do away with not only our firearms but also the sport of hunting. And now, more than ever before, we all need to set good examples which everyone can see. As the saying goes, "A chain is only as strong as its weakest link." We need to work on our weak links. We've come too far to lose out now — hunting's future is in our hands.

Gestation Period In Whitetails

by Kent Horner

Following the breeding of the doe, the length of time the developing fetus spends within the doe's uterus is the gestation period. A correctly-timed gestation period that nourishes the fetus through cold, inclement weather greatly enhances survival of white-tailed deer in northern latitudes.

After breeding, typically in late fall or early winter in many localities, the doe drops her fawn (or fawns) about 187 to 222 days later. On prime deer habitat fully matured does often bear twins. During leaner times, however, that isn't the case. On the average, though, the average number of fawns born to adult does approximates 1.5 fawns per doe.

If the doe is in prime health, living in an area with abundant and nutritious browse, fawn birth dates are usually ten to twelve days earlier than birth dates for fawns born to less robust does. Other natural variables, such as the amount of spring rainfall, may also contribute to early fawning.

But, directly, biologists have found that good health of the doe is primarily responsible for most early fawning.

Thus, the long-range result of a doe in heat during the period of rut, found and bred by a rutting buck, consummates in about a seven-pound fawn delivered when the woodlands and meadows are in full vegetative production the following spring or early summer. This timely breeding enables the doe to provide the suckling fawn with ample, energy-rich milk and within six weeks has the youngster in good condition and looking for green vegetation.

Research wildlife biologists report that does remain in heat approximately twenty-four hours during their monthly estrous cycles. Thus, pheromonal dispersal by the doe and subsequent attraction and detection by the rutting buck really is critical to white-tailed deer survival. This also illustrates that pheromone-based deer lures, at least in concept, should increase the deer

Leonard Lee Rue III

The gestation period for deer is about one-third less than the gestation period for people — a little more than six months in deer as opposed to around nine months in humans.

hunter's chances of fooling a rutting buck.

Not long ago I telephoned a wildlife scientist at a major university where he does extensive research on deer. After a few minutes of conversation my friend, with urgency and conviction in his voice, said, "I've got to run! I've got to go breed a doe!" My biologist friend, of course, meant that he, with the aid of his graduate-student assistants, had to expeditiously tend to the artificial insemination of a doe that possibly had just reached her monthly estrous peak. In such scientific research, the estrous peak can be detected by keeping a sterilized buck with the doe herd. Close observation of their sexual intentions lets the biologist know when the various does come into their estrous peak.

Although does remain in estrus for a relatively short period of time, if not bred they repeat a similar cycle about twenty-eight days later. A doe may go through four or five heat cycles, but the cycles cease after successful breeding. These monthly cycles in white-tailed does broadly span about September through February and are seasonally in phase with the bucks' rutting activities.

However, it's not all that

unusual for hunters in late fall to find newborn fawns roaming the woodland. Such a fawn obviously is headed for almost sure disaster should an early, severe winter storm blow in from the Arctic. Although unusual in the continental United States, when a ripping wind drops the chill factor, temperatures may fall to -100°F. That occurred in states along the Canadian border in late December, 1983. A chill factor of -100°F is deadly.

The comfort range for whitetails ranges from 41°F to 68°F. Wildlife scientists suggest, however, that fawns on a starvation diet reach a negative equilibrium at air temperatures approaching 32°F and a wind velocity of one-half to one mile per hour. The same studies, however, point out that a fawn on full diet can withstand winter exposure to -40°F at a wind velocity of eight miles per hour. This all goes to say that the wind chill factor coupled with the fawn's accessibility to food are natural variables that affect the fawn's likelihood of survival.

To survive drastic chill factors, the white-tailed fawn's body mass is critically important. Thus, for herd survival, importance is placed on seasonal rutting by the buck, well timed estrous peaks in the doe, and an exacting gestation period for their progeny. The timing of these natural events permits the whitetail to reproduce his kind and cheat the cold weather, starvation, and predators that constantly gnaw at herd survival.

Initially, the gestation period tends toward an all-or-none event.

In other words, should starvation conditions hit the herd during early gestation, the doe may reabsorb her fetus.

Nature then permits possibly one deer, the doe, to survive; whereas, should early reabsorption of the fetus not occur, the high probability exists that the doe and the fawn, would succumb to starvation or disease. Also, were fawning not well timed, occurring in summer, the doe would be further drained of vital energy reserves in attempting cold weather milk production, which would be at a bare minimum for hungry, starving fawns. Biologists now know that the doe's milk production, the lactation process, typically stops in January. The doe thus has evolved to protect her own energy reserves in winter. From October toward January the doe's milk production constantly decreases. Quickly it can be seen that winter is not the time for a fawn to be born. Instead, they are better housed in the doe's uterus at that time of year.

Formed during the gestation period, body weight, shape, and body proportions are important for a fawn's survival. Precisely, long spindly legs are soon called upon to evade predators, but not to escape the winter cold. A relatively small body-surface-area to body-mass ratio is important in protecting the fawn's vital zone from the winter's chill. Older, heavier fawns timely born in summer have a greater bodymass to body-surface-area ratio than newborn fawns before growth and weight gain.

Thus, underdeveloped or poorly timed fawns dropped too close to winter usually have a hard go of it. Scientific studies within a known area have shown that about ninety percent of the does become pregnant, but when hard-pressed by lack of food, the mortality rate of their fawns is often quite high. Most fawn mortality occurs within two weeks after birth. Also, it has been shown that even healthy fawns gain very little weight from December through April. As a yearling the next summer, however, they grow rapidly if browse is adequate.

Interestingly, man and the white-tailed deer—the hunter and the hunted—are in the same weight division. For example, the hunter may weigh nearly two hundred pounds (certainly so with all the winter hunting garb on!); so may his favorite quarry, a white-tailed buck. Furthermore, at birth human infants and fawns weigh nearly the same: about five to eight pounds.

The gestation period for deer, however, is about one-third less than the gestation time for people—a little over six months in deer as opposed to around nine months in humans. Deer get the job done in about thirty percent less time. In short, man evolved and adapted to care for and house his offspring through the winter. The deer's only option is for the doe to carry the youngster within her body.

Nature, through eons of animal evolution, pressured and selected the white-tailed deer to breed in

late fall or early winter and fawn in the summer in the temperate regions on earth. These precise natural events in the deer's life are hormonally regulated and mainly triggered over the northern latitudes by day length, the photoperiod. Consequently, the whitetail's breeding and subsequent fawning dates are very close to the winter and summer solstices: the shortest and the longest days in the year.

Wildlife scientists have demonstrated in laboratory experiments that the fawn's genetic material, the chromosomes, half received from the buck in his sperm and half from the doe in her egg, is more variable than the genetic material from other warm-blooded animals. In short, these hetero-genetic (variable) traits provide the whitetail with his high adaptability potentials. Further, these internally adaptable traits translate directly to his field adaptability in being able to evade his enemies. So, we can see how danger from cold weather, starvation, and predators are offset by the whitetail's reproductive abilities, adaptive traits, and physical toughness. It follows then that the hunter pits his own skills against a formidably evasive foe when challenging a white-tailed deer on his home turf. He's good at it. In fact, he is the best of all large game animals in challenging the hunter through evasive tactics.

Prior to and during the gestation of fawns, as with antler growth in bucks, protein intake coupled with adequate supplies of phosphorus ingested by the doe becomes critically important. Wildlife research shows that these organic and mineral components are needed for these two rapid growth processes that periodically occur over and above normal body maintenance and function in deer.

Thus, pregnant does in February are often hard pressed to find adequate food to support the growing fawn within them. The last three months of the gestation period are the most critical for the developing fawn. Failure of the doe to receive adequate nourishment then usually results in a light-weight fawn that dies within a half-month. Winter snows that restrict the search for food even further often are a true debilitating factor for deer in late winter.

Then the whitetail often uses only ten to twenty percent of his normal home range. In the northern states, when the snow is deep, the deer yard up and try to survive the winter. At this time, deer live in a low metabolic state—not in true hibernation but in a much-reduced activity pattern. During this state, the deer's heart rate and other vital functions are geared slower. Further, it is known that most deer in the winter bed about half the time and stand idle about twenty percent of the time. To both the stand and stalk hunter, this is important because of its implication toward the deer's activity patterns.

For example, dense brush, thickets, and canebrakes are common winter bedding sites for idle, ruminating whitetails. Physiologists also know now that a whitetail burns sixty percent less energy when resting as opposed to standing. Also, young deer are often observed running and playing during warm weather. However, during the winter this play activity is seldom observed since deer tend to conserve their energy more in cold weather. Furthermore, trail movement over rough terrain is slower paced for deer in winter as opposed to their summer travel.

In the short run, stop-gap feeding of deer by game managers may save individual deer during a harsh winter. Moreover, correct management practices that hold the herd population below maximum carrying capacity is important for both the deer and the hunter. Hunters then can maximize their sport; and the deer herd is also a long-range benefactor because more healthy deer are ultimately permitted to survive.

In summary, a herd with healthy, well-conditioned does generally drop their fawns on a timely basis amid early summer's greenery. When the Arctic blast swings southward, the fawns have the body mass to survive the freezing onslaught of winter.

❖COOKBOOK❖

Venison recipes reprinted from *301 Venison Recipes*.
Published by *Deer & Deer Hunting Magazine*

Country Fried Venison Steaks

2 pounds venison steak (round or sirloin tip) 1/2-1 inch thick
1/2 cup flour
3 tablespoons shortening
2 cans condensed cream of mushroom soup
Water
Salt and pepper

Trim all fat from the steaks, and cut into pieces approximately 3 inches square. Using a meat mallet, pound flour into both sides of the steaks.

Melt shortening in a large skillet and brown meat slowly and thoroughly over medium heat (15-20 minutes). Season to taste with salt & pepper. As pieces are browned, transfer them to a 2-3 quart deep dish casserole.

Blend the 2 cans mushroom soup in a blender until creamy. Pour this mixture over the steak. Add enough water to cover all pieces of steak. Cover and bake until tender (approx. 2-1/2 hrs) in 350 degree oven, adding water as necessary.

Valorie D. Bailey
Hixon, TN

Smothered Steak

2 to 3 pounds round steak
1/3 cup all purpose flour
1 envelope (1-1/2 ounce) dry onion soup mix
2 10-1/2 ounce cream of mushroom soup
1/2 cup water
3 tablespoons vegetable oil

Sprinkle flour on one side of meat, pound it. Turn meat over and pound in remaining flour. Cut meat into serving pieces. Melt vegetable oil in large skillet, brown meat over medium heat for 15 minutes. Add envelope dry onion soup, 1/2 cup water and mushroom soup. Cover and simmer 1-1/2 to 2 hours, depending on desired tenderness. May add more water if necessary while simmering.

Ron Tate
Bartlesville, OK

Venison Kabob

1 to 2 pounds venison cubed
2 sweet red peppers cubed
1 large onion cubed

Marinade
Juice of 1/2 lemon
3 cloves pressed garlic
1/2 teaspoon oregano
1/2 teaspoon basil
1/2 teaspoon salt
Freshly ground black pepper
2/3 cup brandy
1/2 cup olive oil

Combine all the ingredients for the marinade and marinate cubed
    venison overnight.
Saute peppers and onion lightly in a little olive oil.
Skewer, alternating venison, and pepper and onion.
Broil quickly one to two minutes per side. Serve hot.
    Daryl Lotecka
    Philadelphia, PA

Barbecued Venison Steaks

3-4 pounds venison roast
1 tablespoon garlic salt
2 onions, sliced
1 teaspoon pepper
1 cup brown sugar
2 tablespoons vinegar
1 cup Italian salad dressing

Slice venison roast into 1/2-inch steaks. Coat steaks with brown sugar.
Place a layer of steak in a glass bowl.
Sprinkle with garlic salt, onion slices, and a splash of vinegar.
Pour salad dressing over the top. Repeat with remaining layers of
    meat.
Cover dish and marinate for 8 to 48 hours.
Barbecue on a grill of hot coals.
Thicken marinade mixture with corn starch and brush on meat.
Turn occasionally until meat is done. Serves 6 to 8.
    Joe Bontke
    Long Valley, NJ

Grilled Venison Tenderloin

1 venison tenderloin
pepper
Crushed garlic powder

Remove tenderloin from freezer and thaw "age" in refrigerator for at least five days. Remove from refrigerator two hours before cooking. Sprinkle liberally with pepper and garlic. Meanwhile, start fire. When coals are hot, put tenderloin on grill and cover. Cook for three minutes, turn; cover and cook for another three minutes, turn; cover and cook for another three minutes for a total of nine minutes. Test meat by touching with tongs. If it feels firm, then it's ready. Don't judge by looking at the outside color. It will appear red even when well done. Slice into it if you aren't sure. Let the juices flow out for about thirty seconds before checking. It should be pink on the inside. To serve, slice into thin, round strips.

Camille W. Sewell
West Palm Beach, FL

High Speed Venison

2 to 3 pound venison steak
1 package onion soup mix
1 can cream of mushroom soup
Salt and pepper
2 beef bouillon cubes
2 onions, sliced
3/4 cups milk

Brown meat in skillet. Add rest of ingredients and simmer for 1 hour. Salt and pepper to taste. Serve over rice. Serves 4.

Venison Ribs

3 pounds venison ribs or one rack
2 tablespoons cooking oil
1 teaspoon salt
1/2 teaspoon pepper
2 bouillon cubes
2 tablespoons vinegar
1 teaspoon Worcestershire sauce
2 medium onions, sliced thin

Brown ribs in oil and pour off drippings. Salt and pepper. Add bouillion cubes, vinegar, Worcestershire sauce, onions and 1-1/2 cups water. Cover and cook slowly until meat is tender (about 2 hours). Drain off liquid and make into gravy. Serve over ribs.

Dutch Oven Roast Venison

3 pound venison roast
1/3 cup cider vinegar
3 tablespoons flour
2 to 3 tablespoons bacon drippings
1/2 teaspoon salt
1/4 teaspoon pepper
1/4 teaspoon leaf basil

3 strips bacon
1 onion, sliced and separated
  into rings
1/2 cup hot water
10-3/4 ounces canned tomato soup
1/3 teaspoon garlic salt

In Dutch oven, sear meat in bacon drippings. Lay strips of bacon across roast, securing with toothpicks. Hang onion slices over toothpicks. Add hot water, tomato soup, garlic salt and basil to Dutch oven. Cover and simmer for 2 to 3 hours or until tender. Thicken pan juices to make gravy if desired.

Phil's Deer Camp Venison Stew

3 pounds boneless chuck, cut in 2 inch cubes
1/4 cup salad oil
2 teaspoons salt
1/4 teaspoon pepper
3 cups dry red or white wine
2 cups water
3 white turnips, peeled and cut in pieces 3/4 inches square
1/2 teaspoon thyme, crushed or powdered
2 tablespoons tomato paste
1 large clove garlic, minced
1 large onion, quartered
4 carrots, cleaned and cut in pieces
4 stalks celery, cut in 2 inch pieces
1/4 pound small whole mushrooms fresh or canned
1 bay leaf

In large kettle or saucepan, brown venison in oil. Continue to turn as needed until browns on all sides.
Season with salt and pepper, add the wine, water, tomato paste, garlic, thyme, and bay leaf.
Cover and simmer for 1 to 2 hours, stirring occasionally.
Add carrots and celery and cook for 20-30 minutes. Add turnips and cook another 20 minutes.
Add onion and cook another 15 minutes.
Add mushrooms and cook 10 minutes more. If stew is too thin, thicken sauce with 2 tablespoons corn starch mixed with 1/3 cup water until smooth and keep stirring until thickened and smooth. Serve stew over bed of rice or chow mein noodles.
Phillip J. Mersberger
Sheboygan, WI

Opening Day Chili

5 pounds venison (2 pounds ground, 3 pounds chopped)
2 pounds spanish onions, chopped
1 28-ounce can tomatoes, crushed
1 can tomato paste
1 green pepper, diced
2 cups venison stock (beef stock can be used)
6 garlic cloves, diced
1 stalk celery, diced
2 cups red kidney beans, cooked
6 tablespoons chili powder
1 teaspoon oregano
3 tablespoons cooking oil
Crushed Italian red-hot pepper to taste

Heat oil to hot in a large cooking pot, add garlic. Two minutes later,
  add venison and brown.
Add onions, green pepper and celery; cook until onions are translucent.
Add all other ingredients, except beans; cook 4 hours over low heat.
Add beans last 15 minutes of cooking time.
Use shredded sharp cheddar and thin sliced spanish onion for garnish.
  Joseph W. Yesalonis
  Commack, NY

Venison Stroganoff

2 pounds venison steak or back loin
3 tablespoons butter
3 tablespoons onions chopped
2 tablespoons butter

1-3/4 tablespoons flour
1-1/2 cup cold clear beef
  consomme
1 cup sour buttermilk

Take venison and slice into pieces as thin as possible, or about 1/4 inch
  thick the thinner the better. The pieces should not be more than 2
  inches square.
Salt and pepper to taste.
Put 3 tablespoons of butter into frying pan and 3 tablespoons of onion.
  Add meat, cook on medium heat until meat is tender.
Make a sauce or gravy as follow: Put 2 level tablespoons of butter into
  a large frying pan and melt until it just starts turning brown.
  Remove from stove, now add 1-3/4 tablespoons flour until mixture
  forms a medium syrup consistency, not thick.
Add 1-1/2 cups cold beef consomme and stir well. Place back on stove
  over medium heat and bring to a slow boil. Stir constantly.
  Add 1 cup of sour buttermilk and stir well.
  Pour above sauce into meat and simmer to heat.
  Serve with mashed potatoes, rice or noodles.
  James Chappel
  McFarland, WI

Big Game Pie

4 large potatoes (mashed) or package instant mashed potatoes
1/2 cup celery, finely chopped
1 tablespoon chopped onion
3 tablespoons flour
3 tablespoons butter or oleo
1/2 cup milk
3/4 cup beef broth
2-1/2 cups venison, cubed and browned
1/4 teaspoon browning sauce
1/4 cup grated cheddar cheese

Prepare mashed potatoes according to the package directions. In a skillet, saute celery and onion in butter until tender but not brown. Blend in flour and gradually add milk and broth. Cook and stir until mixture thickens and bubbles. Stir in cooked meat, browning sauce and season with salt and pepper. Pour meat mixture into a 1-1/2 quart casserole and top evenly with mashed potatoes. Sprinkle with cheese and bake at 400 degrees for 20-25 minutes or until brown. Serves 4.

Venison Hungarian Goulash

2 tablespoons oil
2 medium onions, chopped
2 pounds venison, cut into 1-inch cubes
2 tablespoons flour
1 clove garlic, minced
1 tablespoon caraway seeds
2-1/2 tablespoons sweet Hungarian paprika
1 teaspoon Hot Hungarian paprika (optional)
1 teaspoon salt
1/4 teaspoon cayenne pepper
2 quarts beef broth
1 medium tomato, cut into pieces
2 large peppers
4 medium potatoes, cut into small cubes

Heat oil in a heavy Dutch oven. Saute the onions until glossy. Toss the venison cubes with the flour and add to the onions. Cook until meat is lightly browned.

Remove pan from heat. Stir in garlic, caraway, paprikas, salt and cayenne pepper. Immediately after the paprikas are absorbed, add the beef broth. Cover the casserole and simmer over low heat for 1/2 hour.

After 1 hour the meat should feel almost completely tender when pierced with a fork. Add tomato and peppers. Simmer, uncovered 30 minutes, until the consistency of thick soup. Add potatoes and cook until potatoes are tender, about 15 minutes. Taste and adjust seasoning.

Venison Stir Fry

1/2 pound venison steak sliced thin
   or small pieces of venison steak
5 carrots, sliced thin
3 talks of celery, sliced
1 large onion, sliced
1 green pepper, sliced
1 can water chestnut,
   drained and sliced

1 cup mushrooms, sliced
1 can bean sprouts, drained
3-4 tablespoons cooking oil
1 tablespoon sugar
1 chicken bouillion cube
3/4 cup water
4 tablespoon shoyu

Preheat oil in electric frying pan to 300 degrees. Add carrots, celery, onions, mushrooms and green pepper.

Coat with oil and stir. Cover and fry stirring often until crisp tender. Add water, shoyu, sugar, boullion cube, drained sprouts and water chestnuts. Simmer 2-3 minutes. Remove to heated, covered pan. Heat 1-2 tablespoons oil in frying pan. Add pieces of steak and turn them in 1/2 minute. Allow about 1/2 minute more cooking time and remove promptly to heated dish. Immerse them in the sauce of the vegetables. serve immediately on hot rice.
Maren Wegner
Blue Mounds, WI

Venison Burritos

12 10-inch flour tortillas
5-6 pounds venison neck roast
1 medium onion, chopped
2 cups beef broth
2 4-ounce cans green chili peppers
1/8 teaspoon black pepper

1 large onion, chopped
1 cup shredded lettuce
3 cups shredded cheddar cheese
Black olives, sliced (optional)
Sour cream (optional)
Chili-tomato sauce

Put venison neck roast into slow cooker. Add chopped onion, pepper, green chilies and beef broth. Cover and cook on high for 2 hours, then turn to low for 8 to 10 hours, or until meat shreds off bone. Let cool. Shred meet off of bone with fork. Check shredded meat thoroughly for bone and bone pieces.

Refrigerate meat mixture until fat congeals. Remove fat.

Return shredded meat and juice to slow cooker. Heat through; keep warm.

Heat tortillas until warm and flexible before using.

Spoon about 1/3 cup of shredded meat mixture onto each tortilla near one edge. Fold edge nearest filling up and over filling just till mixture is covered. Fold in two sides envelope fashion, then roll up. Place on plate seam side down. Top with cheese, onion, lettuce, tomato, olives and sour cream. Cover with chili-tomato sauce. Makes 12.

Peppered Meat Loaf

2 pounds venison, ground
1 pound pork shoulder, ground
2 medium onions
4 small shallots, minced
1/2 cup minced green bell pepper
1/2 cup minced red bell pepper
1 cup mixed tomatoes and jalapeno pepper, chopped
1 teaspoon basil, chopped
1 cup bread crumbs
1 egg, slightly beaten
2 teaspoons Dijon mustard
2 teaspoons chili sauce
1 teaspoon chili powder
1/2 teaspoon salt
1/2 teaspoon black pepper
1 pinch thyme

Mix all ingredients except mustard, chili sauce and chili powder in a baking dish. Preheat oven to 375 degrees. Combine the mustard, chili powder and chili sauce. Spread evenly over the top of meat loaf. Bake 15 minutes, reduce heat to 350 degrees and bake one hour. Serves 8.

Kuldnis (Dumplings)

1/4 pound ground pork
3/4 pound ground venison
1 egg
1 onion
1/4 teaspoon salt
1/4 teaspoon pepper
1 teaspoon celery seed

1 cup flour
1/8 teaspoon salt
1 egg
1/2 cup water to make into dough

Thoroughly mix the first 7 ingredients and allow to stand while you mix the last 4 ingredients. Roll out dough to pie crust thickness, cut out 4 inch circles, (used a floured large cup) place teaspoon of meat mixture into center of dough, fold over and crimp edge with floured fork to seal in meat.

Boil in slightly salted water and serve.

Charles Bodendorf
Pt. Washington, NY

Venison Hash

1-1/2 pounds ground venison
1 large green pepper diced
1 16-ounce can of tomatoes
1-1/2 teaspoon chili powder
1/2 cup chopped nuts (optional)

3 large onions diced
1 small red pepper diced
2 teaspoons salt
1/8 teaspoon pepper

Preheat the oven to 350 degrees. In a large skillet cook and stir meat, onion, peppers until meat is brown and vegetables are tender. Drain off the fat and stir in tomatoes, salt, chili powder and optional chilies. Heat through and pour into a covered casserole dish.

Bake one hour stirring a couple times while cooking.

Thomas K. Squire
Aberdeen, NC

Summer Sausage

2 pounds ground deer no fat added
2 tablespoons tender quick salt
1 teaspoon liquid smoke
1/4 teaspoon course pepper

1/4 teaspoon garlic powder
1/4 teaspoon onion powder
3/4 teaspoon mustard seed
1 cup water

Mix all of the ingredients together. Put in an air tight container and refrigerate 24 hours. Shape into 2 rolls and bake at 350 degrees for 1-1/2 hours. I use a cookie sheet with a lip and bake the sausage on a cake rack to keep the sausage from setting in the grease.

Darrell Jones
Indianapolis, IN

Venison Jerky

1/2 cup soy sauce
1/2 cup Worcestershire sauce
2 teaspoons seasoned salt
2 teaspoons onion powder
2 teaspoons Accent
2/3 teaspoon garlic powder
2/3 teaspoon pepper
1 pound meat cut into thin strips

Mix all ingredients. Marinate meat over night. Cook on rack, using foil to catch the drippings at 150 degrees for 6-8 hours, until dry. Store in air tight containers. Will keep up to 2 years.

James Chappell
McFarland, WI

Venison Steak and Gravy

2 pounds of venison round steak
1/3 cup flour
1 envelope brown gravy mix
1 envelope onion soup mix
12 ounce can of beer

Cut steak into serving size pieces. Roll in the flour. Set aside.
Put remaining flour, gravy mix, soup mix and beer in Crockpot.
Stir together, then add steak. Cook 10 to 12 hours on low.
Wanda Woosley
Madison, TN

Very Easy Venison Pepper Steak

2 pounds venison steak, cut into thin 1/4- to 1/2-inch strips
3-4 tablespoons oil, fat, or butter
1 large onion cut into 1/8
1 large green pepper
4 cups water
6 beef bouillon cubes
5 tablespoons cornstarch
5 cups cooked rice
Meat tenderizer

Pound tenderizer into meat. Cut into 1/2-1/4 inch strips. Brown in large heavy skillet. Add water and bouillon cube. Simmer 1-1/2 to 2 hours. Add onion and pepper (cut into thin strips).

Cook this over medium heat for a 1/2 hour. Add cornstarch mixed with 3/4 cup water. Simmer until thick. Serve over rice with soy sauce to taste.
Penny Hof
Strongsville, OH

Fresh Grilled Tenderloin

Tenderloin cut in thin pieces
1/2 stick of margarine
2-3 fluid ounces Worcestershire sauce
1 tablespoon lemon juice
2-3 fluid ounces A-1 steak sauce
Salt, pepper, onion salt, and garlic salt to taste.

Need Gas Grill:

Heat margarine on high on the grill, add Worcestershire sauce and A-1 Steak Sauce. Place tenderloins on the grill, add seasoning to taste with lemon juice. Turn meat over once.
William D. Trout, Jr.
Bridgeton, NJ

Venison Rump Roast

4 pound venison roast
1 can cream of mushroom soup
1 clove garlic, slivered
6 small potatoes, peeled
1/2 cup dry red wine
1/2 teaspoon basil
Pepper

Insert garlic slivers in slits cut in the roast with the tip of a sharp knife. Put the roast in a roasting pan and pour the undiluted soup over it. Add wine and sprinkle with basil and pepper. Cover and roast in preheated 350° degree oven for 2 hours, after 1 hour place potatoes in pan basting twice with pan juices during the cooking time. Serve the pan juices in a heated sauce dish and ladle over the meat (mashed potatoes, if you wish). Serves 4 to 6.

Venison Stew

1-1/2 pounds venison stew meat
2 medium onions diced
4 medium potatoes quartered
1 package Lipton beefy mushroom soup
2 cups flour
1/2 cups cooking oil
Salt & pepper

Coat roast with flour and brown in hot skillet with cooking oil. Remove meat from skillet and drain oil. Brown onions and potatoes in skillet. Add venison, package of beefy mushroom mix in pressure cooker and cover with water. Add salt and pepper to taste. Cook for 40 minutes in pressure cooker, or in Dutch oven for 2 hours. Serve with rice or cornbread.

Venison and Rice

1 green pepper, chopped
1 onion, chopped
2 cloves garlic, minced
3 tablespoons butter
1-1/2 pounds ground venison
2 tablespoons flour
1 teaspoon salt
1/4 teaspoon pepper
3 cups canned tomatoes
2 cups cooked rice

Saute green pepper, onion and garlic in butter in deep skillet until onion is transparent. Add venison. Cook until venison is brown, stirring to break venison in small pieces. Sprinkle in flour.
Add Salt, pepper and tomatoes. Mix well, simmer until blended and heated through. Serve over rice.
John W. Swale
Easton, MA

❖ CONTACTS FOR HUNTING INFORMATION ❖

STATE	DEPT/ADDRESS
Alabama	Dept. of Conservation & Nat. Res. District Wildlife Office P.O. Box 993 Demopolis, AL 36732
Alaska	Alaska Dept. Fish and Game P.O. Box 3-2000 Juneau, AK 99802
Arizona	Arizona Game & Fish Department 2222 W. Greenway Rd. Phoenix, AR 85023
Arkansas	Game and Fish Commission HC 71, Box 171 Mountain View, AR 72560
California	California Game Commission P.O. Box 944209 Sacremento, CA 94244
Colorado	Dept. of Natural Resources Division of Wildlife 6060 Broadway Denver, CO 80216
Connecticut	Dept. of Environmental Protection Wildlife Division 391 Route 32 N. Franklin, CT 06254
Delaware	Delaware Fish and Wildlife Division of Fish and Wildlife P.O. Box 1401 Dover, DE 19901
Florida	Game & Fresh Water Fish Commission Division of Wildlife 620 S. Meridian, Farris Bryant Bldg. Tallahassee, FL 32399-1600
Georgia	Dept. of Natural Resources Game and Fish Division 205 Butler St., SE, Suite 1362 Atlanta, GA 30334
Hawaii	Dept. of Land and Nat. Res. Hawaii Div. of Forestry & Wildlife 1151 Punchbowl St. Honolulu, HI 96813
Idaho	Dept. of Fish and Game 600 S. Walnut St, Box 25 Boise, ID 83707

STATE	DEPT/ADDRESS
Illinois Division of Wildlife Resources	Director 600 N. Grand Ave., W. Springfield, IL 62706
Indiana	Dept. of Natural Resources Division of Fish and Wildlife 300 West First Street Bloomington, IN 47401
Iowa	Wildlife Manager Chariton Research Center Rt 1, Box 209 Chariton, IA 50049
Kansas	Wildlife & Parks P.O. Box 1525 Emporia, KS 66801
Kentucky	Dept. of Fish & Wildlife Res. RR 1, Box 309 Williamstown, KY 41097
Louisiana	Dept. of Wildlife & Fisheries P.O. Box 4004 Monroe, LA 71211
Maine	Dept. of Inland Fisheries & Wildlife 284 State St. Station 41 Augusta, ME 04333
Maryland	Dept. of Natural Resources Tawes State Office Bldg. Annapolis, MD 21401
Massachusetts	Division of Fish and Wildlife 100 Cambridge Street Boston, MA 02202
Michigan	Wildlife Division, Michigan Box 30028 Lansing, MI 48909
Minnesota	Dept. of Natural Resources Division of Fish and Wildlife Box 7, 500 Lafayette Rd. St. Paul, MN 55155
Mississippi	Dept. of Wildlife Conservation P.O. Box 451 Jackson, MS 39205
Missouri	Dept. of Conservation 1110 S. College Avenue Columbia, MO 65203
Montana	Montana Dept. of Wildlife 1420 E. 6th Ave. Helena, MT 59620

STATE	DEPT/ADDRESS
Nebraska	Game and Parks Commission Bassett, NE 68714
Nevada	Nevada Dept. of Wildlife P.O. Box 10678 Reno, NV 89520
New Hampshire	NH Fish & Game Dept. Region 1 Office Rd 2, Rte 3N, Box 241 Lancaster, NH 03584
New Jersey	Div. of Fish, Game and Wildlife Bureau of Wildlife Management Nacote Creek Res Stn, P.O. Box 418 Port Republic, NJ 08241
New Mexico	New Mexico DNR Villagra Bldg. 408 Galisteo Santa Fe, NM 87503
New York	Dept. of Environmental Conserv. Wildlife Resource Center Delmar, NY 12054
North Carolina	Wildlife Biologist NC Commission, Wildlife Mgemt 512 N. Salisbury St. Rollie, NC 27604-1188
North Dakota	Game & Fish Dept. 100 N. Bismarck Expressway Bismarck, ND 58501
Ohio	Waterloo Wildlife Experiment Stn Division of Wildlife 9650 State Route 356 New Marshfield, OH 45766
Oklahoma	Dept. of Wildlife Conservation 1801 N. Lincoln Blvd. Oklahoma City, OK 73105
Oregon	OR Dept. of Fish & Wildlife P.O. Box 8 Hines, OR 97738
Pennsylvania	Pennsylvania Game Comm. 2001 Elmerton Avenue Harrisburg, PA 17110
Rhode Island	Dept. of Environmental Mgemt Box 218 West Kingston, RI 02892
South Carolina	Wildlife Resources Dept. P.O. Box 167 Columbia, SC 29202

STATE	DEPT/ADDRESS
South Dakota	Harvest Surveys Coordinator Division of Wildlife Sigrud Anderson Bldg, 445 E. Capitol Pierre, SD 57501
Tennessee	Tennessee Wildlife Res. Agency P.O. Box 40747 Nashville, TN 37204
Texas	Parks & Wildlife Dept. 4200 Smith School Rd. Austin, TX 78744
Utah	Utah Div. of Wildlife Resources 1596 W. N. Temple Salt Lake City, UT 84116
Vermont	Fish & Game Dept. Agency of Environmental Conser. 103 S. Main St., 10 So. Waterbury, VT 05676
Virginia	Comm. of Game & Inland Fish. P.O. Box 11104 Richmond, VA 23230
Washington	Washington Dept. of Wildlife 600 Capital Way N. Olympia, WA 25305
West Virginia	Dept. of Natural Resources 1800 Washington St. E Charleston, WV 25305
Wisconsin	Wis. Dept. of Natural Resources Bureau of Wildlife Mngmt Box 7921 Madison, WI 53707
Wyoming	Game & Fish Dept. 5400 Bishop Blvd. Cheyenne, WY 82006
Canada	Energy & Nat. Res. F&W Div. Main Flr. No. Tower, Petroleum Plaza 9945-108 St. Edmonton, ALB CAN T5K 2 GS
Canada	Ministry of Environment Fish & Wildlife Branch Parliament Buildings Victoria, BC CAN V8V 1X5

DEER &
DEER HUNTING
MAGAZINE

■ State White-tailed Deer Hunting Statistics
Alphabetical by State

State[1]	Estimated Whitetail Population[2]	Resident Hunters[3]	Non-Resident Hunters[4]	Season Bag Limit[5]	Whitetail Harvest[6]
Alabama	1,500,000	200,000	16,000	1/Day	285,000
Arizona	60,000	8,500	400	1	4,567
Arkansas	700,000	217,102	NA	3	113,079
Connecticut	45,000	30,000	1,200	12	8,763
Delaware	14,000	18,000	1,000	2	4,446
Florida	750,000	155,000	1,500	No Limit	107,000
Georgia	1,250,000	415,408	16,002	5	320,000
Idaho	71,000	150,000	10,000	1	15,000
Illinois	No Estimate	195,701	NA	2	66,143
Indiana	No Estimate	126,000	3,000	7	79,318
Iowa	300,000	168,000	931	3	99,712
Kansas	200,000	67,000	NA	5	40,000
Kentucky	425,000	140,000	2,800	3	91,681
Louisiana	650,000	210,000	1,200	6	165,000
Maine	280,000	186,000	35,000	1	30,260
Maryland	150,000	120,000	10,000	6	44,382
Massachusetts	50,000	70,000	1,500	2	7,700
Michigan	2,000,000	710,000	25,000	5	410,000
Minnesota	900,000	468,630	6,757	2	139,480
Mississippi	2,000,000	180,000	30,000	8	268,000
Missouri	750,000	400,000	12,506	4	168,477
Nebraska	180,000	61,311	Combined	2	27,886
New Hampshire	40,000	80,000	13,000	2	7,238
New Jersey	160,000	115,000	2,000	20+	48,526
New York	800,000	750,000	33,000	3	195,398
North Carolina	580,000	260,000	14,000	5	89,264
North Dakota	150,000	68,644	615	2	49,362
Ohio	300,000	300,000	4,000	1	90,000
Oklahoma	225,000	211,719	760	5	38,314
Oregon	715,000	232,045	Combined	1	73,257
Pennsylvania	1,000,000	1,000,000	70,000	3	388,601
Rhode Island	3,100	8,100	419	5	635
South Carolina	750,000	150,000	Combined	No Limit	107,081
South Dakota	22,500	76,760	4,215	11	46,251
Tennessee	650,000	192,000	5,000	11	108,762
Texas	3,500,000	553,000	11,000	4	477,000
Vermont	90,000	89,171	15,125	2	9,343
Virginia	750,000	275,000	10,000	6	135,094
Washington	67,000	180,000	906	1	8,071
West Virginia	800,000	270,000	50,000	6	145,567
Wisconsin	1,300,000	700,000	25,000	2	356,586
Wyoming	60,000	12,870	6,016	2	9,085

1-Western states that provided data for this survey included blacktail and mule deer because hunters generally buy one license that allows them to hunt multiple deer species within the state. These states include NE, ND, OR, WA and WY.

2-Illinois and Indiana do not provide a population estimate. Pennsylvania estimates the state whitetail population in excess of 1-million and declines to be more specific.

3-Based on actual license sales, or best estimates by the respective state Game & Fish Department based on a combination of license sales and hunter surveys.

4-Non-resident hunter numbers are "Not Available" (NA) from some states. Some states provide that data "combined" with the resident hunter numbers.

5-State bag limit is defined here as the general statewide bag limit, or that which is available for the majority of hunters within that state.

6-Whitetail harvest is the actual registered harvest recorded, or the best estimates by the respective state Game & Fish department based on a combination of license sales and hunter surveys.

■ Key Deer Hunting Statistics*
By State in Descending Order

DEER &
DEER HUNTING
MAGAZINE

State	Estimated Whitetail Population	State	Resident Hunters	State	Whitetail Harvest
Texas	3,500,000	Pennsylvania	1,000,000	Texas	477,000
Michigan	2,000,000	New York	750,000	Michigan	410,000
Mississippi	2,000,000	Michigan	710,000	Pennsylvania	388,601
Alabama	1,500,000	Wisconsin	700,000	Wisconsin	356,586
Wisconsin	1,300,000	Texas	553,000	Georgia	320,000
Georgia	1,250,000	Minnesota	468,630	Alabama	285,000
Pennsylvania	1,000,000	Georgia	415,408	Mississippi	268,000
Minnesota	900,000	Missouri	400,000	New York	195,398
New York	800,000	Ohio	300,000	Missouri	168,477
West Virginia	800,000	Virginia	275,000	Louisiana	165,000
Florida	750,000	West Virginia	270,000	West Virginia	145,567
Missouri	750,000	North Carolina	260,000	Minnesota	139,480
South Carolina	750,000	Oregon	232,045	Virginia	135,094
Virginia	750,000	Arkansas	217,102	Arkansas	113,079
Oregon	715,000	Oklahoma	211,719	Tennessee	108,762
Arkansas	700,000	Louisiana	210,000	South Carolina	107,081
Louisiana	650,000	Alabama	200,000	Florida	107,000
Tennessee	650,000	Illinois	195,701	Iowa	99,712
North Carolina	580,000	Tennessee	192,000	Kentucky	91,681
Kentucky	425,000	Maine	186,000	Ohio	90,000
Iowa	300,000	Mississippi	180,000	North Carolina	89,264
Ohio	300,000	Washington	180,000	Indiana	79,318
Maine	280,000	Iowa	168,000	Oregon	73,257
Oklahoma	225,000	Florida	155,000	Illinois	66,143
Kansas	200,000	South Carolina	150,000	North Dakota	49,362
Nebraska	180,000	Idaho	150,000	New Jersey	48,526
New Jersey	160,000	Kentucky	140,000	South Dakota	46,251
Maryland	150,000	Indiana	126,000	Maryland	44,382
North Dakota	150,000	Maryland	120,000	Kansas	40,000
Vermont	90,000	New Jersey	115,000	Oklahoma	38,314
Idaho	71,000	Vermont	89,171	Maine	30,260
Washington	67,000	New Hampshire	80,000	Nebraska	27,886
Arizona	60,000	South Dakota	76,760	Idaho	15,000
Wyoming	60,000	Massachusetts	70,000	Vermont	9,343
Massachusetts	50,000	North Dakota	68,644	Wyoming	9,085
Connecticut	45,000	Kansas	67,000	Connecticut	8,763
New Hampshire	40,000	Nebraska	61,311	Washington	8,071
South Dakota	22,500	Connecticut	30,000	Massachusetts	7,700
Delaware	14,000	Delaware	18,000	New Hampshire	7,238
Rhode Island	3,100	Wyoming	12,870	Arizona	4,567
Illinois	No Estimate	Arizona	8,500	Delaware	4,446
Indiana	No Estimate	Rhode Island	8,100	Rhode Island	635

*Footnotes apply

■Firearms Hunting Information
Alphabetical by State

State[1]	Resident Hunters[2]	Non-Resident Hunters[3]	Whitetail Harvest	Rifle [4]	Shotgun [4]	Handgun [4]	Muzzleloader [4]
Alabama	192,000	15,360	260,000	Yes	Yes	Yes	Yes
Arizona	96,751	2,832	4,411	Yes	Yes	Yes	Yes
Arkansas	NA	NA	97,031	Yes	Yes	Yes	Yes
Connecticut	28,470	852	6,242	No	Yes	No	Yes
Delaware	15,000	700	3,486	No	Yes	No	Yes
Florida	155,000	NA	NA	Yes	Yes	Yes	Yes
Georgia	348,898	16,002	NA	Yes	Yes	Yes	Yes
Idaho	140,000	10,000	15,000	Yes	Yes	Yes	Yes
Illinois	121,751	NA	56,143	No	Yes	No	Yes
Indiana	117,000	2,560	56,521	No	Yes	Yes	Yes
Iowa	122,676	701	81,521	No	Yes	No	Yes
Kansas	50,000	NA	34,000	Yes	Yes	Yes	Yes
Kentucky	98,000	2,000	82,510	Yes	Yes	Yes	Yes
Louisiana	190,000	1,200	155,000	Yes	Yes	Yes	Yes
Maine	194,319	41,216	29,710	Yes	Yes	Yes	Yes
Maryland	102,000	NA	33,320	Yes	Yes	Yes	Yes
Massachusetts	70,000	1,500	5,700	No	Yes	No	Yes
Michigan	710,000	20,000	310,000	Yes	Yes	Yes	Yes
Minnesota	401,962	6,062	129,551	Yes	Yes	Yes	Yes
Mississippi	175,000	30,000	210,000	Yes	Yes	Yes	Yes
Missouri	375,000	11,177	157,507	Yes	Yes	Yes	Yes
Nebraska	54,995	Combined	24,334	Yes	Yes	Yes	Yes
New Hampshire	60,000	10,000	5,409	Yes	Yes	Yes	Yes
New Jersey	110,000	2,000	28,913	No	Yes	No	Yes
New York	750,000	33,000	181,879	Yes	Yes	Yes	Yes
North Carolina	260,000	14,000	77,133	Yes	Yes	Yes	Yes
North Dakota	68,644	615	46,739	Yes	Yes	Yes	Yes
Ohio	240,000	NA	75,018	No	Yes	Yes	Yes
Oklahoma	132,450	NA	29,346	Yes	Yes	Yes	Yes
Oregon	210,705	Combined	68,946	Yes	Yes	Yes	Yes
Pennsylvania	1,000,000	77,000	371,040	Yes	Yes	Yes	Yes
Rhode Island	4,210	93	280	No	Yes	No	Yes
South Carolina	155,000	Combined	NA	Yes	Yes	Yes	Yes
South Dakota	52,000	5,000	43,000	Yes	Yes	Yes	Yes
Tennessee	140,000	5,000	78,500	Yes	Yes	Yes	Yes
Texas	564,000	Combined	465,000	Yes	Yes	Yes	Yes
Vermont	89,171	15,125	8,030	Yes	Yes	Yes	Yes
Virginia	268,119	NA	124,915	Yes	Yes	Yes	Yes
Washington	162,770	756	42,636	Yes	Yes	Yes	Yes
West Virginia	260,000	50,000	123,436	Yes	Yes	Yes	Yes
Wisconsin	639,265	23,015	310,192	Yes	Yes	Yes	Yes
Wyoming	12,500	5,900	8,911	Yes	Yes	Yes	Yes

1-Information "Not Available" (NA) as separate data available from license sales records or harvest totals.
2-Pennsylvania estimates over 1-million deer hunters and declines to be more specific.
3-"Combined" means that non-resident are included with resident figures. In Kansas, hunting permits are not available to non-residents.
4-Indicates types of weapons that can be used to hunt white-tailed deer.

■ Bow Hunting Information
Alphabetical by State

State[1]	Resident Bow Hunters	Non-Resident Bow Hunters[2]	Whitetail Harvest	Crossbows Permitted[3]	Bag Limit[4]	Special License[5]	During Gun Season[6]
Alabama	45,000	3,600	19,000	No	1/Day	No	Yes
Arizona	3,046	104	146	Yes	1	Yes	Yes
Arkansas	NA	NA	7,473	Yes	3	No	Yes
Connecticut	10,033	NA	926	No	2	Yes	No
Delaware	4,800	150	210	Hndcpd.	2	No	No
Florida	51,200	Combined	NA	No	Unlimited	Yes	Yes
Georgia	66,510	2,500	NA	Hndcpd.	5	No	Yes
Idaho	23,000	Combined	NA	Yes	1	Yes	Yes
Illinois	73,950	NA	10,000	Hndcpd.	2	Yes	No
Indiana	56,621	858	16,192	Hndcpd.	2	Yes	No
Iowa	30,815	218	11,857	Hndcpd.	2	Yes	No
Kansas	15,000	NA	5,000	Hndcpd.	2	Yes	No
Kentucky	75,600	800	9,982	Yes	2	No	Yes
Louisiana	23,000	Combined	10,000	Hndcpd.	6	Yes	Yes
Maine	8,233	1,177	416	No	1	Yes	Yes
Maryland	51,600	NA	7,282	Hndcpd.	1	No	Yes
Massachusetts	15,000	NA	1,000	No	2	Yes	Yes
Michigan	270,000	10,000	80,000	No	3	Yes	Yes
Minnesota	66,668	695	9,307	Hndcpd.	1	Yes	Yes
Mississippi	50,000	Combined	25,000	Hndcpd.	8	Yes	Yes
Missouri	81,987	1,329	10,970	Hndcpd.	2	Yes	Yes
Nebraska	12,701	Combined	2,847	Hndcpd.	2	Yes	No
New Hampshire	11,000	2,500	489	No	1	Yes	Yes
New Jersey	48,250	1,750	13,714	No	20	Yes	No
New York	140,000	Combined	12,770	No	1	Yes	Yes
North Carolina	86,000	4,000	4,660	No	5	Yes	Yes
North Dakota	9,565	270	2,337	Hndcpd.	1	Yes	Yes
Ohio	132,000	NA	9,363	Yes	1	No	No
Oklahoma	44,710	NA	4,588	Hndcpd.	2	Yes	Yes
Oregon	19,267	Combined	3,421	No	1	Yes	Yes
Pennsylvania	271,000	NA	11,008	No	2	Yes	Yes
Rhode Island	1,477	176	169	No	2	Yes	Yes
South Carolina	17,000	Combined	NA	Yes	Unlimited	No	Yes
South Dakota	10,625	484	3,081	Hndcpd.	2	Yes	Yes
Tennessee	58,000	NA	13,500	Hndcpd.	4	Yes	Yes
Texas	80,000	Combined	12,000	Hndcpd.	4	Yes	Yes
Vermont	14,284	3,834	1,202	Hndcpd.	1	Yes	Yes
Virginia	65,000	NA	10,179	No	5	Yes	Yes
Washington	18,862	112	3,644	No	1	No	No
West Virginia	86,000	12,000	16,217	No	2	No	Yes
Wisconsin	204,184	6,728	46,394	Hndcpd.	1	Yes	No
Wyoming	1,101	129	174	Yes	2	Yes	Yes

1-Information "Not Available" (NA) as separate data available from license sales records or harvest totals.
2-"Combined" means that non-resident are included with resident figure.
3-Indicates states that allow the use of a crossbow. Many states only permit handicapped individuals to use a crossbow.
4-Indicates the statewide bag limit for bow hunters in that state.
5-States that require the purchase of a special bow hunting license or stamp.
6-States where a bow can be used during the regular gun season.

■ Muzzleloader Hunting Information
Alphabetical by State

State[1]	Resident Hunters	Non-Residents Hunters[2]	Whitetail Harvest	Special Season[3]	Regular Firearms Season[4]
Alabama	20,000	1,600	6,000	No	Yes
Arizona	1,012	110	10	No	Yes
Arkansas	NA	NA	8,575	Yes	Yes
Connecticut	8,108	366	1,595	Yes	No
Delaware	6,000	300	401	Yes	No
Florida	37,600	Combined	NA	Yes	Yes
Georgia	NA	NA	NA	No	Yes
Idaho	11,000	2,000	NA	Yes	Yes
Illinois	4,777	NA	NA	No	Yes
Indiana	40,783	770	6,605	Yes	Yes
Iowa	14,821	20	6,334	Yes	Yes
Kansas	2,000	NA	1,000	Yes	Yes
Kentucky	12,000	Combined	2,250	Yes	Yes
Louisiana	10,000	Combined	NA	Yes	Yes
Maine	2,058	102	134	Yes	Yes
Maryland	29,800	NA	3,780	Yes	Yes
Massachusetts	11,000	NA	1,000	Yes	No
Michigan	110,000	5,000	20,000	Yes	Yes
Minnesota	2,500	Combined	622	Yes	Yes
Mississippi	60,000	5,000	33,000	Yes	Yes
Missouri	7,500	NA	1,881	Yes	Yes
Nebraska	2,478	Combined	705	Yes	Yes
New Hampshire	12,000	1,500	1,339	Yes	No
New Jersey	19,000	Combined	5,899	Yes	Yes
New York	20,000	Combined	749	Yes	Yes
North Carolina	78,000	3,000	7,471	Yes	Yes
North Dakota	667	NA	286	Yes	Yes
Ohio	78,000	NA	4,867	Yes	Yes
Oklahoma	34,559	NA	4,407	Yes	Yes
Oregon	2,073	NA	890	Yes	Yes
Pennsylvania	97,000	Combined	6,553	Yes	Yes
Rhode Island	1,995	150	186	Yes	No
South Carolina	16,500	Combined	NA	Yes	Yes
South Dakota	235	20	170	Yes	Yes
Tennessee	52,000	NA	16,800	Yes	Yes
Texas	NA	NA	NA	No	Yes
Vermont	3,767	Combined	111	Yes	No
Virginia	NA	NA	3,040	Yes	Yes
Washington	5,051	38	1,791	Yes	No
West Virginia	28,000	7,000	5,914	Yes	Yes
Wisconsin	25,000	NA	NA	No	Yes
Wyoming	1,400	150	200	Yes	Yes

1-Information "Not Available" (NA) as separate data derived from license sales records or harvest totals.
2-"Combined" means that non-resident are included with resident figures.
3-Special Season means that a separate season exists in that state as either exclusive to black powder firearms or primitive weapons, which include bows.
4-States where muzzleloaders can be used during the regular firearms season.

■ Muzzleloader Hunting Seasons
Alphabetical by State

State	Season Dates[1]	Special Season[2]	Special Season Days[3]	Hunt Regular Gun Season[4]
Alabama		No		Yes
Arizona		No		Yes
Arkansas	10/21-10/25; 12/16-12/31	Yes	21	Yes
Connecticut	12/10-12/22	Yes	13	No
Delaware	10/12-10/14; 1/22-1/24	Yes	6	No
Florida	10/6-8; 10/27-29; 11/17-19	Yes	9	Yes
Georgia		No		Yes
Idaho	11/7-12/2	Yes	26	Yes
Illinois		No		Yes
Indiana	12/2-12/10	Yes	9	Yes
Iowa	10/14-10/22; 12/18-1/10	Yes	31	Yes
Kansas	9/22-9/30; 11/29-12/10	Yes	21	Yes
Kentucky	10/6-10/7; 12/8-12/14	Yes	9	Yes
Louisiana	12/2-12/8	Yes	7	Yes
Maine	11/26-12/1	Yes	6	Yes
Maryland	12/11-12/23	Yes	12	Yes
Massachusetts	12/17-12/19	Yes	3	No
Michigan	12/1-12/10; 12/8-12/17	Yes	20	Yes
Minnesota	11/24-12/9	Yes	16	Yes
Mississippi	12/2-12/15	Yes	14	Yes
Missouri	11/10-11/18; 12/1-12/9	Yes	18	Yes
Nebraska	12/8-12/23	Yes	16	Yes
New Hampshire	10/27-11/16	Yes	11	No
New Jersey	12/10,11,15,17-22,24,26-29,31; 12/15-12/22	Yes	14	Yes
New York	10/13-10/19; 12/12-12/18	Yes	14	Yes
North Carolina	10/8-11/17	Yes	41	Yes
North Dakota	12/1-12/4; 12/8-12/11	Yes	7	Yes
Ohio	1/4-1/6	Yes	3	Yes
Oklahoma	10/21-10/29	Yes	9	Yes
Oregon	11/25-12/10; 12/2-12/10	Yes	16	No
Pennsylvania	12/26-1/6	Yes	11	Yes
Rhode Island	11/17-11/30; 12/10-12/23	Yes	28	No
South Carolina	10/1-10/10; 10/1-10/6; 11/26-12/8	Yes	23	Yes
South Dakota		No		Yes
Tennessee	10/20-28; 10/27-11/1; 11/5-11; 12/3-9; 12/14-16	Yes	33	Yes
Texas		No		Yes
Vermont	12/1-12/9	Yes	9	No
Virginia	12/18-1/6	Yes	18	Yes
West Virginia	12/18-12/23	Yes	6	Yes
Wisconsin		No		Yes
Wyoming	11/15-11/30	Yes	16	Yes
Washington	9/29-10/12; 11/21-12/9	Yes	33	No

1-Indicates single or multiple season dates within state. Multiple seasons generally means management zones within the state have separate seasons.
2-States having a designated black powder or primitive weapons season.
3-Number of days for the special seasons within each state.
4-States that permit hunting with black powder guns during the regular gun season.

■ Firearm and Bow Hunting Seasons
Alphabetical by State

State	Bow Season Dates[1]	Bow Season Days[2]	Firearm Season Dates[1]	Firearm Season Days[2]	Bow and Firearms Combined[3]
Alabama	10/15-1/31	109	11/17-1/31	76	Yes
Arizona	8/25-1/31	76	10/27-12/31	40	Yes
Arkansas	10/1-2/28	151	11/14-12/9	36	Yes
Connecticut	10/1-12/31	92	11/5-12/8	34	No
Delaware	9/1-1/31	113	11/10-1/20	12	No
Florida	9/2-11/12	72	10/28-2/14	110	Yes
Georgia	9/16-10/20	35	10/21-1/7	79	Yes
Idaho	9/1-9/28	28	10/31-12/9	40	Yes
Illinois	10/1-12/31	92	11/16-12/16	6	No
Indiana	10/7-12/31	65	11/11-11/26	16	No
Iowa	10/1-1/10	85	12/2-12/17	14	No
Kansas	10/1-12/31	80	11/29-12/10	12	No
Kentucky	10/1-1/15	107	11/10-11/19	10	Yes
Louisiana	10/1-1/20	112	11/4-1/17	75	Yes
Maine	10/1-10/26	23	10/29-11/24	24	Yes
Maryland	9/15-1/8	80	11/25-12/2	7	Yes
Massachusetts	11/5-11/24	18	11/26-12/5	9	Yes
Michigan	10/1-1/1	77	11/15-11/30	16	Yes
Minnesota	9/15-12/31	107	11/3-11/23	21	Yes
Mississippi	10/7-12/15	46	11/18-1/17	47	Yes
Missouri	10/1-12/31	83	11/10-11/18	9	Yes
Nebraska	9/15-12/31	108	11/10-11/18	9	No
New Hampshire	9/15-12/16	93	11/7-12/2	26	Yes
New Jersey	9/29-1/25	84	12/3-1/26	10	No
New York	9/27-12/31	101	10/20-12/11	51	Yes
North Carolina	9/10-11/10	60	10/15-1/1	78	Yes
North Dakota	9/1-12/31	119	11/10-11/26	16	Yes
Ohio	10/7-1/31	94	11/27-12/2	6	No
Oklahoma	10/1-12/31	74	11/18-11/26	9	Yes
Oregon	8/26-9/24	29	9/30-10/11	12	Yes
Pennsylvania	9/30-1/6	35	11/27-12/13	15	Yes
Rhode Island	10/1-1/31	120	12/1-12/9	9	Yes
South Carolina	10/1-12/15	31	8/15-1/1	140	Yes
South Dakota	10/1-12/31	92	11/4-12/10	37	Yes
Tennessee	9/29-11/11	40	11/17-1/1	32	Yes
Texas	10/1-10/31	31	11/3-1/13	65	Yes
Vermont	10/6-12/9	32	11/10-11/25	16	Yes
Virginia	10/14-11/11	25	11/20-1/6	42	Yes
Washington	9/15-12/9	47	10/13-10/28	16	No
West Virginia	10/14-12/30	61	11/20-12/2	12	Yes
Wisconsin	9/15-12/31	89	11/17-11/25	9	No
Wyoming	9/1-11/30	89	10/1-11/30	59	Yes

1-Dates for bow and gun seasons as listed are in the broadest context due to space limitations. These dates reflect the first to the last day of that type of deer hunting activity within the state. While some states have statewide seasons, others have varying seasons for different management units within their state.
2-Length of each season is total available hunting days in each state. Some states do not allow hunting on Sundays. Some states break seasons into "early" and "late" seasons, for example.
3-States that permit the use of a bow during the regular firearms seasons. The gun season dates can be added to the regular bow season dates to arrive at total bow hunting opportunity within each state.

■ State Deer Hunting Trends
Alphabetical by State

State	Deer/ Vehicle Collisions	Deer Crop Damage	Youth Hunters	Male Hunters	Female Hunters	Rifle Use	Shotgun Use	Handgun Use	Muzzle- loader Use	Bow Use
Alabama	Constant	Decreased	Increased	Constant	Constant	Increased	Decreased	Increased	Constant	Increased
Arizona	Decreased	Constant	Constant	Constant	Constant	Constant	Constant	Constant	Constant	Increased
Arkansas	Constant	Constant	Unknown	Unknown	Unknown	Constant	Constant	Constant	Decreased	Increased
Connecticut	Constant	Constant	Increased	Increased	Unknown	Increased	Increased	Increased	Increased	Increased
Delaware	Increased	Increased	Unknown	Constant	Unknown	**	Constant	**	Increased	Increased
Florida	Constant	Constant	Unknown	Unknown	Unknown	Unknown	Unknown	Unknown	Increased	Increased
Georgia	Increased	Increased	Unknown	Unknown	Unknown	Constant	Constant	Constant	Constant	Constant
Idaho	Constant	Increased	Constant	Increased	Constant	Increased	Constant	Constant	Constant	Increased
Illinois	Increased	Increased	Increased	Increased	Unknown	**	Increased	**	Constant	Increased
Indiana	Increased	Increased	Unknown	Unknown	Unknown	Increased	Increased	Increased	Increased	Increased
Iowa	Constant	Constant	Unknown	Increased	Unknown	**	Increased	**	Increased	Increased
Kansas	Increased	Decreased	Unknown	Unknown	Unknown	Increased	Constant	Constant	Constant	Constant
Kentucky	Decreased	Decreased	Constant	Decreased	Constant	Constant	Decreased	Constant	Increased	Decreased
Louisiana	Constant	Constant	Constant	Decreased	Increased	Increased	Decreased	Increased	Increased	Increased
Maine	Increased	Increased	Decreased	Increased	Unknown	Unknown	Unknown	Unknown	Increased	Increased
Maryland	Increased	Increased	Decreased	Decreased	Increased	Decreased	Increased	Constant	Increased	Increased
Massachusetts	Increased	Increased	Constant	Constant	Constant	**	Constant	**	Increased	Increased
Michigan	Increased	Increased	Unknown	Unknown	Unknown	Decreased	Increased	Increased	Increased	Increased
Minnesota	Increased	Constant	Unknown	Unknown	Unknown	Unknown	Unknown	Unknown	Constant	Increased
Mississippi	Constant	Constant	Constant	Unknown	Unknown	Increased	Decreased	Increased	Increased	Increased
Missouri	Increased	Increased	Increased	Increased	Increased	Constant	Constant	Increased	Increased	Increased
Nebraska	Increased	Constant	Increased	Increased	Increased	Increased	Unknown	Unknown	Increased	Constant
New Hampshire	Increased	Constant	Unknown	Increased	Unknown	Constant	Constant	Constant	Increased	Increased
New Jersey	Constant	Constant	Decreased	Decreased	Decreased	**	Decreased	**	Increased	Increased
New York	Constant	Constant	Constant	Constant	Unknown	Constant	Constant	Increased	Increased	Increased
North Carolina	Constant	Constant	Unknown	Unknown	Unknown	Increased	Decreased	Increased	Increased	Increased
North Dakota	Increased	Increased	Increased	Constant	Increased	Increased	Constant	Constant	Increased	Increased
Ohio	Increased	Increased	Unknown	Unknown	Unknown	**	Increased	Increased	Increased	Increased
Oklahoma	Increased	Increased	Unknown	Unknown	Unknown	Constant	Constant	Unknown	Increased	Increased
Oregon	Increased	Unknown	Decreased	Decreased	Decreased	Unknown	Unknown	Constant	Unknown	Increased
Pennsylvania	Increased	Increased	Decreased	Constant	Unknown	Constant	Constant	increased	Constant	Constant
Rhode Island	Increased	Increased	Increased	Increased	Constant	**	Increased	**	Increased	Constant
South Carolina	Increased	Constant	Increased	Increased	Increased	Increased	Increased	Increased	Increased	Increased
South Dakota	Increased	Decreased	Unknown	Unknown	Unknown	Unknown	Unknown	Unknown	Constant	Constant
Tennessee	Constant	Constant	Constant	Unknown	Unknown	Constant	Constant	Constant	Increased	Increased
Texas	Constant	Constant	Decreased	Constant	Constant	Constant	Decreased	Constant	Increased	Increased
Vermont	Increased	Increased	Decreased	Decreased	Decreased	Decreased	Decreased	Decreased	Increased	Decreased
Virginia	Constant	Constant	Unknown	Unknown	Unknown	Constant	Constant	Constant	Increased	Increased
Washington	Increased	Increased	Decreased	Constant	Constant	Decreased	Decreased	Increased	Increased	Increased
West Virginia	Increased	Increased	Unknown	Unknown	Unknown	Increased	Unknown	Unknown	Increased	Decreased
Wisconsin	Increased	Increased	Constant	Constant	Increased	Constant	Constant	Increased	Increased	Constant
Wyoming	Constant	Increased	Decreased	Decreased	Decreased	Decrease	Increased	Increased	Increased	Increased

**Use not allowed during the hunting seasons in respective state.

State Deer Hunting Regulations
Alphabetical by State

State	Minimum Hunting Age[1]	Hunter Education Required[2]	Bow Hunt From Tree Stand	Gun Hunt From Tree Stand	Blaze Orange Requirements	Use Food Bait	Hunt Over Salt/Minerals	Hunt With Dogs	Trail With Dogs[3]	Shine For Deer[4]
Alabama	None	No	Yes	Yes	Yes	No	Yes	Yes	Yes	No
Arizona	10	Yes	Yes	Yes	No	Yes	Yes	No	No	No
Arkansas	None	Yes	Yes	Yes	Yes	Yes	Yes	Yes	Yes	No
Connecticut	12	Yes	Yes	Yes	Yes	No	No	No	No	No
Delaware	None	Yes	Yes	Yes	Yes	No	No	No	No	No
Florida	None	No	Yes	Yes	Yes	Yes	Yes	Yes	Yes	Yes
Georgia	12	Yes	Yes	Yes	Yes	No	No	Yes	No	No
Idaho	12	Yes	Yes	Yes	No	No	No	No	No	No
Illinois	No	Yes	Yes	Yes	Yes	No	No	No	No	No
Indiana	None	No	Yes	Yes	Yes	No	No	No	No	Yes
Iowa	None	Yes	Yes	Yes	Yes	No	No	No	No	No
Kansas	14	Yes	Yes	Yes	Yes	Yes	Yes	No	No	No
Kentucky	None	No	Yes	Yes	Yes	Yes	Yes	No	No	No
Louisiana	None	Yes	Yes	Yes	Yes	Yes	Yes	Yes	Yes	No
Maine	10	Yes	Yes	Yes	Yes	No	No	No	No	No
Maryland	None	Yes	Yes	Yes	Yes	Yes	Yes	No	No	Yes
Massachusetts	12	No	Yes	Yes	Yes	No	No	No	No	No
Michigan	12	Yes	Yes	No	Yes	Yes	No	No	Yes	Yes
Minnesota	12	Yes	Yes	Yes	Yes	Yes	Yes	No	No	No
Mississippi	None	Yes	Yes	Yes	Yes	No	No	Yes	Yes	Yes
Missouri	None	Yes	Yes	Yes	Yes	Yes	Yes	No	No	Yes
Nebraska	14	Yes	Yes	Yes	Yes	Yes	Yes	Yes	Yes	No
New Hampshire	16	Yes	Yes	Yes	No	Yes	No	No	No	No
New Jersey	10	Yes	Yes	Yes	Yes	No	No	No	Yes	Yes
New York	14	Yes	Yes	Yes	No	No	No	No	Yes	Yes
North Carolina	None	No	Yes	Yes	Yes	Yes	Yes	Yes	Yes	Yes
North Dakota	14	Yes	Yes	Yes	Yes	Yes	Yes	No	No	No
Ohio	None	Yes	Yes	Yes	Yes	Yes	Yes	No	No	No
Oklahoma	None	Yes	Yes	Yes	Yes	Yes	Yes	No	No	No
Oregon	12	Yes	Yes	No	No	No	No	No	No	No
Pennsylvania	12	Yes	Yes	Yes	Yes	No	No	No	No	Yes
Rhode Island	12	Yes	Yes	Yes	Yes	No	No	No	No	No
South Carolina	None	No	Yes	Yes	No	Yes	Yes	Yes	Yes	Yes
South Dakota	12	Yes	Yes	Yes	Yes	Yes	No	No	No	No
Tennessee	10	Yes	Yes	Yes	Yes	No	No	No	No	No
Texas	None	Yes	Yes	Yes	Yes	Yes	Yes	No	Yes	No
Vermont	None	Yes	Yes	Yes	No	No	No	No	No	No
Virginia	None	Yes	Yes	Yes	Yes	No	No	Yes	Yes	No
Washington	12	Yes	Yes	Yes	No	Yes	Yes	No	No	No
West Virginia	None	Yes	Yes	Yes	Yes	Yes	Yes	No	No	No
Wisconsin	12	Yes	Yes	Yes	Yes	Yes	No	No	No	Yes
Wyoming	14	Yes	Yes	Yes	Yes	Yes	Yes	No	No	No

[1] In many states youth must be accompanied by adult or pass a hunter education course to qualify.
[2] Usually applies to first-time hunters, or all those born after a designated date.
[3] In states that do not allow hunting with dogs, trailing is to recover wounded deer.
[4] Restrictions usually apply in states that permit shining for deer, such as time restrictions and no weapon in possession.

■ State Deer Hunting Trends Breakouts
Alphabetical by State

Deer/Vehicle Collisions

■ Increased
Delaware
Georgia
Illinois
Indiana
Kansas
Maine
Maryland
Massachusetts
Michigan
Minnesota
Missouri
Nebraska
New Hampshire
North Dakota
Ohio
Oklahoma
Oregon
Pennsylvania
Rhode Island
South Carolina
South Dakota
Vermont
Washington
West Virginia
Wisconsin

■ Constant
Alabama
Arkansas
Connecticut
Florida
Idaho
Iowa
Louisiana
Mississippi
New Jersey
New York
North Carolina
Tennessee
Texas
Virginia
Wyoming

■ Decreased
Arizona
Kentucky

Deer Crop Damage

■ Increased
Delaware
Georgia
Idaho
Illinois
Indiana
Maine
Maryland
Massachusetts
Michigan
Missouri
North Dakota
Ohio
Oklahoma
Pennsylvania
Rhode Island
Vermont
Washington
West Virginia
Wisconsin
Wyoming

■ Constant
Arizona
Arkansas
Connecticut
Florida
Iowa
Louisiana
Minnesota
Mississippi
Nebraska
New Hampshire
New Jersey
New York
North Carolina
South Carolina
Tennessee
Texas
Virginia

■ Decreased
Alabama
Kansas
Kentucky
South Dakota

■ Unknown
Oregon

Youth Hunters

■ Increased
Alabama
Connecticut
Illinois
Missouri
Nebraska
North Dakota
Rhode Island
South Carolina

■ Constant
Arizona
Idaho
Kentucky
Louisiana
Massachusetts
Mississippi
New York
Tennessee
Wisconsin

■ Decreased
Maine
Maryland
New Jersey
Oregon
Pennsylvania
Texas
Vermont
Washington
Wyoming

■ Unknown
Arkansas
Delaware
Florida
Georgia
Indiana
Iowa
Kansas
Michigan
Minnesota
New Hampshire
North Carolina
Ohio
Oklahoma
South Dakota
Virginia
West Virginia

Male Hunters

■ Increased
Connecticut
Idaho
Illinois
Iowa
Maine
Missouri
Nebraska
New Hampshire
Rhode Island
South Carolina

■ Constant
Alabama
Arizona
Delaware
Massachusetts
New York
North Dakota
Pennsylvania
Texas
Washington
Wisconsin

■ Decreased
Kentucky
Louisiana
Maryland
New Jersey
Oregon
Vermont
Wyoming

■ Unknown
Arkansas
Florida
Georgia
Indiana
Kansas
Michigan
Minnesota
Mississippi
North Carolina
Ohio
Oklahoma
South Dakota
Tennessee
Virginia
West Virginia

Female Hunters

■ Increased
Louisiana
Maryland
Missouri
Nebraska
North Dakota
South Carolina
Wisconsin

■ Constant
Alabama
Arizona
Idaho
Kentucky
Massachusetts
Rhode Island
Texas
Washington

■ Decreased
New Jersey
Oregon
Vermont
Wyoming

■ Unknown
Arkansas
Connecticut
Delaware
Florida
Georgia
Illinois
Indiana
Iowa
Kansas
Maine
Michigan
Minnesota
Mississippi
New Hampshire
New York
North Carolina
Ohio
Oklahoma
Pennsylvania
South Dakota
Tennessee
Virginia
West Virginia

■State Deer Hunting Trends Breakouts
Alphabetical by State

Rifle Hunting	Shotgun Hunting	Handgun Hunting	Muzzleloader Hunting	Bow Hunting
■ Increased	**■ Increased**	**■ Increased**	**■ Increased**	**■ Increased**
Alabama	Connecticut	Alabama	Connecticut	Alabama
Connecticut	Illinois	Connecticut	Delaware	Arkansas
Idaho	Indiana	Indiana	Florida	Arizona
Indiana	Iowa	Louisiana	Indiana	Connecticut
Kansas	Maryland	Michigan	Iowa	Delaware
Louisiana	Michigan	Mississippi	Kansas	Florida
Mississippi	Ohio	Missouri	Kentucky	Iowa
Nebraska	Rhode Island	New York	Louisiana	Idaho
North Carolina	South Carolina	North Carolina	Maine	Illinois
North Dakota	Wyoming	Ohio	Maryland	Indiana
South Carolina		Pennsylvania	Massachusetts	Louisiana
West Virginia	**■ Constant**	South Carolina	Michigan	Massachusetts
	Arizona	Washington	Mississippi	Maryland
■ Constant	Arkansas	Wisconsin	Missouri	Maine
Arizona	Delaware	Wyoming	North Carolina	Michigan
Arkansas	Georgia		North Dakota	Minnesota
Georgia	Idaho	**■ Constant**	Nebraska	Missouri
Kentucky	Kansas	Arizona	New Hampshire	Mississippi
Missouri	Massachusetts	Arkansas	New Jersey	North Carolina
New Hampshire	Missouri	Georgia	New York	North Dakota
New York	New Hampshire	Idaho	Ohio	New Hampshire
Oklahoma	New York	Kansas	Oklahoma	New Jersey
Pennsylvania	North Dakota	Kentucky	Rhode Island	New York
Tennessee	Oklahoma	Maryland	South Carolina	Ohio
Texas	Pennsylvania	New Hampshire	Tennessee	Oklahoma
Virginia	Tennessee	North Dakota	Texas	Oregon
Wisconsin	Virginia	Oregon	Vermont	South Carolina
	Wisconsin	Tennessee	Virginia	Tennessee
■ Decreased		Texas	Washington	Texas
Maryland	**■ Decreased**	Virginia	West Virginia	Virginia
Michigan	Alabama		Wisconsin	Washington
Vermont	Kentucky	**■ Decreased**	Wyoming	Wyoming
Washington	Louisiana	Vermont		
Wyoming	Mississippi		**■ Constant**	**■ Constant**
	New Jersey	**■ Unknown**	Alabama	Georgia
■ Unknown	North Carolina	Florida	Arizona	Kansas
Florida	Texas	Maine	Georgia	Nebraska
Maine	Vermont	Minnesota	Idaho	Pennsylvania
Minnesota	Washington	Nebraska	Illinois	Rhode Island
Oregon		Oklahoma	Minnesota	South Dakota
South Dakota	**■ Unknown**	South Dakota	Pennsylvania	Wisconsin
	Florida	West Virginia	South Dakota	
■ Not Allowed	Maine			**■ Decreased**
Delaware	Minnesota	**■ Not Allowed**	**■ Decreased**	Kentucky
Illinois	Nebraska	Delaware	Arkansas	Vermont
Iowa	Oregon	Illinois		West Virginia
Massachusetts	South Dakota	Iowa	**■ Unknown**	
New Jersey	West Virginia	Massachusetts	Oregon	
Ohio		New Jersey		
Rhode Island		Rhode Island		

What they say about hunting...

Position Statements On Hunting Of Major Conservation Or Preservation Organizations

In publishing this information, the National Shooting Sports Foundations has assembled, without editorial comment, those varied attitudes toward the hunting sport which are part of the charter, bylaws or self-professed policies of major U.S. associations significantly concerned with the conservation or preservation of our natural resources. They are by no means all the organizations so concerned.

Further, we offer no explanation of anomalies, which are perhaps inevitable in such large groups, where the written policy says one thing and either executive action, or the activities of member individuals, would seem to suggest another. These brief statements may, however, clear up certain misapprehensions in relation to the true policies or attitudes, as written down, of nationally regarded organizations.

Robert T. Delfay,
Executive Director
National Shooting
Sports Foundation

INTERNATIONAL ASSOCIATION OF FISH AND WILDLIFE AGENCIES

Whereas, there is increasing sentiment developing on a national scale to discredit hunting and the harvest of wildlife; and

Whereas, legislation is proposed to ban killing animals on public land; and

Whereas, hunting is a major source of outdoor recreation and participation is increasing annually; and

Whereas, certain documentaries have fostered this anti-hunting sentiment and some groups are creating a misguided emotional reaction among large segments of uninformed urban populations; and

Whereas, the public needs to be presented a counteracting documentation of the true role of the hunter, and hunting, as not only a major form of recreation but an absolute necessity for the proper management and future well-being of many wildlife populations in various areas throughout the country:

Now, therefore, be it resolved, that the International Association of Game, Fish and Conservation Commissioners in cooperation with other State, National, International, private and public agencies involved in managing renewable natural resources, develop a comprehensive program to "Tell it like it is" and provide the public with an accurate portrayal of the role of the hunter and hunting in America.

1412 16th Street NW
Washington, DC 20036
(202) 232-1652

Association of each state or territory of United States, each Province of Canada, the Commonwealth of Puerto Rico, the United States Government and each Government of a country located in the Western Hemisphere as well as individual Associate members whose principal objec-tive is conservation, protection, and management of wildlife and related natural resources.

THE AMERICAN FORESTRY ASSOCIATION

The American Forestry Association believes that, under proper regulations, hunting should be considered as a tool of management by owners of forest and range holdings.

Wildlife management is an integral part of forest and range management. It is of increasing value because of its importance to a growing mobile human population seeking recreation. Because of this, the management of fish and wildlife must be given a higher priority than in the past within the multiple use concept.

1516 P Street NW
Washington, DC 20005
(202) 667-3300

The advancement of intelligent management and use of forests, soil, water, wildlife and all other natural resources. Seeks to create an enlightened public appreciation of these resources and the part they play in the social and economic life of the nation. Created: 1875

THE WILDERNESS SOCIETY

The Wilderness Society recognizes hunting as a legitimate use in wilderness areas, national forests, and certain wildlife areas, subject to appropriate regulation for species protection.

1400 Eye Street NW 10th Floor
Washington, DC 20005
(202) 842-3400

National conservation organization formed to secure preservation of wilderness and proper management of all federal lands, carry on an education program concerning the value of wilderness and how it may best be used and preserved in the public interest, make and mobilize cooperation in resisting degradation of federal lands. Membership: 300,000; Organized: 1935

THE IZAAK WALTON LEAGUE OF AMERICA

The Izaak Walton League of America believes hunting should be considered a valuable management tool, where it is compatible with other resource uses and purposes.

Establishment of hunting and fishing seasons should be based upon the best scientific and biological data which can be obtained. These decisions should not be forced by political pressures, and should be calculated to assure healthy reproducing populations of game species and a balance of predacious animals and birds.

All hunting and fishing license revenues, and taxes on sporting arms and ammunition, should be utilized to enhance wildlife and to protect and restore habitat. Hunting should be characterized by the highest order of humaneness, sportsmanship and respect for species hunted.

1401 Wilson Blvd., Level B
Arlington, VA 22209
(703) 528-1818

Promotes means and opportunities for educating the public to conserve, maintain, protect and restore the soil, forest, water, and other natural resources of the U.S. and promotes the enjoyment and

wholesome utilization of those resources. Membership: 56,000

THE NATIONAL RIFLE ASSOCIATION OF AMERICA

Well-regulated hunting is a beneficial use of renewable wildlife resources which, when left to nature, are finally lost to predators, disease, often starvation and old age. Proper hunting is in complete accord with the moral tenets of man and the historical facts of his existence. Man's hunting heritage predates recorded history for hundreds of thousands, perhaps millions, of years. His reenactment of the chase today is a healthy exercise, both physically and spiritually.

The hunter's interest in pursuing his sport has been the principal factor in nurturing the conservation of our wildlife and other natural resources. Provision for the hunter's harvest provides the indispensible incentive for the hunter's contribution, a contribution without which all else would be lost. The commitment of the hunter and his contribution assures propagation of all wildlife within the framework of income from his voluntary taxing, licensing, and regulation.

Hunting is dominant among American traditions and it has contributed substantially to our sound national character. Its future is a primary concern of the National Rifle Association.

1600 Rhode Island Avenue NW
Washington, DC 20036
(202) 828-6000

Protects and defends the Constitution of the United States, especially with reference to the inalienable right of the individual American citizen to enjoy the use of firearms and to provide the defense of self, family, property, and the Republic; promotes public safety, law and order, and the national defense, trains members of law enforcement agencies, the armed forces, the militia, and people of good repute in marksmanship and in the safe handling and efficient use of small arms; fosters and promotes the shooting sports; promotes and defends safe hunting as a shooting sport and as a viable and necessary method of fostering the propagation, growth, conservation, and wise use of our renewable wildlife resources.

Membership: 2.8 million; Organized: 1871.

THE HUMANE SOCIETY OF THE UNITED STATES

The Humane Society of the United States is strongly opposed to the hunting of any living creature for fun, trophy, or for sport, because of the trauma, suffering, and death to the animals which results. The HSUS also opposes such killing because of the negative effect upon the young who may learn to accept and live with needless suffering and killing. The HSUS believes that a civilized society should not condone the killing of any sentient creature as sport.

The HSUS believes that the characterization of wild animals as "game" denies their intrinsic value and belittles their ecological importance. The Society finds that a great deal of wildlife allegedly killed for management reasons actually is killed as "game" for "sporting" purposes. In such cases, we oppose both the killing and the duplicity. It is the goal of the HSUS to ensure ethical stewardship of wildlife and its environment.

The HSUS recognizes that the welfare and responsible management of animals may, on occasion, necessitate the killing of wildlife. When such killing is permitted, it must be used as a last resort, be demonstrably necessary, be conducted by responsible officials, and methods utilized must result in an instantaneous and humane death.

The HSUS also recognizes that the legitimate needs for human subsistence may necessitate the killing of wildlife. In such cases, killing must be accomplished in a humane and non-wasteful manner and must not involve endangered or threatened animals.

2100 L Street NW
Washington, DC
(202) 452-1100

THE AMERICAN HUMANE ASSOCIATION

The American Humane Association is opposed to the hunting of any living creature for fun, a trophy, or for simple sport. The AHA believes that sport hunting is a form of exploitation of animals for the entertainment of the hunter, and is contrary to the values of compassion and respect for all life that inform American Humane's mission.

American Humane finds that wildlife management often consists of creating habitat that favors "game" species, which creates an overpopulation available for the purpose of sport hunting. We oppose these practices and favor wildlife "management" requiring the least human manipulation, favoring all wildlife in an ecosystem equally. On occasions when all other avenues have been exhausted and there remains a demonstrable necessity to kill some wildlife, it should be performed by responsible officials and methods utilized must result in instantaneous and humane death. American Humane considers sport hunting a violation of the inherent integrity of animals and disruptive of the national balance of the environment through human manipulation, and calls for positive action to prevent such cruelties.

P.O. Box 1266
Denver, CO 80201-1266
(303) 695-0811

A national federation of individuals and agencies for the prevention of cruelty, especially to children and animals. Organized: 1877

THE NORTH AMERICAN WILDLIFE ASSOCIATION

The American system of wildlife administration is the most successful in the world. Fundamental concepts include the public ownership of wildlife. Beneficial nongame wildlife populations and those that are threatened and endangered are given the full protection of the law. Surpluses of game populations can be cropped each year on a sustained basis under strict licensing and regulations.

Hunting regulations based on scientific facts revealed through research assure the yearly survival of adequate breeding stocks of those populations hunted. Similarly, regulations carefully designed and reviewed regularly can be used to adjust populations of browsing animals, such as deer, to optimum and acceptable levels. Through such intensive management, deer populations are maintained in balance with their food supplies and compatible with forestry, agriculture and other human activities. Public hunting is the tool used to achieve such objectives, while simultaneously providing citizens with healthy and enjoyable outdoor recreation.

The majority of funds that support this resource management program come from consumptive users of wildlife — the hunters and anglers. Only in recent years have nonhunting taxpayers, who enjoy bird watching or other nonconsumptive uses of wildlife, started to provide larger financial support for comprehensive wildlife management programs.

The challenge for all citizens interested in wildlife and its proper management is to focus their collective attention on maintaining and restoring habitats required to ensure the survival and reproduction of wildlife populations.

102 Wilmot Road, Suite 410
Deerfield, IL 60015
(312) 940-7776

Helps to sponsor wildlife research through cooperating organizations and promotes conservation, restoration, and management of all natural resources, especially aquatic areas.

THE NATIONAL AUDUBON SOCIETY

The National Audubon Society, since its origin at the turn of the century, has never been opposed to the hunting of game species if that hunting is done ethically and in accordance with laws and regulations designed to prevent depletion of the wildlife resource. We have made this clear repeatedly in official statements of policy and it remains Audubon policy.

Two points need clarification. First, we will advocate restrictions on hunting, including the complete closure of a hunting season, whenever we are convinced that the welfare of the species involved requires it. We would be remiss in our responsibilities as a conservation organization if we failed to implement such convictions. On the other hand, those who have worked with us at close hand know that we insist on sound scientific information before deciding these issues. Secondly, we do not advocate hunting. This is no contradiction, though some people seem to think it is. Our objective is wildlife and environmental conservation, not the promotion of hunting. We think lots of the justifications for hunting are weak ones, and too often exaggerated for commercial reasons, and we do not hesitate to say so when the occasion calls for it. But this does not make us anti-hunting. We are pushing people to think more clearly about these problems.

950 Third Avenue
New York, NY 10022
(212) 546-9100

Among the oldest and largest conservation organizations in North America. Its purposes are (1) to promote the conservation of wildlife and the natural environment and (2) to educate man regarding his relationship with, and his place within, the natural environment as an ecological system. Founded: 1905

OUTDOOR WRITERS ASSOCIATION OF AMERICA

One of today's most important environmental issues is the public's inability to distinguish between the limited purposes of preservation and the broader tenets of conservation. Preservation calls for the total discontinuance of resource-use. Conservation calls for the planned and rational utilization of resources.

The wildlife profession, composed of persons best qualified to make decisions concerning the welfare of fish and wildlife, urges the use of surpluses in fish and game populations for recreation.

They insist that hunting and fishing are not only permissible, but highly desirable, even from the viewpoint of the animal's welfare. Without a regular controlled harvest, many animal populations and the ranges they occupy, would be impoverished. Further, the hunter and the angler, under established season and bag limits, take only a portion of the annual surplus which is going to be lost to other mortality causes anyway.

A fact often overlooked by the protectionists is that the sportsman has carried the burden of financing fish and wildlife management and preservation through the years. His half billion dollars in license fees and voluntary contributions has been spent to conserve and preserve both game and non-game species. The sportsman has been almost solely responsible for funding the endangered species program.

The protectionists and the sportsmen actually have many common goals. Their efforts need to be coordinated for the common good. The outdoor writer can be instrumental in achieving this coordination.

2017 Cato Avenue, Suite 101
State College, PA 16801
(814) 234-1011

We strive to improve ourselves in the art and media of our craft and to increase our knowledge and understanding in supporting the conservation of our natural resources. To this end we pledge ourselves to maintain the highest ethical standards in the exercise of our craft. Membership: 1,500

FRIENDS OF ANIMALS, INC.

The vast majority of Americans do not hunt. We live in the "age of information" and more and more people have come to appreciate the value of our natural heritage. We now know that the web of life is of enormous importance to our own existence, and that there is an urgent need to preserve what is left of the natural world, that wildlife is a vital part of the ecological systems on which all life is dependent.

The premeditated killing of wildlife is abhorrent to most people, particularly when hunting is condoned under false pretenses, under the guise of "wildlife management, overpopulation control," or "protection of crops and public safety."

The age of information is also the "age of information management." Misinformation is the tool of special interests, and perhaps nowhere else is it in use as effectively as in the promotion of hunting.

Friends of Animals believes that the more people are aware of the truths involved, the more right their choices in how our wildlife and wild lands are cared for will be. We believe that wildlife, which by law belongs to all of us, has rights and deserves protection, and that the non-hunting majority needs a voice, an active advocate.

Ours is a point of view based on natural values, one that draws on what has been learned in the scientific studies of biology, ecology, and zoology. It is drawn from a very large and growing body of knowledge that has become increasingly important to the survival of all animal life, including humans.

P.O. Box 1244
Norwalk, CT 06856
(203) 866-5223

An international not-for-profit animal welfare and protection organization that seeks to reduce an eliminate animal suffering wherever it exists. Established: 1957 Membership: 104,000

THE WILDLIFE LEGISLATIVE FUND OF AMERICA

The Wildlife Legislative Fund of America believes that hunting, fishing and trapping are rights, not privileges. They are honorable pursuits that can be defended by our Constitution. These oldest of heritages are treasures that can and should be defended as we defend other legacies that weld us to our roots and remind us from where we came.

These rights can be taken away only by breaking the laws and regulations designed to protect wildlife.

The Wildlife Legislative Fund of America is the nation's principal sportsmen's rights organization and through its associated organization represents over one million sportsmen. It is a firm believer in scientific wildlife management and supports regulated hunting, fishing and trapping.

Founded to combat the animal rights movement, the WLFA is proud to have served sportsmen for over a decade. The staff is comprised of professionals with backgrounds in the fields of public relations, legislative lobbying, natural resource management and law.

The WLFA is an association of organizations ranging from national groups like Ducks Unlimited, the Foundation for North American Wild Sheep, National Wild Turkey Foundation and others to hundreds of state and local sportsmen clubs. It provides money and manpower to sportsmen under attack anywhere in America. The ALFA operates in all 50 states and Washington, DC.

Sportsmen are America's greatest conservationists. Because of their concern for wildlife and their support of the nation's dedicated wildlife managers, America's wildlife is thriving. No species of wildlife in the United States has been endangered by modern sportsmen. On the contrary, the sportsmen's concern for wildlife, backed up by $950 million annually through license fees and self-imposed taxes, is the reason wildlife is thriving. Sportsmen provide a service by harvesting surplus animals. This can be crucial for many wildlife species' populations. Scientific data collected by biologists from the sportsman's game bag provides invaluable information that wildlife managers use to formulate wildlife management plans to ensure wildlife's health and abundance.

To combat a growing anti-hunting/animal rights movement, the WLFA recently launched a nation-wide public education program called "Protect What's Right". It is designed to carry the sportsmen's message to the non-hunting public. It is currently operational in hundreds of communities in 48 states.

50 West Broad Street
Columbus, OH 43215
(614) 221-2684

The Wildlife Legislative Fund of America and its companion organization, The Wildlife Conservation Fund of America, are national organizations whose purpose is to protect the heritage of the American sportsmen to hunt, to fish and to trap ... and to promote and protect scientific wildlife management practices.

public about wildlife habitat and management. To this end, Ducks Unlimited encourages of ethical conduct among all who enjoy the outdoors.

National Headquarters
One Waterfront Way
Long Grove, IL 60047
(312) 438-4300

DUCKS UNLIMITED

Ducks Unlimited supports the concept of regulated sport hunting as an integral part of sound wildlife management, and as a wise and prudent use of renewable natural resources.

For more than half a century, Ducks Unlimited has held fast to its singleness of purpose: to develop, preserve, restore and maintain waterfowl habitat on the North American continent. As a result, more than five million habitat acres have been brought under DU's wing.

Waterfowlers are the cornerstone in Ducks Unlimited's habitat building program. They provide the volunteer support and the dollars that reach across socioeconomic and political barriers into the breeding, staging and wintering habitat that sustains the resource. America's hunters are the progenitors and financiers of the most scientific wildlife management ever conceived. Hunters have been and continue to be the champions of wildlife conservation around the globe. Waterfowlers and other hunters identified the need and filled it long before the words "conservation" and "ecology" became fashionable. And regardless of attempts to persuade them otherwise, the general public owes America's hunters a large debt of gratitude for their pioneering achievements on behalf of habitat and wildlife conservation.

Because Ducks Unlimited was chartered as a conservation organization, it is not a "hunting" organization per se. But as a part of its singleness of purpose, Ducks Unlimited attempts to educate the

THE NATIONAL WILDLIFE FEDERATION

The National Wildlife Federation is composed of millions of members and associates whose primary interest is in the conservation of our nation's renewable resources. Although our members and affiliates have many and varied opinions on how these resources might be best utilized, hunters and non-hunters alike support our broad conservation objectives.

We support hunting because, under professional regulation, wildlife populations are a renewable natural resource that can safely sustain taking. Although we understand the moral philosophy of those who feel that hunting is wrong and that wildlife populations should be protected completely the real and fundamental problem facing wildlife is not hunting but instead is habitat degradation and destruction. The National Wildlife Federation therefore, is committed to conserving wildlife habitat.

To accomplish this objective, hunters and non-hunters should unite efforts to preserve wildlife habitat, the key to wildlife variety and abundance. We are hopeful that those having a true interest in meeting this objective, like millions already, will continue to support the National Wildlife Federation and its efforts.

1400 Sixteenth Street NW
Washington, DC 20036-2266
(202) 797-6800

To create and encourage an awareness among the people of this Nation of the need for wise and proper management of those resources of the earth upon which the lives and welfare of men depend; the soils, plant life, and the wildlife. Organized: 1936

DEFENDERS OF WILDLIFE

Defenders of Wildlife is neither an anti-hunting nor a pro-hunting organization, but most of its 80,000 members are non-hunters and their concern is with the restoration and protection of all species of wildlife and their habitats. Defenders' goal is to win permanent protection for the homes of every native plant and animal species through political action to save representative examples of all plant and animal communities and wildlife dispersal corridors between them.

Defenders' traditional special campaigns include restoration and protection of the mammalian predators — the wolf, the mountain lion, the coyote and others — and reduction in the use of the leghold trap and wildlife-killing agricultural chemicals. It views the National Wildlife Refuge System as the core a national network of diversity maintenance areas where wildlife reproduction success is given top priority over human uses of all kinds — consumptive and nonconsumptive. It has opposed hunting of some species — sandhill cranes (where they could be confused with whooping cranes), tundra swans (where they could be confused with trumpeter swans), mountain lions (with dogs, in California's fragmented habitats) — and proposed reductions in bag limits to leave more prey for the wild predators (e.g., to leave more deer for Florida panthers in the Big Cypress Preserve).

Its "bottom line" goal is sustained populations of all native wildlife species for the enjoyment of all and for their intrinsic value.

1244 Nineteenth Street NW
Washington, DC 20036
(202) 659-9510

WILDLIFE MANAGEMENT INSTITUTE

The Wildlife Management Institute supports and encourages recreational hunting and harvests within (1) prescribed scientific guidelines, (2) essential standards and traditions of fair chase and (3) laws and regulations established and enforced by state, provincial and federal wildlife management agencies.

The Wildlife Management Institute does not recognize as recreational hunting any pursuit of taking of wildlife outside prescribed and promulgated guidelines, regulations and laws. Those who violate hunting laws and regulations and ethical tenets are considered outlaws and despoiler, not hunters.

Hunting designated wildlife populations legally and responsibly is a legitimate, healthful and otherwise worthwhile recreational activity. It can help regulate wildlife numbers on a sustainable basis, within seasonal and year-round habitat carrying capacity limits of those populations. Therefore, besides being an enjoyable recreational endeavor when conducted legally, responsibly and ethically, hunting is a viable and practical means of maintaining healthy and productive wildlife populations and reducing conflicts with people, such as minimizing crop depredations, highway accidents, etc. Revenues from hunting licenses and permits provide essential economic support for managing all forms of wildlife for the benefit of those resources and all people.

Recreational hunting is a significant boon to many local and state economies, as well as the nation. In some areas, hunting provides subsistence for native people. Through contacts and observations when afield, hunting serves as an important link to improve participants' understanding and appreciation of natural resources and the critical roles of stewardship and management of those resources and human activities.

1101 Fourteenth Street NW
Washington, DC 20005
(202) 371-1808

A national, nonprofit, private, scientific, educational membership organization, supported by corporations, groups and individuals, and promoting improved sustainable use of natural resources for the welfare of the Nation.

THE WILDLIFE SOCIETY

Hunting has co-evolved with the needs and cultures of mankind. Archeological evidence indicates that early cultures were dependent upon wild animals for subsistence. As skills in animal husbandry and agriculture were acquired, dependence on hunting for subsistence decreased. Today hunting is principally useful for recreational purposes, for utilization of the harvestable surplus to benefit man, and for controlling populations.

Most wild animal populations produce more animals than their habitats can support. These surplus animals are removed by mortality factors that regulate population numbers within the limits of the habitat. Hunting can be used to remove a portion of these excess animals that would otherwise be lost to natural mortality.

Professional wildlife managers are charged with the responsibility of managing wildlife populations in an ecologically sound and socially acceptable manner. Hunting, when based on biological information and properly regulated, can be used effectively to satisfy this responsibility. In addition, hunting through licenses and taxes, provides the major source of financing for habitat acquisition, law enforcement, research, and management programs for wildlife, both game and nongame species.

The policy of The Wildlife Society, in regard to hunting, is to:

1. Assist decision makers so that judgments on hunting and the welfare of wildlife are guided by both biological and societal consideration.

2. Endorse the principle that hunting, when properly regulated, is a biologically sound means of managing wildlife populations.

3. Encourage expansion of programs for hunters to increase their knowledge of wildlife ecology and management and to emphasize hunter ethics and responsibilities.

5410 Grosvenor Lane, Suite 200
Bethesda, MD 20814
(301) 897-9770

Association for those professionally employed in the biological or related fields of wildlife conservation. Aims to establish and maintain the highest possible professional standards; to develop wildlife conservation and management along sound biological lines; and to prepare and disseminate information to effect these ends. Membership: 8,400; Organized: 1937

THE FUND FOR ANIMALS

The Fund for Animals is unalterably opposed to the recreational killing of wildlife. Besides being a piteously unfair and cruel slaughter of innocent animals, sport hunting is also ecologically destructive. Despite claims to the contrary, hunters take a heavy toll on endangered and threatened animals. Last year alone, they killed dozens of bald and golden eagles and grizzly bears and even such extremely rare animals as Florida panthers and whooping cranes. Despite dire warnings about the future of duck populations, hunters annually position themselves along the migratory flyways and massacre, often indiscriminately, millions of ducks. And while the black bear cannot yet be considered endangered, hunting is leading to regional scarcity of the bears in many parts of its range. In addition, hunters have littered the environment with toxic lead shot which animals will be living and dying with for decades.

There are also more subtle ecological processes that hunting disrupts, such as natural selection. Hunting by humans does not ensure the survival of the fittest animals, but precisely the opposite — individuals who would not normally have reproductive success will have it because hunters do not select the weakest animals as nature does. By often killing the ablest, hunters downgrade the quality of the gene pool. It's no surprise that some ecologists refer to hunting as "evolution in reverse."

Much of the problem is a consequence of how our government wildlife agencies operate. Rather than being concerned about the needs of wildlife, they cater to the desires of hunters.

It's a fact that the prime function of the state wildlife agencies is not to protect individual animals or biological diversity, but to propagate "game" species populations for hunters to shoot. The agencies' expenditures demonstrate the bias. On average, they spend well more than 90 percent of their funds on game species projects, even though non-game animals constitute the vast majority of each state's fauna. State agencies spend millions manipulating habitat for "game" species by burning and clearcutting forests. They penrear and stock "game" animals to increase "shooting opportunities." And they pour millions of dollars into law enforcement of game regulations and into hunter education, which includes the construction of target shooting ranges. The fact is, they're out to conserve hunting, not wildlife.

And it's not just an issue of animal rights, but one of the public's rights as well. As a consequence of widespread hunting, non-consumptive wildlife enthusiasts cannot safely walk in the woods during the hunting season. They get fewer opportunities to view wild animals, who become skittish or nocturnal for fear of being shot by humans. And most importantly, they are denied an equal voice in determining how our wildlife is treated. A mere seven percent minority of the public — the hunters — has 100 percent control of our wildlife.

For these reasons and others, The Fund for Animals opposes sport hunting and seeks a restructuring of state wildlife boards and commissions to ensure that all parties legitimately concerned about wildlife are proportionately represented.

200 West 57th Street
New York, NY 10019
(212) 246-2096

THE SIERRA CLUB

The Sierra Club is not opposed to sports hunting outside of appropriate sanctuaries such as national parks, provided it is regulated. It cannot help wondering, though, whether debate over hunting doesn't dominate too much of our discussion of policy for wildlife. Admittedly, sports hunting serves to check unrestricted propagation of those species that used to be controlled far better by natural predators (which, too often, have been tragically destroyed). But wildlife policy should not revolve about hunting.

Wild animals should not be valued principally in terms of whether they can serve as targets. Wildlife, in its most abundant diversity, should be viewed as a vital feature of the natural world, as part of the earth's genetic legacy. As members of the family of life, we should respect the moral right of all creatures to exist, to maintain basic and successful breeding stock, to have essential habitat protected, to be free of unnecessary predation, persecution, and cruel and unduly confining captivity. Our attention particularly should be directed to the plight of rare and endangered species, and so called non-game species that our culture neglects.

In the context of these aims, regulated sports hunting may have a place for those who choose to pursue it, but there are more pressing concerns. And more and more people are finding ways to value wildlife in other terms.

730 Polk Street
San Francisco, CA 94109
(415) 776-2211

To protect and conserve the natural resources of the Sierra Nevada, the United States, and the World; to undertake and publish scientific and educational studies concerning all aspects of man's environment and the natural ecosystems of the world; and to educate the people of the U.S. and the World to the need to preserve and restore the quality of that environment and the integrity of these ecosystems. Founded: 1892 by John Muir

NATIONAL SHOOTING SPORTS FOUNDATION

Since the National Shooting Sports Foundation was created "to foster in the American public a better understanding of and more active participation in the shooting sports," its position on hunting as properly defined is one of strong support. NSSF believes that sport hunting is a desirable part of modern recreational patterns. NSSF feels that Americans have a right to hunt but to do so on private land is a privilege extended by the landowner.

Hunting with proper controls is an effective and needed tool of that game management which has become the responsibility of modern man everywhere. It is the function of the hunting-interested

to transfer their knowledge and their understanding of the hunting ethic to the younger people just as it has always been their function, at times theirs alone, to finance the conservation of both game and non-game wildlife. Over recent decades, such support, public and private, has amounted to some 7 billion dollars, with another 1 billion dollars being added every year.

No game species has been moved toward serious threat of extinction by sport hunting alone. On the contrary, numerous species have been returned to healthy numbers through hunter-sponsored, hunter-financed habitat management. NSSF believes that, in the ecological and environmental future of this nation, hunting has an important role, just as the hunter himself has played a vital part in its past.

555 Danbury Road
Wilton, CT 06897
(203) 762-1320

Non-profit educational trade-sponsored association intended to foster in the public mind a better understanding of and more active participation in the shooting sports and in practical conservation. Founded: 1960

WORLD WILDLIFE FUND

World Wildlife Fund is dedicated to preserving endangered wildlife and habitats throughout the world and to protecting the biological resources upon which human well-being depends. Its activities are scientifically based, aim to produce immediate and long-term conservation benefits, and provide models for natural management techniques and policies.

Since its founding in 1961, the Fund has allocated over $50 million to more than 2,500 conservation projects around the globe and has helped rescue many species from extinction. It has supported 260 national parks and equivalent reserves on five continents and continues to promote international, regional and national action to protect living resources.

As with most charities of its kind, there are widely divergent views on the issue of hunting among the supporters, board and staff of World Wildlife Fund; however, the organization itself takes no position, either pro or con, on hunting.

World Wildlife Fund recognizes that responsibly conducted hunting can be an appropriate wildlife management tool, particularly for abundant game that is maintained on a sustainable basis. On the other hand, given the irrevocable consequences, World Wildlife Fund opposes hunting which might adversely affect the survival of threatened or endangered species.

It is unfortunate that adversarial relations between organizations over the issue of hunting have been to the detriment of a broader common interest in maintenance of the biological heritage of the globe. It is toward the latter objective that World Wildlife Fund devotes its efforts.

World Wildlife Fund — U.S.
1250 24th Street NW
Washington, DC 20037
(202) 293-4800

Private, tax-exempt international conservation organization. Makes grants to qualified scientists, government agencies and other organizations based on a set of global priorities established in cooperation with the International Union for Conservation of Nature and Natural Resources. Funds are used for research, for habitat management and protection, to encourage sound environmental policy, administration and law, and to provide training and grassroots conservation education. One of 27 independent national affiliates of World Wildlife Fund — International Gland, Switzerland. Established: 1961

❖DEER HUNTER'S CHECKLISTS❖

GEAR
- ❏ License
- ❏ Permits
- ❏ Maps
- ❏ Compass
- ❏ Hunting Knife
- ❏ Butcher Knife
- ❏ Hacksaw/Meat Saw
- ❏ Drag Rope
- ❏ Matches
- ❏ Watch
- ❏ Alarm Clock
- ❏ Game Carrier
- ❏ Game Bag
- ❏ Packet Knife
- ❏ Walkie Talkie
- ❏ Extra Battery
- ❏ Ear Plugs
- ❏ Binoculars
- ❏ Sporting Scope
- ❏ Range Finder
- ❏ Belt Shell Holder
- ❏ Gun Cleaning Equip.
- ❏ Back Pack
- ❏ Tent
- ❏ Sleeping Bag
- ❏ Air Mattress
- ❏ Air Pump
- ❏ Cot
- ❏ Blankets
- ❏ Pillow
- ❏ Camp Chairs
- ❏ Camp Heater
- ❏ Camp Stove
- ❏ Stove Fuel
- ❏ Mess Kit
- ❏ Kettles
- ❏ Coffee Pot
- ❏ Can Opener
- ❏ Ice Chest
- ❏ Camp Axe/Saw
- ❏ Water Jugs
- ❏ Rifle (lg.bore)
- ❏ Rifle (sm. bore)
- ❏ Shotgun
- ❏ Pistol
- ❏ Ammunition
- ❏ Clips or Magazines
- ❏ Bow/Arrows
- ❏ Arm/Finger Guards
- ❏ Deer Tags/Back Tags
- ❏ Back Tag Holder

CLOTHES
- ❏ Cap
- ❏ Face Cap
- ❏ Coats
- ❏ Gloves
- ❏ Mittens
- ❏ Shirts
- ❏ Trousers
- ❏ Suspenders
- ❏ Underwear
- ❏ Insul. Underwear
- ❏ Boots, Leather
- ❏ Boots, Rubber
- ❏ Felt Liners
- ❏ Dress Shoes
- ❏ Dress Clothing
- ❏ Mosquito Netting
- ❏ Camo Face Mask
- ❏ Sweaters
- ❏ Vests
- ❏ Blaze Orange Clothes
- ❏ Handkerchiefs
- ❏ Rain Wear
- ❏ Camo Clothes

MISC. EQUIP MENT
- ❏ Money
- ❏ Hunting Chair
- ❏ Tow Rope
- ❏ Grunt Calls
- ❏ Rattling Horns
- ❏ Tree stand
- ❏ Extra Bow
- ❏ Extra Bow Strings
- ❏ Came Calls
- ❏ Scents/Lures
- ❏ Decoys
- ❏ Brushcutter
- ❏ Camo Paint
- ❏ Plastic Cloth
- ❏ Carcass Cloth
- ❏ Deer Buggy
- ❏ Camp Lantern

- ❏ Flashlight
- ❏ Penlight
- ❏ Spotlight
- ❏ Toilet Articles
- ❏ Port. Toilet
- ❏ Camp Matches
- ❏ Tools
- ❏ Tire Chains
- ❏ Gas Can
- ❏ Scissors
- ❏ Safety Pins
- ❏ Needle/Thread
- ❏ Tape
- ❏ Pencil/Pens
- ❏ Notebooks
- ❏ Logbooks
- ❏ Shovel
- ❏ Flares
- ❏ Glasses
- ❏ Sun Glasses
- ❏ Shooting Glasses
- ❏ Gun Cases
- ❏ Extra Gun Cases
- ❏ Deer Bag
- ❏ Hunters Hoist
- ❏ Knife Sharpener
- ❏ Snake Bite Kit
- ❏ First Aid Kit
- ❏ Insect Repellent
- ❏ Boot Dressing
- ❏ Camera/Film
- ❏ Video Camera
- ❏ Sling Shot
- ❏ Thermos
- ❏ Playing Cards
- ❏ Radio

- ❏ Money
- ❏ Credit Cards
- ❏ Handwarmer
- ❏ Water
- ❏ Canteen
- ❏ Lunch Pail
- ❏ Tobacco Products
- ❏ Gum
- ❏ Reference Material
- ❏ *Deer & Deer Hunting Magazine*

FOOD

- ❏ Beans
- ❏ Biscuit Mix
- ❏ Pancake Mix
- ❏ Syrup
- ❏ Bread
- ❏ Cereal
- ❏ Coffee (Regular)
- ❏ Coffee (Instant)
- ❏ Cookies
- ❏ Eggs
- ❏ Snacks
- ❏ Juices
- ❏ Milk (Dry)
- ❏ Milk (Regular)
- ❏ Soup
- ❏ Peas
- ❏ Corn
- ❏ Potatoes
- ❏ Pickles
- ❏ Hot Chocolate
- ❏ Margarine
- ❏ Butter
- ❏ Salad Dressing

- ❏ Mustard
- ❏ Ketchup
- ❏ Crackers
- ❏ Potato Chips
- ❏ Peanut Butter
- ❏ Jam/Jellies
- ❏ Candy Bars
- ❏ Pop
- ❏ Mix
- ❏ Soda Water
- ❏ Beer/Liquor
- ❏ Ice
- ❏ Donuts
- ❏ Sugar
- ❏ Salt/Pepper
- ❏ Cooking Oil
- ❏ Lettuce
- ❏ Tomatoes
- ❏ Oranges
- ❏ Apples
- ❏ Onions
- ❏ Hamburgers
- ❏ Hamburger Buns
- ❏ Hot Dogs
- ❏ Hot Dog Buns
- ❏ Bacon
- ❏ Ham
- ❏ Steaks
- ❏ Sausages
- ❏ Paper Towels
- ❏ Knives/Forks/Spoon
- ❏ Hand Soap
- ❏ Dish Soap
- ❏ Alka Seltzer
- ❏ Aspirin
- ❏ Personal Medicines